ALONE IN SILENCE
EUROPEAN WOMEN IN THE CANADIAN NORTH
BEFORE WORLD WAR II

It has been estimated that over 500 European women travelled or lived in Canada's Northwest Territories before 1940. They came as visitors, journalists, and artists, or worked as nurses, scientists, and missionaries. In *Alone in Silence* Barbara Kelcey describes the women who lived and worked in the north and the unique situations they faced.

Kelcey details their struggles with the domestic realities of setting up a home or living in the hostile conditions imposed by the geography, as well as their need to adjust the way they worked. For instance, the rich sources left by Christian missionaries provide details of missionary women caught up in the zeal of their vocation but held within the confines of a paternal church. The letters and reports of the Grey Nuns who worked alongside the Oblate Fathers in the Mackenzie indicate the hardships imposed by their situation but also show how driven they were by their missionary purpose.

Alone in Silence is the first book to address the anonymity of European women in the north. Kelcey draws from a diverse field of sources, making use of published and primary sources so scattered that there has been no previous sense of collective memories. By giving voice to this neglected group she offers a unique perspective on the vast literature on life in the north.

BARBARA E. KELCEY is a historian living in Winnipeg.

MCGILL QUEEN'S NATIVE AND NORTHERN SERIES
BRUCE G. TRIGGER, EDITOR

Alone in Silence

European Women
in the Canadian North before 1940

BARBARA E. KELCEY

McGill-Queen's University Press
Montreal & Kingston • London • Ithaca

© McGill-Queen's University Press 2001
ISBN 0-7735-2197-6 (cloth)
ISBN 0-7735-2292-1 (paperback)

Legal deposit third quarter 2001
Bibliothèque nationale du Québec

Printed in Canada on acid-free paper

This book has been published with the help of a
grant from the Humanities and Social Sciences
Federation of Canada, using funds provided by
the Social Sciences and Humanities Research
Council of Canada.

McGill-Queen's University Press acknowledges the
financial support of the Government of Canada
through the Book Publishing Industry Development
Program (BPIDP) for its activities. It also acknowledges the support of the Canada Council for the
Arts for its publishing program.

**National Library of Canada Cataloguing in
Publication Data**

Kelcey, Barbara Eileen, 1949–
    Alone in silence: European women in the Canadian
    North before 1940

    (McGill-Queen's native and northern series; 27)
    Includes bibliographical references and index.
    ISBN 0-7735-2197-6 (bnd)
    ISBN 0-7735-2292-1 (pbk)

    1. Women—Canada, Northern—History.
    2. White women—Canada, Northern—History.
    3. Europeans—Canada, Northern—History.
    4. Canada, Northern—History. I. Title. II. Series.

HQ1459.N58K44 2001   971.9'02'082   C2001-900211-4

Typeset in 10.5/13 Palatino by True to Type

For my sons Sean and Brian

Contents

Acknowledgments

The documents used in the research for this study were spread across a continent. The white women who lived in the Canadian north before the Second World War took their diaries, letters, and memorabilia with them when they went "out" to their scattered homes further south. I am therefore indebted to archivists and librarians in both large and small depositories across Canada and the United States for their enthusiasm and the alacrity with which they offered their help as I pursued these women. I would particularly like to thank the archivists at the Hudson's Bay Company Archives at the Provincial Archives of Manitoba, the Prince of Wales Heritage Centre in Yellowknife, the Yukon Territorial Archives in Whitehorse, the National Archives of Canada, the General Synod Archives of the Anglican Church of Canada, and the Sisters at the Grey Nuns Convent at Edmonton.

I travelled to so many places to find these records that Canadian Airlines made me a member of its President's Club during the initial research year. But I never would have been able to undertake all that travel without the generous financial support provided by the University of Manitoba Faculty of Graduate Studies, a doctoral fellowship from the Social Sciences and Humanities Research Council of Canada, several Travel and Research Grants from the Northern Scientific Training Program of the Department of Indian and Northern Affairs, and two J.S. Ewart Travelling Fellowships. St John's College at the University of Manitoba provided office space and a very collegial atmosphere, including inspiration from experienced writers and researchers.

A number of individuals should be singled out for special thanks, including my thesis supervisor, John Kendle of the Department of History, University of Manitoba, and, for his insights, John Matthiasson of St John's College. Special thanks also go to Anne Morton at the Hudson's Bay Company Archives for her suggestions and to Dorothy

Kealey at the General Synod Archives. Last but not least, I wish to thank my husband, Nelson, for his patience, and for finally understanding that not everyone works at a tidy desk.

Helen Sowden, nurse at Aklavik, 1938,
as drawn by Kathleen Shackleton for her series for the
Hudson's Bay Company.
(Hudson's Bay Company Archives, Provincial Archives
of Manitoba, 1987/363–s–24/65)

The staff at Shingle Point, June 1934. Left to right, back row: the Rev. Harry Shepherd, the Rt Rev. Archibald Fleming, the Rev. Thomas Umoak. Front row: Ethel Hewer, Mabel Jones, Grace Somers, Adelaide Butler (Anglican Church of Canada/General Synod Archives, P0314–454 Arctic Collection)

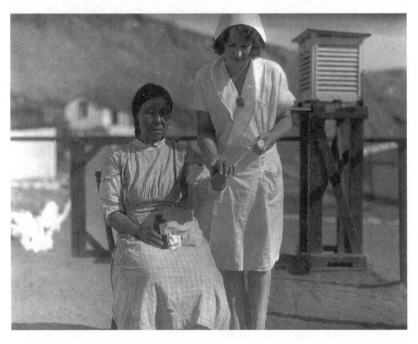

Carolyn Soper nursing an Inuit woman, Lake Harbour, Baffin Island, August 1930. (JD Soper/National Archives of Canada, PA 101457)

Florence Giles and Major David McKeand on board the *Nascopie*,
probably 1937. (DIAND/National Archives of Canada, c8307)

Lake Harbour, Baffin Island, early March, 1931. The Hudson's Bay
Company store in the foreground, Department of Interior building beyond,
and the Anglican Church in the middle.
(JD Soper/National Archives of Canada PA 101479)

Christmas at the Reindeer Station near Aklavik, 1932.
The Porsilds with wives and children of Lapp herders. Note the tree ornaments. (AE Porsild/National Archives of Canada, PA 101114)

Going north on the *Distributor*, 1929. Left to right: Florence Hirst,
Reta Ritchie, Elizabeth (Bessie) Quirt, Major Ritchie, Rev. Shepherd, Ethel
Catt, Lucy Ball, G.D. Murphy.
(DIAND/National Archives of Canada, PA 75899)

Charlotte Selina Bompas with Native child.
(Anglican Church of Canada/General Synod Archives,
P75–103 S5–684, MSCC Collection)

Mary Lyman (Kost), at that time Aklavik store and hotel keeper at Yellowknife, 1939. (R. Finnie/ Northwest Territories Archives, N–1979–063: 0013)

The founders at Fort Providence, left to right, first row:
Sr Bousier (Boursier), Sr Colombine, Sr Boisvert (Boisvers);
second row: Sr Aigle (D'Aigle), Sr Brunelle, Sr Ward, Sr Michow, Sr Masse.
(Catholic Mission [Fort Providence]/NWT Archives, N–1984–001 2/1)

The Rev. and Mrs Anna Rokeby-Thomas's wedding, 1935. "The most northerly white wedding in the British Empire." (Fleming/NWT Archives, N–1979–050:0071)

The wedding of Gladys Fosterjohn and H.C.M. Grant,
Hay River, 1923. Canon Vale, Rev. Stottard, and Rev. Westgate were named
but not identified.
(Yukon Archives/ACR McCallum Collection, 86/61 N1)

The mission and church at Shingle Point, Yukon, 1925. (Yukon
Archives/ACR McCallum Collection, 86/61 A1–6)

Overleaf: map of Northern Canada, 1939

MAP OF NORTHERN CANADA 1939

Shipping route to the
Eastern Arctic

GREENLAND (Denmark)

Craig Harbour

Baffin Bay

Dundas Harbour

Pond Inlet

Arctic
Bay

Davis Strait

To St. John's

Pangnirtung

Foxe Basin

ARCTIC CIRCLE

*ATLANTIC
OCEAN*

Frobisher Bay

Cape Dorset

Lake Harbour

Southampton Is

from Montreal

Baker Lake

Wolstenholme

Sugluk
West

Port
Burwell

Chesterfield Inlet

Stupart's
Bay

*Ungava
Bay*

Cape Smith

kimo Point

Hudson Bay

Fort Chimo

Port Harrison

Churchill

QUEBEC

MANITOBA

ONTARIO

James Bay

Charlton Depot

Anne Lynagh copyright 2001

ALONE IN SILENCE

Introduction

Miss Florence Hirst, known to her friends as "Flossie," was a seasoned Arctic veteran when she took up duties as house matron at the Anglican mission hospital at Pangnirtung on Baffin Island in 1935. Acquainted with as many male heroes of the north as anyone, she had served on the staff of the Shingle Point school between 1929 and 1933 and was not new to the Arctic and its ways when she wrote in her journal about an unfortunate episode at the hospital. An Inuk, she reported, had become violent. The local doctor and Royal Canadian Mounted Police (RCMP) had remanded the insensible and uncontrollable man to the custody of the two women at the hospital. The women were decidedly unhappy at having to care for him in their small cottage hospital. "Of all places in Baffin Land to put a crazy man," Miss Hirst noted, "this was the limit, to dump him in the one and only place on the whole of Baffin Isl where there was no man in residence and where the girls in charge had a hospital of sick people to care for. "Strong – Brave – Silent (men?) of the North," she wondered about the white men in charge.[1]

Miss Hirst's question was a commentary on the image of the Arctic regions of Canada at the time: a masculine domain, where European men fearlessly cracked whips across the backs of dog-teams as they and their native guides rode carioles across the ice packs and through the scrub forests of the subarctic. To the wider world, white men in the Arctic were hardy trappers and shrewd fur traders who mingled with intrepid explorers, salty whalers, dauntless Mounties, and long-suffering missionaries. The feats of these men figure prominently in the white, European legends of the north but, as Flossie Hirst and her female associates might have attested, these were ordinary men even if their circumstances were not. Like many North American pioneers, they called on personal resources and a little courage when the situation demanded.

The white, masculine, Eurocentric nature of the history of Canada's north is not unique in the historical tradition. The masculine focus of northern history can be attributed to the usual reasons for the omission of women, including the misconceptions of many men about the domestic duties performed by women and the lack of importance attached to this work. In the northern case, such delusions have perpetuated the myth that women lived passive lives even while putting up with the same privations and hardships as men engaged in more active pursuits. In the northern case, it is often assumed that because there were so few white women anyway, incorporating their experiences into the record wasn't worth the bother.

In the initial endeavour to address the inevitable questions about the size of the sample in this study, I kept a record of every woman encountered along the path of research. Eventually I stopped counting as the numbers climbed, because the purpose of my search was not to prepare a census. For the period between 1867 and 1939, my records showed that at least 500 white, European women resided in the Northwest Territories (NWT) of Canada, or passed through as travellers for a long enough period to make some impact on the north, or for the north to have had some impact on them.[2] The nature of the Canadian census data for the period makes it impossible to determine exact numbers, but the names of about 130 Sisters of Charity of Montreal (Grey Nuns) are documented in the Order's records, along with selected details about the place and time of service. More than seventy wives of Anglican missionaries or Anglican mission workers were identified by carefully sifting through Anglican Church of Canada (ACC) documents and letters published in *The Living Message*.[3] Many of these Christian missionary women stayed in the north for some time. Also identified were wives of traders, women who acted as independent traders alongside their husbands, and wives of government agents and Royal Canadian Mounted Police officers. Some women attempted to settle in the inhospitable region, providing homes for their families and often working with their husbands on trap lines. Entrepreneurial women opened businesses. Others were employed by the Hudson's Bay Company (HBC) as stewardesses on their northern supply vessels or as housekeepers at isolated posts. A few women were scientists in their own right, while a significant number travelled into the north on excursions that were recorded and published for posterity. It was not really all that difficult to locate the women: not only are true bachelor societies rare, but the remoteness of the region and the controlled access at the time meant that I could identify and examine the lives of a significant number of *individual* women, even though the identification and location of these white European women resulted inevitably in a confirmation of their anonymity.

The recorded history of the north[4] reflects the image portrayed at the beginning of this introduction; it is primarily a tale relating the impressive feats of explorers and Company men, based on countless pages of HBC Post journals, RCMP patrol reports, and exploration diaries. Indigenous people and white women have not surfaced in these records because they are rarely mentioned among the game tallies, fur statistics, and heroic actions recorded by these men. Women and Aboriginals do appear briefly when they came to the attention of the authorities, but very little evidence documenting white European women's lives is located in the extant political and economic records made by men. So a history of these women in the Canadian north must be assembled from the bits and pieces left behind by the women themselves. Many of those pieces came from disconnected sources; the fragmented nature of the evidence imposed theoretical restrictions, necessitating the creative use of material to produce some form of collective memory. With no continuous or extensive manuscript base available, both the narrative and analysis had to be constructed from a plethora of unconnected threads. This has resulted in gaps, but there are glimpses that enabled me to identify what was important to the lives of white women in the north. The same themes recur, consistently addressing the cross-cultural encounters and domestic issues that figured so prominently in the white women's daily existence. And the volume of the material is substantial enough, even though the nature of these sources often prevented my making connections across time.

In some historical studies, the lack of a strong chronological pattern would be problematic. In this case, it was not limiting: the pattern was one of movement rather than change, and of the exigencies of northern existence that characterized northern living. Living conditions did not change substantially before the Second World War. This meant that transiency was a constant theme affecting my research and subsequent conclusions. Transiency in this sense is understood to encompass not only the movement of these women in and out of the region as immigrants (not as nomadic indigenous peoples), but also their anticipation of those moves, and the attention such transiency received from institutional organizations in the south. Tracking these women as they moved "in" and "out" of the north, or from one settlement to another, was a challenge. I soon realized why traditional historians have preferred to focus on one individual explorer or a set of Post journals housed neatly in the Hudson's Bay Company Archives.

By way of explanation, consider the fictitious but representative Mrs Smith, Mrs Green, and Mrs Jones. In 1911 the imaginary Mrs Smith resided at Fort Good Hope and in 1926 at Fort Resolution and her annual letters to the "outside" about her mission home have survived in the archives of the mission society. Mrs Green lived with her Indian Agent husband and their family at Fort Norman in 1915 and at Aklavik in 1927 and later wrote an article for a popular journal. The fictional Mrs Jones worked at Fort Simpson as a nurse for two months in 1925, because she missed the sailing of the steamer that would have taken her on to Fort Resolution and her husband at the RCMP detachment. Her experience and the problems she encountered while travelling were recorded in official documents. From this kind of disjointed evidence I learned about travel options, family adaptation, marital considerations, and working conditions, as well as official attitudes about women in the North, although I was not always able to obtain biographical data with which to explain class issues, or understand how education and family had prepared these women for their northern sojourns. Nor could I extrapolate to some connecting point or overlap lives in any decisive way.

In effect, I had all the outside pieces of the many jigsaw puzzles that made up a larger unit; missing were the loops and knobs from many important connectors inside the puzzle itself. It was a very large puzzle, with lots of pieces. The quantity of material made the project viable, and allowed me to readily identify the landscape, even if the sources did not allow an accumulative, comprehensive picture and an analysis that might have paralleled events already recorded. What emerged was a picture that showed how these women had had to change their outlook to adapt to the living conditions imposed by the north. They simply could not escape from necessity, nor was it possible for them to enjoy the living conditions afforded by their southern homes.

The paucity of complete records coupled with the varied nature of motive and source did not immediately signal a conceptual framework, despite the breadth of the data and what might appear to be the obvious, given current research trends. Recently, historians have used the ideological concepts inherent in feminist thought to try and understand women's lives in relation to the society around them. At first, this seemed to be an attractive and timely approach. Of course, those who study imperialism and colonialism accurately recognize the Canadian north as representative of the imperialist exercise and I contemplated some of this post-colonial perspective too.[5] But there were additional considerations, such as how to resolve the dilemma of studying women in a unique situation requiring a significant independence on their part, separated from family support networks and enduring geographic isolation within what they regarded as a foreign culture, while simultaneously pursuing some sense of analysis that would harmonize with my own philosophy and life experience. In other words, how does one apply fashionable frameworks while recognizing the weakness of the overarching structure of ideas? Feminists will understand how women instinctively appreciate other women and the problems they face, what is important in their lives, and the decisions they make. They should also appreciate the confidence of some women that allows them to ask questions that fall outside the mainstream of current thought.

For me, it seemed the critical point was that these women were not feminists of the late twentieth century, nor women's studies students. For the most part, they had been socialized by their culture to accept their domestic, subservient role. Whether that was right or wrong is moot. It cannot be changed. It just was. Moreover, the framework of imperialism in particular – and of feminism in general – directs the analysis toward understanding a male rather than a female world, judged from the perspective of those who "know better." In other words, the analysis itself is clothed in the guise of objectivity and scholarship, often eschewing common sense. Let me offer a northern symbol that underlines my idea and signals some of the problems I encountered.

Inukshuk rise from the Arctic Tundra like sentries marking the boundaries of traditional Inuit hunting grounds, helping to manoeuvre the caribou herd towards the hunter. They are ingenious structures, unlikely to disintegrate under harsh conditions. The piles of rock that take on the human shape with a discernible head, body, and legs are built from the meagre materials available on the almost barren land.[6] In Inuit culture, the male is the hunter, so by definition *Inukshuk* are representative of man, silently declaring for perpetuity that some human hand has commandeered this as his domain. In fairness, it must be assumed that the Inuit saw *Inukshuk* as meaning not caribou and not necessarily not woman. This is a point not lost on me as an historian in pursuit of women's stories, but *Inukshuk* are foreign to the landscape, much like the white women who ventured north, and there are gaps between the stones because nature does not readily supply symmetrical rocks that will fit together like manufactured bricks. The documents left by these women do not fit together either, and do not allow for smooth, seamless stories like those provided by Arctic explorers, Anglican missionaries, or Company men. Like the scattered *Inukshuk*, located in barren wastelands and not readily accessible to any but those familiar with the terrain, the records left by white women are found where the women retired, away from their temporary northern homes. This is why there are gaps in this northern story.

There are *Inukshuk*-like markers that directed the research and analysis to a comparison with colonial and pioneer settings in North America, and to the outposts of the British Empire, especially since the women I write about were a part of that Empire and identified themselves as such, and as occupants of its farthest reaches. Mena Orford, when writing about her four years on Baffin Island, remembered Baffin Island as "the promised land. In the flesh it was something very different." Recalling how friends and family had referred to the Orfords "pushing back the frontiers of Empire," she added that "whoever [had] thought that one up had never seen the east coast of Baffin Island."[7] The *sense* of Empire lingered across the Canadian north long after Canada achieved political independence. Like Winifred Marsh who began her 1935 Christmas circular letter from Eskimo Point with the phrase "continuing the Empire Broadcast,"[8] white European residents identified where they lived or visited with such phrases as "the most northerly post office in the British Empire,"[9] or the "farthest north customs post in the British Empire."[10] Some were sure their marriage represented the "most northern white wedding in the British Empire,"[11] while others spoke of serving at the "most isolated hospital in the British Empire." [12] An anonymous teacher describing her post at Shingle Point entitled her article in a woman's journal "The Most Northerly Residential School in the British Empire."[13] "If only King Edward VIII could have known how concerned we, his northern subjects, were over his love life," remembered Anna Rokeby-Thomas after the abdication crisis.[14] A year later, the *Chroniques* of the Grey Nuns at Chesterfield Inlet recorded that the radio carried "l'ècho fidèle des fêtes du courronnement de notre nouveau Roi Georges VI." It was "une rejoussaince quais universalle. Pour notre part nous hissons les drapeaux et prions Dieu benir ce nouveau règne. Dieu sauve le Roi."[15]

The burgeoning literature that deals with women and the British Empire includes studies about lady travellers, professional women, and women as helpmeets. Christian mission and racism are central issues in this literature, and by extension the culpability for imposing European culture on indigenous societies. Following the direction offered by these studies, I discovered parallel patterns, but was unable to clearly relate my material to that available for Africa, for example. I soon became convinced that the conceptual framework offered by this approach was really the same as *Inukshuk* – rocks of man – disguised like women, steering historians into false hunting grounds, away from a more meaningful and worthwhile hunt. Since I was more concerned with the women themselves, I used these patterns as guides, knowing that general conclusions cannot be drawn from disparate situations, but hoping that some kind of comparisons could be made even while the unique setting of the Canadian north put such patterns awry.

Because white women were identifiable primarily by their race, and not as a particular group or class, race is what singled them out for examination. I did not look specifically for racist behaviour, knowing that within the historical context, such expectations would be verified. It was more constructive, I thought, to assess women's interaction with other races on their own terms, pointing the discourse away from a negative focus. People cannot be separated from the times in which they live, and these women did not share the choices available in a more enlightened era of feminist consciousness. Since the white European women who went north before the Second World War carried with them all the cultural baggage of the time, bulging as it was with bias and expectations, I was not surprised to discover that they had assumed native culture was primitive or that they believed they were racially superior. Neither did they change those views substantially during their stay. The evidence before *them* merely confirmed their preconceptions that these people were dirty, unteachable, and primitive. They were frustrated by what they saw as a lack of co-operation – a refusal on the part of the indigenous people to understand that for the cultural imposition to be a success, they had to accept all of it, not just take what they wanted (which is what they did). Clara Vyvyan remarked on this condition in her field notes, when she described the Inuit form of Christianity as the "incorporation of white man's medicine with his own, taboo added to taboo."[16] No evidence from either cultures suggests that the indigenous peoples of the north absolutely absorbed the cultural lessons taught by white European women. There is only evidence it was taught, leaving me pause to wonder how the impact of racist behaviour is measured when defined in contemporary academic terms. Overall, white European women in the north acted in *accordance* with the racial views of the time. My initial premise was never that how they acted out those views was wrong; it was more that *current* thought interprets those actions as poor choices.

It was not a revelation to discover that white women settling down to their familiar domestic lives had reinforced those views. They adapted where necessary, but preferred their own rituals. I wanted to know what things were important to them and which were the rituals they worked hard to maintain. The question was not why they had done it – I already knew that – but *how* they had done it. I discovered the answer to that question was sometimes with panache, often with simple perseverance, but mostly with alacrity, because for the most part they were ordinary women, with the skills learned for the gender roles they understood. Exposing white women's culture disproves the myth that this was no place for a woman, but it also means accepting the women's domestic role as the norm and understanding that motherhood was usually inevitable for all but the religious, whose destiny also included domestic duties. Alternatives were few. The domestic arrangements of the women's homes, as well as their occupations, show they could adapt, would adapt, and, on occasion, could be humble about it in the harsh environment.

I expected a certain degree of independence and courage from these women. Deciding to go north, particularly at the turn of the nineteenth century, had profound emotional and physical ramifications. Augusta Morris, for example, wrote in her diary how she would write about her first Christmas, if she lived. But as I read through letters and diaries, I learned that white women who undertook the challenge discovered, like the Grey Nuns, that courage is not the same as strength.[17] The evidence shows how strength reinforced by faith was far more conspicuously present than courage, which is a greater complement to the women's ability to redefine their social milieu. Because their homes and the places these women visited were located in a region cloaked in romance and inaccessibility, the circumstances were synonymous with adventure; yet their lives were clearly not adventurous in the sense that they sought out danger (except for the travellers who were a breed unto themselves). Their lives were often directed by the environment, and certainly shaped by the need to adapt to that environment. But the environment did not determine the direction of their lives. The distinction is a subtle one. The women only repacked their cultural baggage, they did not replace it. In other words, these women did not milk the musk-ox, rather they ordered canned milk or *Klim* from the supply vessel,[18] or learned how to substitute water from the Hay River. And they did not give up their recipes.

That independent nature also translated into some resistance directed toward men and their bureaucratic barriers rather than general institutions. I think it is important here to remember that if not for the institutions, most women would not have gone north in the first place. Any resistance was more likely a reflection of the geographic situation, for it was relatively easy to make decisions on the spot and to set aside momentarily the outside directive. There was no suffrage movement, no temperance objectives, nor calls for equal rights in the north before the Second World War. But why would there be? There was some indication that the women were concerned about the consequences of sexual exploitation and miscegenation, but there was no movement towards change, beyond suggesting Christian marriage and marital responsibility – the options they themselves understood.

Along with transiency, religious faith was the most constant theme throughout the sources, for all these women, not just the missionaries. It is their Christian faith that stands out above all else. It was their faith that made the experience tolerable, even exciting. Those with a strong faith saw the good in their situation, no matter how difficult it all seemed. Those whose lives are controlled by more secular forces might find such faith incomprehensible, even alarming, and difficult to appreciate that like *Inukshuk*, this faith was solid and tangible and symbolic of optimism. For them, their God's presence was almost palpable in the northern emptiness. In *North to the Rime-Ringed Sun*, Isobel Hutchison echoed other Arctic writers when she declared:

We are alone in silence here,
Her ample footsteps throng –
The Peace of God breathes all around,
And fills this place with song. (Frontispiece)

The focus of my analysis, then, became the personal situations and relationships, whether with God and the north, men in the north, or with other women and other cultures, rather than the ideological frameworks of another time. That focus also had an impact on the presentation of the findings, and several points concerning terminology must be clarified. The first is that where possible I have chosen to allow the women's words to speak for them, so direct quotations abound. I have also retained the use of Miss and Mrs throughout the text. This is not because I wished to identify the women in relation to some man, although in some cases it is important to know whether the woman was married or unmarried; nor does it reflect a lack of feminist consciousness. Rather, I know that these women would have been deeply offended by the male-defined usage of their surnames only, and even more insulted by the familiar use of their given names. The women under study are referred to as white Europeans rather than non-native, recognizing them as a part of one group, rather than not of another; remembering them for what they were, not what they were not. That definition is integral to my analysis, an approach that historians bent on correcting old wrongs by creating new definitions might do well to consider.

Although I use the terms "north" and "Arctic" throughout the text, my geographical boundaries are more specific. They include the Northwest Territories as they were defined before the Nunavut agreement, and the part of the Yukon that lies north of Old Crow. This demarcation allows for the use of materials from women who lived in the border regions or were migrants within the area, and those that lived at Shingle Point and Herschel Island (settlements located in the Yukon but administered as part of the Northwest Territories [NWT]). This is an arbitrary geographical boundary, one that does not include the northern prairie provinces or northern Quebec, for example. But the artificial margins demarcate an enormous region and, for research purposes, kept the study from getting out of hand.

Finally, in order to maintain historical integrity, I have retained the word *Eskimo* in those direct quotations where it appeared originally. Occasionally, the white women of this period referred to the Inuit along the Arctic coast as *Huskies*.[19] This appears to be their response to their understanding that the Inuit were uncomfortable with the term *Eskimo*. In my text, these people are referred to as *Inuit*, or in the case of a single man, *Inuk*. The native people of the Mackenzie Valley are properly referred to as *Dene*.

Chapter 1 describes the problems of supply, climate, and isolation faced by the white women in the north. Until the arrival of regular air service, dog teams were the principal means of communication during the winter months. Supplies were ordered on an annual basis and everyone lived with the fervent hope that new supplies would arrive aboard next year's ship in the Eastern Arctic, or on the HBC paddle wheeler along the Mackenzie River.

These conditions set the stage for a look at the domestic life of white women, which is the focus of chapter 2. Geography, and the fact that this was not a settlement frontier dictated a somewhat different domestic economy and structure for white society. In particular, viable female networks did not develop in many communities because the white population was never large enough to allow anything remotely resembling "a group" of women. Chapter 2 describes the effect of Christmas on northern inhabitants. Judging from the extensive comments in the sources, the quintessential Christian and "southern" festival was one of the pivotal events for northerners in the annual cycle of their lives.

Chapter 3 examines Victorian and Edwardian travellers in the region. The emphasis is on four women who published accounts of their travels. The observations of these four are used to consider change over time in the north. In chapter 4, the experiences in the

1920s and 1930s of three women with some professional purpose are outlined. The available documents permitted a somewhat more detailed study of the women's encounters with men in the north, and with male decision makers in the south. These women were very independent. When the north began to open up to travellers generally, they seized the opportunity to broaden their personal interests. But they found their trips could be hampered not so much by ice and privation as by administrative barriers.

Chapter 5 takes advantage of the largest cumulative record left by European women. With only a few exceptions, female Anglican Church missionaries were educated and literate. Part of their commitment was to writing letters and keeping records, many of which have survived. In this chapter, I offer a view of the Anglican mission from the perspective of these women, rather than from the dogma itself.

Chapter 6, in contrast, examines the largest single, identifiable group of white European women in the north. Unfortunately, evidence providing personal views from the Sisters of Charity of Montreal (Grey Nuns) is not as abundant as those available in the Anglican documents. So rather than assess the mission itself, the chapter presents a brief history of the development of the Roman Catholic missions established by the Grey Nuns, while exposing some of the attitudes and vocation that sustained it.

Chapter 7 addresses such issues as race, racial distinctions, and cultural differences. This was a difficult section to research and write, given the lack of indigenous sources. The result is a survey of how the women studied addressed those issues. Since I would argue that racism offers an anachronistic, value-laden, and troublesome framework, I concentrated more on cultural distinctions and noticeable connections. The final chapter presents a case study of one woman's experience, illustrating many of the themes raised in the previous chapters.

Touches of the fabled romance and mystery of Arctic living, at least before aeroplanes and modern communication systems made the region accessible to a new generation of explorers and exploiters, permeate the book and go some way to explaining why this study ends at the beginning of the Second World War. That was the juncture at which technology changed transportation and communications enough to ensure that the Canadian north emerged from its isolation, and the war brought an influx of military and engineering specialists into the region. Their interests included exploiting natural resources on a large scale, as well as building towns, roads, and airstrips, and their values differed markedly from those of the Bay, the Church, and the RCMP. Undoubtedly, thrills and romance can divert attention away from a difficult reality. For those who lived in the north before 1940 however, this was home – even though there may well have been another home somewhere else. And for white European women living in the north and going about their daily lives, this home was quite likely more chilling than thrilling.

CHAPTER ONE

A Long While Between Dog Teams: Climate, Communications, and Isolation

Canada's Northwest Territories stretch northward to the Pole across 1.3 million square miles of some of the most inhospitable geography on the planet. The NWT constitute 34 percent of the area of Canada. In 1988, there were estimated to be only 57,298 residents, or one person for each 22.7 square miles. In 1911, the population numbered 6,507, or one person for each 200 square miles. One Anglican Bishop of the Arctic described this vast and empty land as so remote that there was an "un-get-atibileness"[1] to the place. The letterhead of one of the Anglican missions underlined the isolation:

ANGLICAN MISSION
Lake Harbour, Baffin Island
c/o The Hudson's Bay Co., 100 McGill Street
Montreal, Quebec, Canada
(One Mail a Year, Leaves About July 1st)[2]

The NWT is not a land of eternal ice and snow, although freezing temperatures can occur in any month in the Arctic region and the winters are undoubtedly cold. In the Mackenzie River Valley temperatures fall below zero degrees Celsius for at least seven months of the year, and temperatures of minus fifty-seven degrees Celsius have been recorded. In the Eastern Arctic, where some of the islands are covered by a permanent ice cap, the temperatures are more variable and often related to the proximity of Hudson Bay and the Arctic Ocean. January thermometer readings range between minus twenty-five degrees and minus fifty degrees Celsius. But it is not just the interminable cold that figures in the climate, contributing to the bleak image of the north. At the summer solstice the sun never sets across much of the region. And in the depth of winter, it does not shine at all.

Winter, coupled with the effects of the isolation and remoteness that distinguished life for European women in the Arctic, only added to the strain of stretched communication lines. If a woman's health deteriorated, or a difficult birth was anticipated, it was not simply a matter of waiting for the next boat to travel to civilization and medical care. In the Eastern Arctic, there was but one boat to wait for, and it arrived only if conditions allowed. In the Western Arctic along the Mackenzie River, the HBC supply ship took two trips if ice conditions permitted, and after the ship had travelled "down north" it had to return south along the same route to its home port. This allowed inhabitants of settlements along the river to visit with friends in communities along the route.

Residents of Shingle Point and Herschel Island waited for ideal ice conditions before a schooner could supply them from Aklavik, or from the west around Cape Barrow, Alaska. On the Arctic coast there is one long winter and a short summer, but according to one observer, the local Inuit enjoyed four seasons: the "time of ice, ice going, no ice, and ice coming."[3] Lack of contact with the outside world left residents feeling "like a colony of Robinson Crusoes,"[4] and Adelaide Butler wrote from Shingle Point about how the white women there watched their visitors leave on the last supply boat of the season. They felt stranded and "forlorn – standing in the mud and rain, waving wet handkerchiefs." It was, after all, "a long while between dog teams."[5]

On Easter Sunday 1921, the women at Hay River saw the first aeroplane land at their settlement. It would be some time yet before regular air service was initiated in the Mackenzie and before aeroplanes became reliable, if expensive, ways to travel in the north. Even after planes could be counted on for occasional visits, communication and travel throughout the region was slow. Before the Mackenzie River Air Mail Service was instituted in December 1929, mail was delivered regularly only once a year. Until that time in the Western Arctic – and until later in the Eastern Arctic – mail delivery was otherwise sporadic, dependent on the RCMP patrol or other official visitors.

In the north, it was the supply ship which moved the goods and brought the news and *shiptime* played such an important part in the lives of Arctic residents that many viewed the boat's arrival as the beginning of their year. The supply boat brought the food and supplies for the next year's physical sustenance. It was also a time of spiritual renewal, whether that took the form of personal mail, the arrival of the bishop (both Roman Catholic and Anglican), or the incoming alcohol ration. "The impact of the supply ship on Arctic dwellers had to be experienced" explained Anna Rokeby-Thomas; it was not only the security of another year's supply and fuel that the ship brought, it was "the tangible link with civilization" that came with it. Arctic residents "became intoxicated with happy excitement and talked with the crew like many magpies."[6]

While the supply ship represented a tangible link with the outside, it was also a once-a-year event and, ironically, symbolic of transiency in the north. Because many white residents, and certainly white women, were merely sojourners in the north, the boat contributed to a condition described by Richard Finnie as "psychologically camping out."[7] Once a year, the constant flux and impermanence were figuratively tied up at the dock, or waiting out in the harbour. Never mind whether the women of the settlement were about to embark or not. Shiptime was crucial, and it was fleeting, leaving those along the route exhausted – first from the waiting, then from the socializing.

Along the coast of Hudson Bay and Baffin Island, supplies arrived on the HBC supply ship out of Montreal. After the ice started moving out of harbours in early summer, anxious European residents would scan the horizon daily for signs of a steamer moving slowly through the ice floes. Flossie Hirst at Pangnirtung wrote about her inability to explain her feelings the moment the boat was seen: "It is one thing to expect the boat but when expectations are finally realized, the feeling is altogether *awful*. It is both joyous and frightening for us because we know that mail and news are actually within sight – and frightening because we wonder what news is contained in our mail after such a long silence."[8]

Decisions of some importance to one's life came with the boat. Who was aboard could signal the need for some speedy packing. At Pangnirtung, as the ship appeared on the horizon the hospital staff would run up the flag, then watch through field glasses for signs of the bishop and, more significantly, for a mission uniform at the ship's railings. A uniform might mean a replacement, a departure, perhaps even an additional nurse. By 1932, nurses travelling under the auspices of the Woman's Auxiliary (WA) of the Missionary Society of the Church of England in Canada (MSCC) were required to wear a red-lined, hooded, blue Grenfell cloth coat with red shoulder straps. The blue felt hats with a "dash" of red made nurses easily distinguishable from teachers, whose similar uniform had pale blue decorations.[9] In her 1933 diary, Flossie Hirst confessed that she was glad no missionary uniform had been sighted on the deck of the *Nascopie* because she was afraid that she or her companion might be replaced.[10] Later, they knew that the new nurse had arrived because they "discerned the familiar garb of an Arctic Missionary, trimmed with red,"[11] that lent a special Arctic accent to new orders.

The procedure at shiptime followed a pattern similar at all outposts in the Eastern Arctic. After the ship was sighted, everyone started running; it was summer and the ship could be seen at any time of the day or night. White residents and Inuit alike would visit the supply ship in small craft, swarming over the decks, shaking hands with everybody and looking for mail.[12] Long letters from home contained a whole year's news, but it was impossible to sit back and read them leisurely. First of all, one just *had* to know the news. Who had married or given birth? Who was ill or had died? While these were important bits of news, there was always the possibility that something might need a reply, and the letter had to go on the ship about to leave. Some women kept annual diaries so they would be prepared to write their letters when the ship arrived; some simply sent the journals home intact. Keeping the journals meant real self-discipline. Besides, as Augusta Morris apologized in an early entry in her journal, although she had allowed a long interval between writing, "it augers ill for my resolution, but there is nothing to write about but the weather."[13] More than one woman noted it was easy to put off recording daily events, knowing the ship would not arrive for months. There was almost a universal scramble to write letters before the ship left. "Why had we not done all this before?" asked E. Wallace Manning. "I cannot very well explain, but if you were to live in the Arctic a few years, doubtless you would understand. We always made good resolutions about *next* year"[14] when the next mail arrived. Like Christina Fry at Herschel Island, some women who had the equipment resorted to mimeographing letters, apologizing for the use of the machine. Not only did they have to say the same thing over and over again, they had only a few days in which to do it.[15] This use of the mimeograph was a remarkable breach of etiquette for some, yet it represented an example of adaptation and initiative under remarkable conditions.

The panic to get the latest news on to the returning ship was also a reaction to isolation. As the only white woman at Chesterfield Inlet in the early twenties, Luta Munday associated the arrival of the mail with a feeling of "utter aloofness." It seemed as if she had been cut "off from everyone and everything with the realization that letters were months old, most of them as much as five months, and that almost anything could have happened since. Those feelings [she] never could describe, it seemed almost that [she] had died and all the world was left behind."[16]

In one sense, no communication with the outside portrayed the independent nature of the white women's lives in the north. In another sense, it signified their loneliness and their isolation from the comfort traditionally supplied by the support systems of friends and family. This created a paradoxical existence. Just facing the ensuing tensions became an important part of living in the north for European women. Witness Mena Orford's reaction to hearing news of the sighting of the first supply ship in to Pangnirtung after her arrival the year before: "I stayed where I was, cold shivers running up and down my spine. For the first time since the ship had sailed away, I was admitting to myself that I had never really believed it would come back again."[17]

The supply ship with the attendant receipt of mail is one of the recurring themes in Arctic memoirs. Keeping in touch from places a thousand miles from anywhere was crucial for day-to-day existence and maintaining an identity with the women's own culture. Trying to comprehend both the excitement and the accompanying tension is difficult and leads to the temptation to dismiss comments such as those of one Anglican missionary's wife at Aklavik who, in 1928, wrote: "Life is just full of thrills and interest here. I was never so thrilled in my life, I think, as getting the winter's mail."[18] Consider too, the impact of the mail's arrival for Sophie Porter and the other wives of whalers at Herschel Island in 1895. "Those who each morning impatiently listen for the postman's ring can scarcely picture the eagerness and anxiety with which we receive our one solitary yearly delivery," Mrs Porter wrote from the Arctic coast, "where the conditions of life and environment are utterly opposed to all that makes existence comfortable to us within the bounds of civilization, culture and modern improvement."[19]

By 1918, Christina Fry at Herschel Island was receiving two mails a year – a number considered the "height of modernism" by one trader's wife at Fort Good Hope.[20] One of those deliveries came overland by dog team, probably via the west coast and the Yukon. Of the intervals, Mrs Fry commented that it was like living in "Wonderland. Then it is we wonder – how you are, where you are, what you are doing, and when good news of Peake will come. However, we never allow our wonder to drift into worry, for that isn't worthwhile."[21] Acceptance of the situation was a necessity for white women in the north. There really was no other alternative until the next vessel appeared. When the ship came in, women who lived along the route knew that no further contact could be made with the outside, except for the occasional mail delivery by dogteam. They knew that if anything was forgotten in a letter ordering supplies, for example, it might be some time before they could even reorder. When the supply ship came, "it would be a strenuous day indeed, hard to keep cool and collected" when there were so many things to think of.[22] Staying cool and collected while living in the Arctic was a challenge at any time, for anxieties were exacerbated by harsh environmental conditions and difficult communications. Maintaining mental equilibrium required some effort. It is no wonder that ships bringing visitors, supplies, and mail had such an impact.

Not surprisingly, winter weather was an almost universal feature of letters and memoirs from the Arctic. By describing climatic conditions, writers portrayed hardships in terms that relatives and friends could understand, without actually whining. Descriptions such as those of Dorothy Page at Hay River in 1914 are commonplace: "Half of our winter is past now and it has not been nearly so severe as last year. It has registered forty-six degrees below zero at two different times, but [that] lasted only a few hours. Of course, it is below zero nearly all the time, but we do not call that severe here."[23] From Fort Norman in 1903, Rose Spendlove told *Letter Leaflet* readers that "the thermometer had read between fifty and sixty degrees below zero for some time. Please excuse my scribble, my fingers are cold and the ink has frozen."[24] Earlier, Mrs Spendlove had thanked the WA for the supply bale; she added "the tea cozy is so very pretty and will keep our tea from freezing which is frequently the case during the winter."[25]

An Arctic winter required proper clothing. Some women though, were reluctant to wear the native costume, which was the most suitable garment for the climate. In an era when women still wore long, heavy skirts, white women in the north probably eschewed native garb for reasons of practicality and Victorian modesty. With the addition of a fur wrap or coat, their skirts and the petticoats underneath gave some protection from the elements. This costume would have served the women in the settlements and missions along the Mackenzie River well. The styles also distinguished these women from their native neighbours, providing a visible racial and class distinction and lending, in their minds, an authoritative air.

Along the Arctic coasts, these women soon recognized that keeping warm was more important than looking like a respectable European lady. Luta Munday recognized that native clothing was suitable for the outdoors but complained that the garments were a nuisance because all the "house clothes" had to be removed before the "deerskins" could go on, even for a fifteen-minute walk. "The hauling, pushing, and shoving to get into the *kool-le-tang* (coat) and out of it again was maddening, and oh, the condition of my hair," she noted.[26] Now if Luta Munday had lived in a snowhouse, she would not have removed her furs until she retired for the night, just before she crawled onto the fur-lined sleeping platform with the entire family. But Mrs Munday lived in a heated cabin, which separated her culturally from the Inuit women at Chesterfield Inlet. Although she realized that outside the cabin her life depended on native dress, inside the cabin she needed to retain her own cultural and feminine identity. Luta Munday described native dress as being very similar for men and women, although the women's *kool-le-tang* or *atigi* had a large hood in which to carry infants. It was tied at the waist to provide a safe seat. While fawn skins made the best clothing, summer skins had the necessary short, fine hairs. This clothing was worn without underclothing; the fur was soft so it did not irritate the skin. The suit was doubled: one part was worn with the hair next to the skin, the other with the hair facing out. The coat slipped over the head and over wide short trousers, deerskin stockings, and sealskin boots. Some white women added bearskin mittens. The clothing, sewn together with sinew, was windproof.

Boots, or mukluks made with a layer of fur inside to keep the feet warm, featured hair on the outside sole to prevent slipping on the ice. The soles had to be constantly replaced as the hair wore away quickly. In contrast to native women, whose principal role was to prepare skins and sew clothing for their family, white women found this constant maintenance of skins a nuisance. Sadie Stringer observed with some understatement that the Inuit had learned that in cold weather "it did not pay to allow holes in their clothing"[27] and that centuries of tradition had provided the Inuit women with the skills and the impetus to chew skins until they were soft and malleable enough to be used for clothes. However, this was a domestic art unfamiliar to white women. It was also a profound cultural difference. Gladys O'Kelly recalled how Inuit women had looked into her mouth with interest and decided that she was very lazy: obviously she had done little sewing since the edges of her teeth were still intact.[28] Wallace Manning learned to prepare and sew the skins she and her husband needed to perform their scientific work in the Cape Dorset region, although she drew the line at some native preparations. For example, Mrs Manning recalled that sinew was used to sew sealskin boots because when wet, it swelled and filled the needle holes. Caribou sinew was preferred, and, after being stripped from the long backs of the beasts, it was cleaned of large pieces of meat, soaked, scraped, and allowed to dry. The native women "removed the meat by sucking it," she noted, "but I found a knife was quite as effective."[29]

The constant repair to native clothing posed problems to European women culturally conditioned to the virtues of cleanliness. Winifred Marsh at Eskimo Point remembered the white sealskin boots made for her son by a native woman that were washed in warm soapy water, and then hung up to dry. After the treatment, not surprisingly, the boots always became stiff.[30] Mrs Marsh learned to chew the boots to soften the skins and to replace new ones as needed.

Just because these women lived a long way from fashion centres does not mean that they were unconcerned about appearance, even though winter and the intense cold may have forced them to accept what they perceived as an unorthodox and unfeminine appearance. These women had heard such fabulous tales of the northern climate that one does not wonder at their dressing to suffocation, wrote Selina Bompas. A parka, she noted, "made of deerskin with hood and mittens all in one, is the finest garment ever invented for the purpose."[31]

Even though an *ategee* made her ready for the worst weather, Susan Quirt pointed out that it was "dreadfully long and sloppy" and felt precisely as if she were outside in her nightdress and bedroom slippers. Miss Quirt resigned herself that she would get used to it like everything else.[32] Mhairi Fenton described the parka made for her at Lake Harbor in 1937 as an "Eskimo garment like a dress (with a hood), but comes down to the hip only and has no waist, and no allowance for the bust as it is very full."[33] Mhairi Fenton's comment that her parka was made by an Inuit woman who was "sweet and much cleaner than the rest" reveals another reason for white women's reluctance towards the garments.[34] European women, confessed Sophie Porter, had to "overcome" their "disgust" at the sickening odour of deerskins, and if her "wholly elegant outfit, decorated in the most approved style," had developed the same smell, heated cabins would have been unendurable for European noses.[35] Because of the intense cold and primitive heating systems, it was not easy to air out stuffy cabins.

One missionary remembered asking Mrs Fred Jackson at Inman Harbour whether her home was warm in winter; allegedly she replied: "cold as hell! cold as hell! cold as hell!"[36] – a reply that unfortunately cannot be substantiated but is indicative of how the cold permeated even well-built cabins. One woman explained that she and her husband had to sleep with the blanket over their heads. Another recalled how every night the bedroom fire had gone out, so she was always frozen when she was alone. Her nose was numb, her eyelashes were frozen together, and she dared not move, she said, explaining that there was only one warmed spot in the bed.[37] It was possible to heat homes with a good stove, and in the Mackenzie Valley wood was available. On the coast, coal was imported as wood was scarce. Of course, heat generated in cozy cabins could cause a nightmarish predicament for anyone already suffering from claustrophobic conditions. "The heat of the room, meeting the cold air from outside, froze the condensed vapour all around the door," recalled Addie Butler, so that in addition to freezing to death outside, it was possible to be frozen *in* as well.[38]

Selina Bompas, a missionary wife of long-standing in the north, maintained that Arctic winters were healthful and invigorating." Even while you shiver you enjoy," she claimed. "While feeling that you have a strange resemblance to a bear with your shaggy coat, and eye-lashes thickly laced with icicles, you cannot help laughing and are ready, in spite of all, to thank God that you are alive."[39] Well, perhaps. Mrs Bompas probably wrote those observations with missionary recruitment in mind. She might have added Christina Fry's portrayal of forty-six degrees below as an enhancement. "To experience something similar you will have to stand on a bridge as a train is passing underneath puffing up smoke and steam, blinding you. Freeze that steam, put a big wind behind it," she added and you might be able to imagine the cold. "Still, I suppose it might be worse."[40] And she was right. It was not so much the interminable cold of winter that was the biggest environmental problem in the north. It was the climate together with the "season of no light" as Mena Orford called it, which produced the living conditions that led to "cabin fever."

Winter did not mean total darkness in most of the Arctic, for there was a dull twilight of about two hours duration at noon. The lack of sunlight and fresh food meant everyone became "languid," with the physical effects translating into psychological ones.[41] Women became irritable and edgy, often succumbing to fits of grumps. Even "candles or other lighting did little to dispel the winter shroud that had folded over us," explained Anna Rokeby-Thomas; the darkness "held the strange power of quenching the human spirit."[42] Even the anticipation of the dark period caused anxiety. When Addie Butler described the incessant sound of ocean waves pounding the spit at Shingle Point, it reflected her concern about the impending winter. The "break, break, break, lulled us to sleep, but when freeze-up comes, it will be us who will break," she wrote, "from the silence and the cold."[43] "The awful silence" was not easy to describe. Luta Munday recorded that her pen was inadequate for the task, although she ventured that: "it seemed to descend upon us and enfold us, the grave itself could not be more quiet. Very occasionally there came the howl of a wolf or the bark of a fox. I would say sometimes to [my husband] Walter, I must scream. It was to avoid the sensation of being buried alive."[44]

It was a silence northern residents could almost feel, "a silence not only physical, but often one that became a silence within their minds."[45] The silence provided a metaphor for the isolation, although few women would admit, like traveller Clara Vyvyan, that "to a certain extent, the north" was a prison, from which one "may not easily get out, being held there by some individual weakness or by the grip of a force too great for definition and defiance."[46] Two dimensions characterized this force. The simple inability to go anywhere else during the winter was the first. The second was more complex: a package of acceptance, all tied up with the ribbons of duty and the women's own understanding of their role. It was unlikely that any white European woman travelled into the Arctic without a specific goal in mind, unless she had convinced herself that she could at least make an effort. Wallace Manning explained how she "shrugged mentally and said goodbye to clean white sheets. After all, it wasn't the end of clean white sheets. There would still be clean sheets," when she went outside.[47] Another woman divulged that she "wasn't a bit in a hurry to get to Aklavik." In fact, she said she "rather dreaded it; didn't expect to like it much [and] my hunch was right – I didn't like it, and I don't like it yet, and I'm sure I won't, at least until winter is here. But all that doesn't matter really; we didn't expect to come here to enjoy the scenery, nor the social life. There are other things to take our time and interest."[48]

Keeping busy was important. Selina Bompas insisted that constant occupation was a cure for faint-heartedness in women in the north. Sadie Stringer recalled that what with "helping the school, caring for the sick, and playing the organ for our little services and caring for my babies I did not have time to sit and pine."[49] Her situation at Peel River and Herschel Island was not unique. Gladys Clarke echoed her sentiments from Fort Norman, "We are kept so busy that time goes – well I can't describe how quickly."[50] Those with specific employment such as nurses and teachers often remarked on how little time they had for themselves; seldom did they comment on loneliness, except for acknowledging homesickness. Many of these women shared the conviction that prayer was an active, powerful force in their lives, and if there is one strong influence which is evident throughout the records, it is unwavering faith that God would protect them, and that He would provide. Rose Spendlove wrote that it was "through God's mercy we have endured nearly a quarter of a century,"[51] while Reita

Latham declared: "This is a great adventure, and we're glad we're on it. All the world over, Jesus is revered, is the King, imagine the great joy of being one of His apprentices, so we do rejoice and daily strive to show him in our life – preaching is necessary, but living Christ is essential to make a success of what we are trying to do."[52] From Shingle Point Mildred McCabe wrote: "During my term of office in that northerly hospital offtimes the unseen world seemed very near, and I was reminded of the presence of the risen Lord."[53] She, like Christina Fry, *knew* she had been "watched over, guarded and safely brought through many perils known and unknown."[54] Even those who were not missionaries felt guided by the same hand. Isobel Hutchison was a Scottish botanist who travelled along the Arctic coast during the winter of 1933. Although not in the Arctic to prose-lytize or preach, she maintained that she never took chances because God always blazed her trail.[55]

The trials of isolation were made easier to endure with God's help, but it was critical for European women to develop strategies for dealing with obstacles and problems posed by the environment. Some used their imagination, like Flossie Hirst who fantasized, "Oh to be in England now that April's here, but with the warm sunshine pouring through the window it isn't hard to imagine that England is not far away."[56] For some, it was an endurance test simply not to have another white woman in the vicinity. "I have no white women to speak to, the nearest being 300 miles away," wrote Rose Spendlove. "The loneliness is extreme."[57] In her diary, Mrs Spendlove recorded, "I am a woman alone but I have been for so many years that I am used to it."[58] Her diary and letters to the WA acknowledge encounters with Dene and mixed-blood women, so being the only white women was what she meant by being alone. This does not suggest a bigoted attitude as much as it does the understanding of a bond shared by women of common cultures, and the belief of white women that they would be a comfort to each other in the isolation of the north.

Sadie Stringer once stated in an address that, for five years, she had not the company of another white woman.[59] She explained that she "learned to understand men during that time," and that the men around her were very appreciative of what she did for them.[60] Her presence provided the men she encountered with a "soft" aspect to their harsh environment and a visible link with the wives and fami-lies left in the south. She nursed them when they were sick and enter-tained them when they came to visit. She also taught shorthand to sailors wintering at Herschel in the mission school. What Sadie Stringer did for these men was domestic and feminine in nature; it was what the men would have expected, and what she would have expected of herself. Mrs Stringer once wrote that she had heard people say it was cruel to ask a white woman to go north, but that she thought it more cruel to leave her behind.[61] She saw her place as beside her husband; he was already an Arctic missionary when she married him, and they shared a mutual vocation.

Luta Munday simply learned to get along without other white women, although she noted that others always had difficulty with the idea. "When I explain why I do not miss them, questioners always say aren't you funny or aren't you queer until now I am sure I must be," she wrote, adding that it was a plus that the men she encountered were all interesting.[62] When Mary Ferguson, a trapper's wife living near Fort Providence, petitioned the government in 1933 for a hunting licence, loneliness and isolation were among the reasons she gave for a privilege to which she was not legally entitled. She wrote:

> My husband runs a long trapline and is away from home for eight to fourteen days each trip. During this time it is necessary that I remain alone. It is common knowledge that but few persons accustomed to life on the outside can for so long maintain their mental equilibrium amid the solitary silence and loneliness of the far North without they have something with which to keep the mind occupied and the body busy. It is just that which I seek! The legal right to get out in the open with some definite incentive designed to furnish both the body and the mind with the necessary exercise which is also a relaxation – a lessening of the nervous system's high tension – a counter-irritant for long days and weeks spent alone in comparative idleness during the cold months of winter.[63]

Shooting and trapping small game probably provided Mrs Ferguson with limited entertainment, but she recognized that she had to get out of that cabin. She worried about staying alone and what might happen to her while her husband was away.[64]

In one way or another, white women alone learned to live without other white women. It would be easy to put this down to "the stuff of which pioneer women were made," but that explanation is too general. It ignores realities and damns those who could not bear the strain – and there were certainly some of those. Annie Card allowed that even though her husband was fascinated with his job as an Indian Agent, she herself could not tolerate the isolation. With the nearest doctor 700 miles away she was afraid her young daughter might succumb to the diseases prevalent among the Indians. After two years she left the north, one year after the departure of the farming instructor's wife who had arrived at the same time at Fort Simpson.[65]

Mrs Card's concerns about health and the availability of care were magnified by the remoteness of the north, but no more so than for women on the settlement frontier, or even for working-class and poor women in the city. Put into perspective, white women in early northern settlements may have been denied access to modern facilities and technologies as they developed, but there never seemed to be a shortage of trained or experienced nurses to assist during epidemics of influenza or measles, or for those diseases for which, wherever one lived, there was little treatment obtainable besides competent nursing.

The threat of emergencies was more likely responsible for the fear generated by the lack of medical facilities and doctors, and the sad experience of Margaret Clay only reinforced those anxieties. It was a particularly northern tragedy. On 21 September 1924, Mrs Clay died from wounds sustained two days earlier when she was viciously attacked by sled dogs in the community of Chesterfield Inlet. The circumstances "of this misadventure, which emphasized the degrees attending life in [those] inhospitable latitudes, were distressing in every particular," declared the RCMP Commissioner in his 1925 report. The RCMP statement provided to the press, in order to stave off undue publicity, described how Mrs Clay was walking alone near houses at the post when she was set upon by the dogs. It was surmised that one of the dogs had snapped at her in play and accidentally drawn blood, prompting the other dogs to attack. Two members of the police post were alerted by the commotion and beat the dogs off, but one of Mrs Clay's legs had been so badly lacerated it was amputated at her request the day after the accident. The surgery was performed by an Oblate priest at the settlement, the closest surgeon being at The Pas. Four men were in attendance to treat Mrs Clay: the two Mounties, the priest, and the HBC man. Although anaesthetics and morphine were available and the operation itself was successful, Mrs Clay apparently died of shock due to blood loss. The RCMP report noted that Mrs Clay was familiar with northern conditions, implying that she had accepted the risks and therefore presumably absolved the RCMP of any blame. "She had gone North to be with her husband, but in her darkest hour she was deprived of his presence," pointed out one story, because her husband was out on a long patrol.[66]

Sergeant Clay's absence prompted the men who rendered the first aid to put their signatures to a statement outlining the desperate situation and their intentions. It is difficult to determine if this was standard practice at northern posts since no similar files could be located; however, the document appears to be singular. Corporal O.G. Petty, in charge of the detachment, assumed all responsibility and assured Father Duplain that under the Criminal Code, no responsibility would rest with him.[67] Two reasons probably accounted for this action. The men may have felt compelled to record the circumstances since Sergeant Clay was not available and since it was the practice at the time for a husband to grant consent for surgery on his wife. It may also be that because Mrs Clay was the only white woman at Chesterfield, the four men saw their position as tenuous after administering medical treatment under anaesthesia and without a chaperone. Whatever the case, the declaration is a striking document inasmuch as it illustrates the kind of issues that arose in the north due to isolation. It reads:

In the case of Mrs Clay:
1. We do not see any chance that the leg of Mrs Clay can be saved
2. We seriously fear that gangrene will start in, the whole leg from the knee to ankle being chewed up
3. Mrs Clay is under intolerable pains
4. We seriously think that we can succeed, and we see in the amputation the only way to save the woman's life
5. The person is quite willing to have her leg amputated knowing perfectly well the existing conditions
Signed: O.G. Petty Cpl; H.W. Stallworthy Cst; N.W. Snow; E. Duplain OMI

Margaret Clay's death provoked some action on the part of the RCMP administrators in Ottawa. One officer recommended that, in settlements, all dogs not working should be kept tied up. A new dog ordinance was drafted to provide the RCMP with the authority to compel owners to keep their dogs tethered. The ordinance elicited some dissenting opinion, undoubtedly because it would have been difficult to enforce among the Inuit along the coast.

Dogs represented one of the hazards that white women regularly mentioned. In part, this was because Aboriginals did not treat their dogs the way white people did. If the dogs were not working during the summer, owners tended to ignore them. Luta Munday, while she trusted and was fond of her own dogs, recognized the dangers of dogs reared by both the Inuit and Dene; she believed they were cruel to their animals, never giving them any affection. As a consequence, she said, "their dogs never expected anything but a blow, from which they were ever trying to escape."[68] Northern dogs were also dangerous because they were territorial in nature. "If the company's dogs passed within half a mile all our dogs would fly at them," Mrs Munday remembered. "Then [ensued] such a battle royal." Although the dogs were all strong and willing workers, Luta Munday tempered her fond memories with those of the attack on Mrs Clay. The Clays had replaced the Mundays at Chesterfield Inlet, and Mrs Munday recalled that Margaret Clay had told her how much she disliked the idea of going to Chesterfield, how she disliked the settlement and the Inuit. "I could hardly bear to leave her behind feeling as she did, and the whole of the following winter she seemed to haunt me. I think we both must have had a premonition."[69]

Wallace Manning and her husband depended on their dogs and understood the Inuit could not afford to keep dogs that were unable or unwilling to work. But an Inuit hunter, she explained, rather than shoot a dog with a cartridge that could be saved to kill a caribou, might leave the dog to starve. The Inuit believed that if the dog were shot, it would bring bad luck. If the animal only died from starvation, they reasoned, the owner could not be blamed.[70] The treatment and behaviour of northern dogs shocked observers like Isobel Hutchison, who made the absurd suggestion that there should be a northern equivalent of the RSPCA.[71] In the end, as in most situations, the women learned to deal with the dogs.

When visiting the sick, Valenis Ottaway, a nurse at Hay River carried her little brown bag as well as a big stick to ward off any trouble with the dogs.[72] Native dogs are "awfully fierce and chew strangers," claimed Addie Butler without further example. She added that sometimes dogs got loose and fight furiously, "and if we know of it, we don't go out unless we are armed with a thick stick."[73] Dogs were one of the necessary evils that made northern existence bearable. They pulled the *komatik*, which carried the mail, the law, the sick, and the visitor, and enabled communication across the frozen wastes. The general understanding was that residents put up with them.

The experience of Mrs Clay is exceptional – not because of the dogs, but because of the medical implications brought about by her location at Chesterfield Inlet. While accidents, and the resulting injuries, often presented serious medical problems in the north, three physical ailments, though not unique to the region, were commonly experienced by all residents. Addie Butler's complaint of her eyes being overworked because of the continual use of oil lamps during the winter was typical.[74] Reading and letter writing were favourite activities during the winter season, and winter meant vitamin deficiencies caused by a lack of fresh fruit and vegetables which left the body without resistance to diseases that affect the eyes. In summer, the prolonged glare of the sun's rays often produced snow blindness, adding further distress to eyes already at risk.

Medical investigations undertaken during the Eastern Arctic Patrol in 1937 determined that dental decay, however, was the "most prevalent objective disturbance to be found in white women in the area."[75] Dental disorders were commonplace among white residents, but since pregnancy trebled the rate of tooth decay, women were at greater risk. Delaying treatment of dental caries only made the condition more severe. During her 1922 trip along the Arctic coast, Gladys O'Kelly noticed that dental problems were a serious drawback to living in the north. She observed that the Inuit had splendid teeth while the white men invariably lost all of theirs. Was this caused by using ice for drinking water, she wondered. She had noticed that "civilized Eskimos who follow this practise [of melting ice] have not so [sic] good teeth as those who use more animal blood than water."[76] What concerned the government doctor was not so much the tooth decay itself, however. Government medicine chests were supplied with enough supplies and instruments to deal with toothaches, but deterioration of the teeth led to such muscle and joint manifestations as neuralgia, myalgia, neuritis, and perhaps even arthritis.[77]

The 1937 study determined that the most common complaint was "bad stomach," which included hyper and hypo acidity brought on by the continuous consumption of food prepared in tins, and gastritis caused by overeating and a sedentary life. It pointed out that some digestive ailments originated with nervous disorders and emotional upsets.

Emotional stresses and strains were intensified in the Eastern Arctic concluded the report, a view shared by Flossie Hirst. Based on her experience in both the Eastern and Western Arctic, Hirst concluded that the isolation of the east required a more determined effort than that of the west.[78] Strangely, this contention is not supported by available evidence for the period, although the Royal Northwest Mounted Police (RNWMP) reported in 1906 that for one woman, "three years in the Arctic [was] an important contributory factor in bringing about her present [insane] condition."[79] No name is mentioned and no further explanation was forthcoming.

Indeed, only one set of official records have survived that relate to what might be considered the stresses and strains of isolation. In April 1925, Minerva Sophia Oulton, who lived in a cabin at Point Brule on the Slave River near Fort Smith, shot her sixteen-month-old baby with a ten-gauge shotgun. The RCMP report understated the carnage at the Oulton home: Mrs Oulton had shot up the house, killed the cat and dog, and fired on her ten-year-old son, Cecil. She had also attempted to kill herself with an axe because she had decided the world was coming to an end. In his deposition to the inquest, the examining doctor disclosed how Mrs Oulton "complained of being kept alone last fall with the baby for nine weeks at Great Falls, when she thought she would go crazy with loneliness." In his evidence, Cecil Oulton stated that it was the first time he had noticed his mother acting "that way; she was worrying the day before about my two brothers whom she had not seen lately; it was a week since my father had left. She said she thought they had all drowned."[80] At the time, Minnie Oulton was thirty-five years of age and had five children. The police report listed her as Presbyterian; Minnesota born; imbecilic; and, most importantly, poor. Poverty meant she was unable to escape her situation, unlike Annie Card who could leave the north before she felt her world was coming to an end; Minnie Oulton simply resided close to what some considered to be the ends of the earth during the long winter months.[81]

Not to be forgotten in this account of the frost and gloom of northern winters are the distinctive situations associated with the short Arctic summer. Imagine the emotion when, after three months of darkness, the Grey Nuns at Aklavik could record in their *Chroniques* that they "saw the sun, rather his eye only, for the first time since November. What a pleasant wink he did give us, and then disappeared again, assuring us he would remain longer with us tomorrow."[82] As the summer solstice approached, night turned into day; in the far north, the sun just rested on the horizon, never setting. During the summer, the long hours of daylight curtailed sleep and produced a strange kind of lethargy caused by exhaustion. Fatigue resulted from the inability to ignore the temptation to keep going as if the nights were, in fact, days. It was hard to go to bed, and life carried on as if it were one long afternoon. With little to distinguish day from night, women became disoriented, unaware of the date and time. Reita Latham wrote of a holiday at Herschel Island in 1932, when she and her companions visited the HBC Post for tea. They had a "ripping good time" she remembered. But she also noted that they had not the slightest idea of the time of day, which turned out to be quite late.[83] Travellers like Elizabeth Taylor remarked how it "hardly seemed the thing to do to go botanizing at one o'clock a.m." It was quite an experience for her to attend a midnight mass at Peel River while the sun streamed through the windows.[84]

When the sun returned, everyone felt healthier and had renewed vigour. Positive comments replaced those of dread and foreboding, which were used to describe winter. Gladys O'Kelly's description illustrates the sense of restoration that summer produced: "The short Arctic nights cast an enchantment over this land where the atmosphere of the long brilliant days, like champagne, makes laughter and song the easiest thing in the world. At midnight the sun sinks regretfully to rest and a band of molten red rims the world."[85] Nature in her own way provided the perfect cure for the winter blues. The unlimited sunshine was nonetheless enervating, especially when it coincided with the business of shiptime, which began the yearly cycle for women in the north.

With all the problems posed by isolation, climate, and weak communication links, it is understandable that the advent of radio and aeroplanes changed the lives of women in the region. Radio transmission was established across the Arctic by the mid 1930s. Ironically, while it speeded up communication with the south, it also emphasized the isolation of the north and added to the sense of loneliness. For British women on the shores of Hudson Bay, and even as far west as Shingle Point, the nightly sound of Big Ben evoked intense nostalgia: "Through the frosty starlight of this Arctic Region his chime rang with the uncanny sound, bringing sudden visions of wet streets and umbrellas, emptying theatres and the hoot of the taxi."[86] Apparently, the London news was usually easier to tune in because of fog and Atlantic depressions. According to Winifred Marsh it was often possible to hear ten different stations at Eskimo Point.[87] But the radio was not a panacea for the communication ills of the north. As one Cambridge Bay resident acknowledged, "Troubles can get out" by radio, "but in no way could help get in."[88] Nevertheless, when transmission radio came to Pangnirtung on Baffin Island, Mena Orford was thrilled. For the first few months, words costing forty cents each "poured over the air like water,"[89] lifting spirits and providing one of the real changes to northern life.

The atmosphere that carried those radio waves and the very location of the NWT afforded residents the opportunity to view one of nature's outstanding displays – the aurora borealis, one of the small, yet exciting pleasures of living in the north. "One would feel sorry for the man or woman who could not watch the flickering movements of its magic radiance without emotion," said Selina Bompas,[90] who often shared evening walks with Augusta Morris at Fort Norman and Fort Simpson. They watched the pink and green lights in the sky moving "with the rapidity of lightning"[91] thanks to an electrical discharge that creates a current carried mainly by electrons. The lights, which usually appear in the shape of a curtain 80 kilometres above the earth, are the result of emissions caused when atoms and molecules in the upper atmosphere collide with the current.[92]

Christina Fry's description of the curtain is far more poetic and certainly less intimidating than this scientific one. As she put it, the aurora borealis is "simply grand. They [the lights] dance and swing and flutter, drop so low you could take a handful. Some people think they can hear a rustling." She related how Mrs Bompas and Augusta Morris were sure they had heard the rustling, but her own disappointment is unmistakable when she concluded "as yet I cannot."[93] In an article entitled "The Beauty of the Arctic," Luta Munday depicted some of the natural wonders of the NWT, emphasizing the "growing community" and the rewards nature dispensed to those who found the strength to persevere through the trials of Arctic winters and its isolation. She wrote:

> Then there were the Northern Lights. A single silvery shaft shoots across the heavens and changes to a riot of brilliant Collor [sic]. I have seen one half of the sky dyed blood red, no other shade mingled with it at all while at the same instant the opposite arch of the heavens showed every Collor of the rainbow. Sometimes those swift dancers of the air seem to advance and recede to a lilting measure then suddenly disappear, and as we draw a breath of wonderment thinking the spectacle is over, they burst on us again in all their radiance. At times I have laid myself flat on the snow in my deerskins to watch the full arc of their ghostly dance braving the intensity of the cold rather than lose a moment of that vision.[94]

The intensity of the cold and the difficult conditions of northern climate and isolation does not qualify these women for any kind of heroic status; nor should they be placed upon a pedestal because of the hardships they faced and the self-sacrifices they made. Such ideals only obscure the everyday occurrences that affected their lives and explain the immediate strategies they devised to help them live within a harsh environment. Nevertheless, as Canadian historian W.L. Morton wrote: "In the North, environment is a fact of life, and a factor in historiography. Life is possible in the North, but depends ever and always on the conditions imposed by it."[95] Despite some bleak conditions that controlled the very essence of their lives, many women found elements of the northern climate and its isolation actually vitalized and inspired. The aurora provides but one example.

Meatless, Wheatless, and Sweetless Days: The Domestic Arrangements of a Northern Home

For any woman living on European frontiers, "home" had a double meaning. The concept of home is important to understanding how the women retained their own customs and is crucial to appreciating the northern experience. Home embodied their roots and extended families – in the case of white European women in the north, this meant those who were *outside*. This was the home they had left behind and, for the most part, where they returned to (or perhaps more importantly, where they hoped to return). It was where they were personally grounded and where the customs they endeavoured to sustain were rooted. For most women of the period, however, home was also a construct of the moment, in which the domestic plays of each woman were acted out on a daily basis. It was not just a physical space, although the actual building did engender real consequences for these women. In the north, the homes were isolated; primitive; and had almost always belonged to someone else in the past, transferred by the institution or agency responsible for their location. In this home, the remoteness and extremes of climate meant that both daily and special activities were dominated by the environment, shaped by the continual effort to adapt to the exigencies of daily life in the north, rather than the everyday routines the women had learned in the south. In the northern home of a white European woman, thoughts of home more often than not had to be put aside, or at least placed on hold; women's domestic role was intensified. Romantic illusions regarding the Arctic situation soon withered. For most white women, life was simply "more chilling than thrilling."[1]

The domestic situation of women provides a focus with which to examine their daily activity, allowing some study of how women reconstructed what passed for a southern "society" in the north. White women perpetuated in their homes the social customs they brought with them from the south. Women bore the responsibility of introducing "civilization" into the north: the expectation was that they would introduce a softer edge into an otherwise bleak world. Although critics may view the recreation of white society as a destructive force responsible for discrimination, what alternatives were available to white women? Indeed, what else could be expected? Women sustained familiar customs in isolated settings because they needed to remember who they were, where they came from, and what standards to maintain after the arrival at their destination. There is a subtle distinction between that perspective and the understanding that women ventured into the Canadian north knowing there would be difficulties. The former view suggests powerlessness and a reaction to it. The latter indicates adaptation; it allows for versatility and personal initiative. Before the northern visitors left the south, they had personal goals and guidelines clearly established; they simply altered them to meet the situation.

Some historians have suggested that the advent of white European women – and in particular British women – into colonized regions contributed to the distance between the community and the white men who controlled it. They view this development as the result of a social hierarchy closely aligned to the political order of the ruling elite, the type of activities in which women engaged as a group, as well as the use of servants in most of their homes.[2] In the north, the reality was that women's lives were contained within a cycle of annual ordering, feeding of families and traveller guests, storing and preserving for the following winter, adapting to available local provisions, and cleaning of homes, washing of clothes, and bathing of babies or mission charges. There were variations on all those themes, but it is noteworthy that none of the women saw this domestic role as changed or changing in any way, whatever their function in the community.[3] Food and supplies, obtaining water, and household chores are among the themes that dominate the women's letters and memoirs. Although essential to everyone's existence, food and water may be considered trivial to traditional history; household chores, on the other hand, probably fall somewhere short of trivial. Since isolation and environment affected the supplies available in northern kitchens, household management was critical to the northern experience. More important, because of the domestic nature of women's work, ideas about food and home economics are gender-specific themes. Consequently, when white women write about the food they cook and the food they consume of necessity, they write about their *self*.

Men living in the north did not care any less about their food, and many of their memoirs mention the monotonous fare of bachelor kitchens. But women expressed their concerns more often and in greater detail: they wrote about the food they cooked and ate because they were ice bound and psychologically kitchen bound by gender expectations. Activities associated with meals were closely tied to their daily schedules and domestic occupations. Deprivation has always been part of the northern folklore, so a knowledge of how housewives coped in northern kitchens and their thoughts about their domestic circumstances should be part of the historical record – without producing a northern cookbook that describes one hundred and one historical ways of preparing seal meat and fog berries according to southern standards.[4] The north was not always a land of plenty; it would be wrong to cling to the illusion of abundant game in the woods, or fish in the lakes and seas. Grand banquets and social events with elaborate gastronomic menus were not common, although, not surprisingly, hospitality and celebrations were characterized by the consumption of food – a reflection perhaps of the conditions imposed on white society by the supply system, as much as a reflection of custom and culture.

Women described food and food supplies to friends and family because they knew the women to whom they wrote could visualize the difficulties of supply and preparation and sympathize with the monotony. It was all part of the sacrifice, and describing the associated problems of food preparation subtly conveyed that message south, where, it should be remembered, there were no supermarkets or convenience foods either. When in 1918 Christina Fry wrote from Herschel Island about the lack of variety in the family's diet, she noted that fresh fruit and green vegetables were out of the question; but it was her description of the "meatless, wheatless, and sweetless" days that summed up the extent of Arctic victuals in terms any housekeeper could understand.[5] Northern tables required one to keep what Sister Elizabeth Ward at Fort Providence recorded as "Lent by anticipation" for often there were only fish and potatoes to eat – when there *were* fish and potatoes.[6]

Fish provided a staple protein and, as Minnie Hackett explained, during "open water season" near Aklavik fresh fish were usually available daily. Even fish frozen in the fall and kept all winter tasted better than canned food,[7] but dried fish was not necessarily the most palatable alternative for those who relied on it. Louisa Camsell Mills, born at Fort Simpson, recalled that as a child the main course for most meals was fish; if people did not like fish, they went hungry. Since the dogs were fed fish exclusively as well – there were five or six dog trains in Simpson at the time – the men of the community spent three weeks each autumn fishing in Great Slave Lake. Twelve thousand whitefish represented a good catch. To preserve the harvest, the whitefish were hung ten to a stick on a fish stage. "If the weather had been warm, these fish got rather 'high', and after coming all the distance from Great Slave Lake in two scows, uncovered and tramped on by men and dogs, one can imagine what [the fish] would be like."[8] It is not difficult to imagine why Annie Card remarked that they always hoped for cold weather when the boats returned from fishing.[9]

Country foods such as seal meat, polar bear, walrus, and muktuk (which is the inner layer of whale skin) provided fresh meat in coastal settlements, as did caribou when available. Moose, caribou, deer, bear, mountain sheep, and rabbits augmented the diet further inland "on rare occasions," wrote Minnie Hackett. Any shortages were due, in part, to the men who worked at the missions and trading posts; they considered their occupations and vocations as their principal responsibilities. They were usually not hunters in the traditional sense. Traders, missionaries, government officials, and policemen had other things to do, which were neglected only under conditions of dire need. Inuit and Dene were often hired to hunt and fish if game was present in the area. This explains why, in 1928, Miss Hackett described to *Living Message* readers the good fortune of St Peter's Mission the previous winter to have had a good supply of caribou, noting that the legs were hung in the storehouse and could take several days to thaw out even when brought into a hot kitchen.

Obtaining and preparing country meat was often less of a challenge than actually eating it. Witness Sadie Stringer's account in an 1897 letter of how Inuit had killed two polar bears at Peel River. The next morning at the mission they had bear steaks for breakfast, but one meal of the rich meat was enough for it left them *feeling* like polar bears. Witness too, traveller Clara Rogers's description of a scene after her guides had killed a bear. It was the only fresh meat they had eaten for some days. "As we sat there, close to the reeking corpse, consuming fried bear steaks and rice and treacle," she confessed, "we tried to regard this revolting scene as a matter of course."[10] Luta Munday considered seal and walrus to be very good eating, but she liked the walrus best. She described walrus as a very fat, dark meat and especially the flippers of a young animal as really quite good, although she disclosed that not all white people in the community were enthusiastic about eating either one.[11] Mena Orford recalled how her husband and children liked seal meat, but she could only manage to eat the liver, and then only because it tasted a bit like calf's liver when fried with bacon. Mrs Orford's dislike of the dark, fatty seal meat became so strong that she eventually was unable either to cook or even touch it: she confessed "at the first sight of the black flesh, [she would] have to go and lie down."[12] But unfamiliar tastes and smells were often the means to survival, as Clara Rogers reminded herself when she sat and ate fresh bear meat. "Sometimes life catches you up and whirls you into the strangest experience from which there is no escape, and you just bow your head and wait until it's over."[13]

Although harvesting eggs, geese, and ducks in the spring allowed for fresh meat when supplies of all kinds were running low, strict regulations about shooting waterfowl out of season evolved over time. These regulations presented some social difficulties in small communities when everyone was just short of starving and geese and ducks were the only available food. At Cambridge Bay, the RCMP felt it necessary to inform the residents of the law. Anna Rokeby-Thomas related how these visits from the local constabulary often created an uncomfortable situation because every time the Mounties appeared at her home to deliver their stern warning, she had a duck in the oven.[14]

Even Mrs Rokeby-Thomas, who claimed there "were ways of disguising the monotonous food" supplied in the Arctic, "considered it a real victory when a day passed without having to use army beans for either the noon or evening meal."[15] Fresh meat or not, the mainstay of the northern kitchen was beans, often referred to euphemistically in correspondence as "dried vegetables," which fooled no one. Christina Fry, who called beans "Mackenzie River Strawberries," noted that any fresh food at all was a treat after a winter of beans, beans, and beans.[16] Beans even figured in the folklore about white women in the north. One Anglican missionary recalled how the white wife of an HBC trader was ill and "of a delicate stomach." There was country food and dried meat available, but a traveller who had spent a short time at the post, noting the condition of the wife and taking "courage to advise his host," asked whether he could not order some luxuries for her. "Luxuries? is it?" asked the trader. "Do you no ken that I get 600 pounds of beans every year?"[17] The accuracy of this tale cannot be verified, but it indicates how luxury in northern kitchens often meant quantity and not quality, as well as how the supply of provisions was often determined by another hand. And a situation is certainly put into perspective when beans can provide a measure of social status.

At least beans could be prepared with some flair if the cook was versatile. Not so canned meat, recalled Luta Munday, who described it as so salty as to be unpalatable. The saltiness meant it needed to be boiled beyond recognition so it contained no nourishment whatsoever. Mrs Munday preferred cold boiled bacon, though it was not altogether appetizing either – particularly when it had been stored at the detachment for two years, having been shipped into the Arctic rolled in a creosote preparation so the chemical taste permeated the whole thing.[18]

Dry food supplies such as beans and sugar had to be shipped in bales or boxes, and there was often a chance that foodstuffs would get mixed. Insignificant as this may seem, such inconveniences meant daily challenges rarely encountered by a southern cook. In a letter of gratitude to the WA for sending supplies north in 1898, Mrs Reeve at Fort Simpson tactfully suggested that groceries should be sewn up separately in strong cotton bags. She had learned from experience that pearl barley, oatmeal, and pepper were not a very serviceable mixture. Any blending meant the contamination of an entire year's supply. Moreover, there was no way to replace the goods until the boat returned in twelve months time.

To supplement the monotonous diet, northern women planted gardens wherever there was a little soil, although the fickle climate and poor growing conditions meant that harvests were unpredictable. Take the Grey Nuns' garden at Aklavik, which yielded lettuce leaves three inches in length, four to six leaves to a plant. The lettuce was so tough, the staff at the mission resorted to boiling the leaves; the radishes and spinach went to seed because of rapid growth due to continuous daylight.[19] Sister Ward wrote one year how the barley crop at Fort Providence was ruined by locusts, the potato crop was very poor, and the previous year's wheat had been destroyed by frost. In addition, the lake had frozen over before fish could be caught. The nuns in charge of the gardens managed to harvest just one carrot. Even the onions were a disappointment; it "appears they were so bad that the locusts disdained them." In the early years at Fort Providence, the Grey Nuns faced severe hardships; their gardens were essential because supplies were not shipped to them with any regularity, and barley was used as a coffee substitute so a lost crop was nearly catastrophic.[20]

Even if the northern gardens yielded a bounty, the supply of fresh vegetables did not last through the long winter. That absence weighed heavily on the minds of white women in the Arctic. Winifred Marsh wrote from Eskimo Point in July of 1936 that she was "crazy for something fresh" for she had had no fresh food for days.[21]

Mena Orford described how a calendar picture of a bowl of fruit "provided the last straw to [her] hungry cravings." Every time she saw the picture, her "mind would flood with poignant yearnings for bananas and [with] nostalgic memories of apples ripening on a tree."[22] Bananas were not unknown in the NWT; they could sometimes be purchased at Fort Smith where the Connibears were independent traders. It seems Mrs Ada Connibear was not afraid to order goods that no one else would bother with, including shipments of green bananas. Her first order spoiled because it was not loaded on the boat in time, but the next year's supply arrived intact. The shrewd Englishwoman obviously understood what would sell the fastest in her store.[23]

While Mena Orford had to make do with a picture on the wall, Flossie Hirst and Florence Giles at Pangnirtung were engaged in window-box gardening, with some amusing results. Having planted potatoes in a box, they decided to have a dinner party and surprise their guests with a treat. They dug up the potatoes, all the while concerned that the bowl they held in hand would not be big enough. In her journal, Miss Hirst divulged that they had previously cut off the tops and eaten them as a green vegetable, which might explain the following description of the harvest: "Our expressions must have been rather comical when we had all the obvious result of the total crop on the floor. There were about 3 potatoes the size of an egg, and the rest were the size of marbles – and smaller!! We set them on the floor and laughed – and laughed – and laughed. There was a surprise all right, but it was ours, and we were not the invited guests."[24] They did not wait for the guests, but cooked the potatoes immediately. They were delicious, and the women rationalized that there were more in the box garden for the HBC traders when they next came to dinner. The garden also provided these two women with a little game of colonial one-upmanship. Miss Hirst planted Canadian seeds on one side and declared them to be Miss Giles's. Seeds planted on the other side were claimed for herself and England. "Canada and England are going to it, neck and neck," recorded Miss Hirst – although Miss Giles had insisted if the Canadian seeds started to gain, it would be proof of Canada's superiority over England.[25]

Elizabeth Howard told *Letter Leaflet* readers in 1915 that cooking in the north was somewhat different to what it was in a southern home. She explained in a letter to the WA that before they were able to get fresh milk, eggs, and butter at St Peter's Mission, "there was nothing to do but substitute *Hay River*. Really, it is marvellous what one can do with water," she wrote, and for thrifty and stretched housekeepers, it was highly recommended.[26]

Water may have been inexpensive as an ingredient in small amounts, but securing sufficient quantities of water in the north was labour intensive. The mechanics of melting snow and ice in the winter occupied considerable time and energy. The constant need for water was a reflection of the white woman's understanding that despite the conditions in which she lived, a clean home, clean bodies, and clean clothes were still important. Of those southern conventions that clashed with the Arctic environment, cleanliness and cleaning were the most difficult to adapt. As a result, the women's obsession to maintain sanitary conditions comparable to their southern homes was at times almost perverse. To their eyes, clean clothes and bodies separated them from their native neighbours. Cleanliness may have provided an immediate visual distinction between the races, but it would be wrong to assume that European women engaged in the southern rituals of cleanliness in order to maintain that distinction. They would have done so anyway. Not only did they view such chores as part of their everyday occupation, but their fastidiousness was culturally ingrained and personally desirable, even if this meant cracking the layer of ice on the water pail every morning just to wash.

If cooking in an Arctic household challenged a housewife, washing and laundry was one of her bitterest trials, concluded Isobel Hutchison, after describing how a tub of snow was placed on the stove to melt. Her washing "froze stiff as boards the moment it was hung on the line to dry."[27] Christina Fry told *Letter Leaflet* readers that although she liked to put clothes out on the line, it was not always the best plan in winter.[28] Mary Ferguson, who washed clothes with melted snow in the winter, found that even in summer, the hard river water made doing laundry difficult. Except for woollen garments, which were hung in the house to keep their softness, clothes were hung out on the line until much of the moisture was gone. The laundry was then hung inside, which meant endless lines of damp clothes cluttering already cramped cabins.[29]

Melting snow in any quantity was a tedious job. The usual method was to fill large pots and reduce the snow to water on the stove. If hot water was needed, the wait could be interminable. Fuel supplies were scarce, although the never-ending cold meant that a stove was probably lit for most of the day and could do double duty. In the missions and schools, bath night and laundry routines were strictly enforced. Mary Crocker wrote from Aklavik in 1938 that the climax of the week began when bath water was hauled in pails from the laundry tanks in another building. "It's quite a business by the time you get to the thirty-eighth bath," she recalled. In the end, she considered it "rather a lark."[30]

Water could be obtained in a number of ways during the winter months. At Cambridge Bay, huge slabs of ice were sawed out of a freshwater lake to be used for drinking water during the winter. (Ice yields more water than snow and salt water loses its salinity with freezing.) The slabs were stored close to the buildings where "they stood like a sparkling forest as they waited their turn to pinch hit for the water tap."[31] Ice in the vicinity such as at Shingle Point residential school on the Arctic coast did not always mean it was available for immediate use. Bessie Quirt longed for an easier way to transport snow into the house from the single remaining large drift located some distance away from the dormitory at Shingle Point. Her solution was to place an old stove with a pipe near the drift, light a fire in the stove, and stick the stovepipe into the snow. Within hours, she had a whole tub of water. Delighted, she used the stove to melt snow until the drift was gone.[32]

At times, men delivered ice slabs or carried in tubs full of snow, but for the most part, women took care of the water themselves and had little help from servants. Some white women in the north had native servants and there is some sense of their presence in letters and diaries, although they might more properly be called "home help" than servants. Often a government official or missionary would hire an Inuit assistant as a guide, to help with dogs and boats, and to build ice houses when travelling out on the land. Such expertise was essential, and few men had any illusions about who was in control in those circumstances. When an Inuit guide was taken on though, it usually meant that his dog team and his family were part of the bargain.

In 1930, Roly Soper engaged an Inuk named Moosa in this capacity at Lake Harbour; his wife Carolyn acquired the services of Neve, Moosa's wife. Mrs Soper called Moosa, Neve, and their two children her "attached Eskimo family." The Sopers were responsible for the Inuit family's welfare, which included weekly rations. The Inuit family lived in traditional housing close to the Sopers, and Moosa was paid a monthly wage, plus food and tobacco, to accompany the scientist husband on all his trips. Neve's primary job was to provide Arctic clothing for the Sopers.[33] Employing native women in this way was not uncommon; it suited most white women, who preferred to get on with the housework themselves.

There were a number of reasons for doing the housework themselves. First, it was usually unnecessary to have a number of servants in a two-room log cabin or glorified tent structure, and for women disciplined to domestic work, the familiar drudgery of housework kept them busy enough to offset depression and loneliness. Servants were not a symbol of status in the north; there was no one to impress.

White women did not normally compete for social position. Although a "class distinction" might exist between Europeans and Natives, distinctions between white women were less meaningful. This does not mean there was no pecking order, but if a white woman were the only one in the settlement, why would she need to be superior? In a community where a woman's very survival depended on a good rapport with all the other women in the settlement, there was little room for social snobbery.

Only one recorded incident could be located to disprove the notion of an "uncontentious" female society. According to Ethel Catt, who wrote to Bishop Stringer in 1933 from Fort Smith, Mrs Godsell had had a tea party and set the settlement in a flap – she did not invite either the police or the government ladies such as Mrs Gagnon. As Fort Smith was the centre of administration, a number of white women were married to men with some status in the community. Mrs Godsell, for instance, was the wife of a flamboyant and aggressive Factor at one of the Company's major trading posts. In response to Mrs Godsell's snub, Mrs Gagnon hosted another party and invited every lady in the settlement, including the mixed-blood women, but not Mrs Godsell. This, declared Miss Catt, set the settlement "jangling." Unfortunately, no further observations were offered. The Factor's wife was served notice about how she ranked among the civil servants and Mrs Gagnon's message was equally clear about how white women in the north treated those who believed themselves superior. Fort Smith's status as a settlement with a large white population permitted some deviation from other northern white societies,[34] but this appears to be an isolated incident resulting from one woman's failure to recognize her neighbours as peers. It was not usually a mistake made among the women.

Most white women were wives of missionaries, salaried traders, or policemen and could not really afford domestic help. In one of her letters home, Winifred Marsh told how she had hired a woman to assist her after the birth of her first child. The woman's duties included turning the wringer, bringing in the coal, scrubbing floors, and getting the water. Her main references seemed to be that she had lived with a white man for some time and was clean and strong.[35] Within three weeks, Mrs Marsh was disillusioned. Her house help had left. "Women up here get spoilt," she declared, noting that the pay of six dollars per week (at a time when a maid in Winnipeg was paid fifteen dollars a month) had been considered insufficient. "She didn't figure the pay was worth the work," wrote Mrs Marsh, and she worked "only from 10.30 till 2.00, and everything [I] had to teach her."[36]

Mrs Marsh's experience was typical. Women who attempted to train Inuit and Dene to do the housework had little success. The explanation lies partly in the difference in housing and in the understanding of what housekeeping required, especially in the coastal regions where Inuit lived in skin tents in the summer and variations on tented ice houses in the winter. For example, the aboriginal women could not understand why Christina Fry felt compelled to shovel snow from the roof of the storehouse as part of her spring-cleaning ritual.[37] Luta Munday tried hard to teach some of the Inuit at Chesterfield how to clean her house and wash the clothes, but it was futile. "The Esquimos first of all had never seen a white woman's clothes, nor used soap. They had not the haziest idea how to use the latter," she explained.[38] Luta Munday and her white sisters could comprehend why the Dene and Inuit had never used soap, particularly after the women had spent a winter in the north and had developed some awareness of living conditions and native clothing. The compulsion to keep their own homes clean or to practise personal hygiene interfered, however, with any sensitivity to native traditions; yet it is difficult to expect that white women would replace their own traditions with those of the Natives.

Domestic employment was also at odds with what northerners referred to as *Indian time*. This attitude had less to do with hours and minutes than with responsibilities and duties, not to mention structured schedules. It was hard to persuade domestic servants to stay on the job when their families were returning to hunting or fishing grounds. Employment and commitment held different meanings for whites and the local population. For example, it was impossible to convince young, single, native or mixed-blood women to stay on as domestic help after an eligible man had proposed marriage. Native custom and economics left no doubt as to which alternative was most desirable. Where young women were employed, there was also a matter of propriety. Missionaries were always distressed by the possibility that their female charges were being led into a life of immorality (never actually defined, immorality apparently meant living with a man outside of Christian marriage). Irene Biss Spry reported that at Fort Rae the local priest did not permit individual women to work alone in a house that had no resident white woman.[39] This meant that the resident white women in a community may have enhanced the possibility of employment for young women in a region where jobs were otherwise non-existent.

While it is obvious that white women attempted to secure help in their homes in the north, few details of the ensuing relationships are mentioned in the sources. Missionaries often reported the presence of an adolescent orphan or older child who attended school at the mission and helped around the home. The departure of the children always engendered expressions of sadness, and apparently the missionaries made some attempt to keep track of them. Usually, this is the only time servants are mentioned, except for Inuit and native guides hired by males. While this absence of remarks could reflect an attitude of complacency, given the conditions, it is probable that servants were an insignificant factor in the domestic environment. White women may have had expectations of hiring the locals and exercising some prerogative over indigenous domestic help, but any such plans were probably scuttled by northern attitudes. Since native women had different domestic priorities, both sides were no doubt somewhat intolerant of each other. To add to the mix, there was no local tradition of service in a domestic sense.

Women who had other white women as neighbours in the settlement, did occasionally help each other. Childbirth in particular offered an excuse for closer social contact, contact which might otherwise have been thwarted in northern communities by the danger of wild animals, roaming dogs, and bitter weather. Attending a sister in need was one domestic duty everyone understood, even if it meant packing a suitcase and moving to the other woman's quarters for the duration. The rituals of birth also emphasized some of the domestic consequences of housewifery in the north. In one of her letters, Winifred Marsh described the situation at the HBC trading post when the white wife of one of the traders gave birth. "There I did miss an abundant water supply, every drop of water I used had to be melted from ice. The men thought they were heroes to supply me with two kettles each half full of boiling water," she lamented. "For a fortnight, I slept with the [mother and child], and cooked for the mother each day. The weather was very cold and I found that oiling the baby was the safest means of cleansing."[40]

Necessary environmental adaptations were often presented in the same matter-of-fact way. Rarely were they complaints. Agnes Cameron observed it was a point of honour in the north not to whine, whatever happened.[41] Miss Cameron does not elaborate, except to describe how Mrs Harding smiled bravely as the scow carrying half a year's provisions broke away from the steamer and smashed against the shore. This dearth of protest signals an acceptance of the conditions; there was not much point in griping about something that could not be changed, although it must be remembered that pre–Second World War women probably had more humble expectations. Historical attitudes and expectations also partially explain the omission in the sources of comment about what Jean Godsell recorded as "the complete lack of privacy and the lack of sanitary accommodation" when she journeyed north on her honeymoon in the 1920s. She described her bridal chamber as a "tarpaulin covered mountain of freight."[42] Sadie Stringer noted the same lack of privacy in a 1955 article in *Maclean's*, where she described how sick sailors off the whaling ships slept alongside Inuit and the Stringers, in bunks built for that purpose in the Stringer's mission home.[43] Neither women divulged how that lack of privacy affected their lives and the rare mention of things private underscores the sense that these women did not reveal personal secrets because they were, indeed, personal.[44] The historian hoping to discover whether the environment affected sexuality, for example, would be disappointed. Jean Godsell's remark was the only one to address that issue, even in an oblique way, although Wallace Manning did describe her first year of marriage, which was shared with an Inuit family in a snow house. She wrote: "Had I been an Eskimo all would have been well – or at least much better – for they are accustomed to live with one or two other families in the same dwelling. Since I was not Eskimo, and unaccustomed to lack of privacy, I found it an effort to adjust myself to a life where practically every movement was open to inspection by one, two, or three pairs of eyes."[45] Like all the brides who travelled north, Mrs Manning likely assumed it was none of her reader's business how her conjugal arrangements were affected by the situation. Curious historians will have to live with that attitude, because no useful evidence exists.

What did receive considerable attention from white women in the north was Christmas. Aside from shiptime, which has already been discussed in a previous chapter, the celebration of the Christian festival at Christmas was a social occasion of some import in northern settlements. Like shiptime, when mail from home was delivered in quantity, Christmas in the north – amidst the Christmas card atmosphere of the Arctic landscape – was both public and private. The ritual procedures of European Christmas customs represented the definitive endeavour to impose European culture on the indigenous population; it also required an unconscious attempt not to recall too poignantly the seasonal gathering of relatives and friends outside the north. This meant creating memories of Christmas present – a task attacked with some relish and a certain amount of zeal.

Christmastime was *Nerriwigycoak*, wrote Winifred Marsh. This was the time of a big feast, and of *Kowee-enarktok*, the time of rejoicing.[46] It was a time, too, when nostalgia and homesickness could cloud the excitement, especially after the advent of the Northern

Messenger radio broadcasts in the thirties. Those messages reinforced the separation from families, even as they drew them closer together through a sense of personal contact. Because there was often only one radio in each community, or one resident with a radio receiver superior to all the others in the settlement, listening to these broadcasts became a social event. While profoundly personal, these events evoked emotional responses in even the most seasoned of Arctic residents.

Mena Orford received three messages during her first Christmas at Pangnirtung. She heard very little of them. "The tears which [she] had been holding back so long took quick advantage at the first sound of [her] Mother's voice." Her husband handed her a handkerchief, but "no one else appeared to notice, or for that matter hear anything unusual, though [her] tears were noisy that night as well as wet."[47] At Pangnirtung too, Florence Hirst listened to messages directed to all her companions. Despite the disclaimer about how much she enjoyed listening to all the other messages, a single statement in her journal, set off in a paragraph of its own, conveys her true feelings. She wrote: "I didn't receive any message at this time."[48] Louise Buffum, a young bride at Fort Rae at the beginning of the Second World War, told a writer that during the Buffum's first Christmas there "it was thrilling to hear my mother speak to us from Winnipeg, but it made me homesick with the knowledge that we were so far apart.[49]

The group gathered at Cambridge Bay in 1938 were disappointed when their radio failed. The routine for messages had been standardized by this time: the Maritimes was heard from first, then Quebec came on the air, followed by Ontario messages. Friends received messages in turn. But on this occasion, when their host adjusted the volume of the radio, Toronto was lost. "I was sure that the whole world must know that our radio had faded at the most critical time," Anna Rokeby-Thomas recorded, and she waited in vain for a return to Toronto and her messages.[50] Winifred Marsh wrote from Eskimo Point in 1938 about the CBC broadcasts, pointing out that those in "the empire's outposts [were] privileged to hear mothers and dear ones speaking personally to their own sons and daughters and loved ones. It [was] intensely moving to hear each voice vibrant with emotion speaking some message straight from the heart."[51] Winifred Marsh was to begin another Christmas circular letter from Eskimo Point with: "Continuing the Empire Broadcast. This is Eskimo Point Calling," reminding her correspondents that "part of our Christmas we spend with you because we are members of the GREAT EMPIRE FAMILY. We did not hear the broadcast too well," she continued, "but we heard every word of the King's speech."[52] Her comment was an attempt to link distances too staggering to comprehend, but she understood that all her correspondents had heard the same broadcast.

It is evident that Mrs Marsh kept British customs in other ways for she continued her Christmas greetings by making "Eskimo Point's broadcast a little longer than most." She wanted to take her readers to a party given for both native and white children at Eskimo Point. This is how she described the 1938 Christmas Eve:

At 3.00 pm the school door burst open. The intense cold outside as it met the warm air of the schoolroom created a great inrushing fog, out of which emerged our little breathless and excited friends. By the time the fog had cleared tumbled hair was straightened, and a row of rather awestruck and shy children, stared and gaped and pointed at the decorations. Now, let me tell you what they saw. Down one side of the room we had a long table set ready for the approaching onslaught with jellies, buns, biscuits, puddings and tea. By the side of each plate was a gaily coloured paper hat. The whole of the room was festooned with green and red wood chip decorations. Father Christmas's sitting on paper balloons were hung from the ceiling. (You know the sort of thing made from concertiny paper.)

In order to facilitate the clearing of the table, we told the children to line up at the side of the room. My eyes were blindfolded and a huge assortment of lovely balloons was put into my hands. They really were glorious. Each child coming forward received a balloon which I drew from the bunch. (We did this [so] that there [would] be absolute fairness, as the balloons were of various shapes, colours and sizes.) Well! Really I thought that children "outside" loved balloons, but you can imagine what a thrill those kiddies got when they saw and handled them, some for the first time in their lives. The ages of the children ranged from 3 years to 12 years, while we had three mothers with babies. Now believe it or not! at the end of the party, every child's balloon remained intact.[53]

There were lots of games such as pin the tail on the donkey, hide-and-seek, and blind man's buff – games with little meaning to the guests. According to Mrs Marsh, musical bumps was popular because the deerskin pants worn by the children provided some padding, but it is more likely that the Inuit children could actually understand the point of the game. Each child received a parcel and a squeaker before they went home. The party itself came to an abrupt end when three children had violent nosebleeds, which Mrs Marsh noted was a common occurrence among the Inuit. Nevertheless, "it was a time of great happiness, of gleaming eyes and flushed laughing faces." In her letter, she thanked those who had sent the gifts and balloons from the south and remarked how "great and lovely was their share in making Christmas such a wonderful time" for their Inuit guests as well as themselves.[54]

The wonder and amusement of the children who were guests cannot be doubted. Winifred Marsh failed to explain however, what happened to the balloons when they left the warm, friendly atmosphere of the schoolroom for the frigid exterior blasts and the icy walls of snow houses, or the disappointment of the Inuit children startled by the bang of inevitably bursting balloons. It reveals more about Winifred Marsh than the children, for what she had arranged was a very secular event, more reminiscent of a European childhood party than a sacred Christian festival.

Anglican missionaries and those who left chronicles about their lives in the north throughout the early decades of the twentieth century depict Christmas in much the same way. Naturally, the exact shade of religious overtones depended on the target audience. But the goal was to replicate the European celebration, and everyone tried to make Christmas an event to remember. Mrs Rokeby-Thomas recorded in one of her stories how white residents in the north recycled Christmas cards received from the outside. However, not only the cards were reused, so too were the inhabitants' memories of the past. Such activities were important to their own ability to cope with Christmas in a remote region away from home.

Christmas at Fort Norman is 1881 was not an easy time for Augusta Morris. She faced not just loneliness but the very real prospect of never seeing home again. In her journal she wrote: "Christmas Day, 1881, Sunday. I am going to write an account of today, perhaps in a few years time, if I live. I may like to remember how I spent my first Christmas in the far north. I have been thinking a great deal of them all at home all day & also of dear Mary & Harry & I am longing very much to hear from them all."[55] She had slept late that morning and had to hurry. Instead of school lessons, Bishop Bompas gave the children a special address and Indian prayers followed. After a walk with Mrs Bompas, the mission family ate their Christmas meal – baked fish, cakes, and blueberry jam. Things were a little different the following year at Fort Simpson; her 1883 journal does not reflect the same melancholy and remorse about leaving her family. Bishop Bompas was away that year, but Selina Bompas woke Miss Morris with a tin of marmalade as a gift. Christmas dinner 1883 included beef sent from Fort Providence, followed by plum pudding. At both Fort Norman and Fort Simpson the Bompas mission celebrated New Year's Day with much more frivolity, including dancing.

At Peel River, Sadie Stringer wrote about the Christmas-week activities of 1896. It was the first year the Stringers spent at that remote post.

This week we had no school. We had singing practice with the white men for the Xmas carols and with the native children singing their hymns for Xmas. We had them sing in groups. Baked Xmas cakes and tarts. XMAS DAY. In the morning Mr Stringer had service with one hundred natives. The children sang the hymns we had practised with them. After service we gave them a treat consisting of biscuits and butter, raisin cake, caraway cake, tea and sugar, taffy and pop-corn. It was their first celebration of Xmas Day and they all seemed as though it were a Merry Christmas. Had English service at 2pm. Sermon by Mr Stringer. Christmas decorations were "Glory to God in the Highest on earth peace good will towards men." "Merry Christmas'" "Welcome" and "Happy New Year." In the evening, had a spread for the white men. Menu as follows: oysters, cold venison, cold fowl, pickles, cheese, bread, butter, tea, coffee, sugar, jelly tarts, mixed cakes, and two Christmas story cakes with icing. Afterwards we had a few addresses, recitations, and some singing.[56]

Note that sugar was listed as a separate item on both menus. Christmas was one of those special occasions when its generous usage was the rule.

Rose Spendlove spent Christmas at Holy Trinity Mission, Fort Norman, in 1902. Despite a devastating epidemic of measles in the Mackenzie River valley, Mrs Spendlove reported that the service was delightful and the Christmas celebrations were happy. As was the custom at that time, the Dene who gathered at the mission were provided with a "a good dinner of Arctic Region fare," with "plum pudding and plenty of tea. This, with the Christmas tree and gifts, well paid the Indians who had come long distances, on *snow shoes*, to hear the joyful news of our Saviour's birth."[57] A cynic might wonder if the Dene were being bribed to partake in the religious celebrations, or if the Christmas festival with all its trimmings was not being used as a focal point for the continuing process of conversion. In any case, the exchange was a fair one and both parties probably enjoyed themselves

At St Peter's Mission School in Hay River, Miss Frances Harvie wrote about the Christmas of 1917 in her annual report. It was a happy time for all at the school, she concluded, and although it was her first Christmas away from home, she declared it the happiest she had ever spent. At six in the morning the mission bells rang out to signal ten minutes of silent prayer. This was followed by visits to staff

members and an exchange of holiday greetings. Cards were distrib-
uted to all the children at breakfast, and Holy Communion was celebrated for the native congregation in the morning. Miss Harvie
explained further:

> Then the children look forward to candies being given them. This one
> day in the year, school and staff dine together, much to the delight of the
> children. After supper comes the event of the day, our Christmas tree.
> The little ones for weeks have been making presents to be put on this
> tree for the staff and others. Besides these are added toys sent in by
> friends outside, together with moccasins and mitts sent by parents to
> their children. The tree last year surpassed any I have seen outside. One
> of the builders of the school dressed up as Father Christmas and dis-
> tributed the toys and gifts. It was not until after the children were
> tucked safely in bed that we looked at our own presents and had light
> refreshments.[58]

Whether the Dene population of the Mackenzie Valley ever really
grasped the true meaning of Christmas is never addressed. It appears
from Miss Harvie's account that the indigenous residents had caught
on to the gift-giving aspect of the festival, although they were probably curious as to why such generosity was confined to a short period
of time during the winter solstice. Luta Munday thought that Christmas was a strange celebration for the Inuit at Chesterfield Inlet,
astutely noting the Roman Catholic Mission directed their conversion
attempts to the children of the community. Children were the ideal
constituency for all the festivities; if there was also a message to be
conveyed, it was easier to rationalize any excess.

Mrs Munday, who was not a missionary, focussed on the white residents when describing her first Christmas at Chesterfield Inlet. She
described a parcel arriving with the annual supplies marked "not to
be opened until Christmas." Since this is how all Christmas gifts
arrived from the south, Christmas spirit was in plain sight in small
cabins for over six months. Mrs Munday's parcel contained crimson
butterfly crackers, ultimately the only decoration at her table.
However, her guests were Roman Catholic priests who had never
seen such crackers – Mrs Munday implied that that indicated a
serious shortcoming in their life experience – yet "when [the crack-
ers] were pulled, the rhymes read, and the caps put on, we waxed
quite merry," she recalled. They ate plum pudding and enjoyed the
meat of two small caribou brought in the day before. This was the
first fresh meat they had enjoyed for some time, so Christmas was
extra special that year for the white residents of Chesterfield Inlet.[59]

Christmas at Shingle Point residential school off the Yukon coast meant enjoying the festivities on a desolate icebound spit. "It does not seem possible that tomorrow is Christmas Eve," wrote Priscilla Shepherd in 1929. "All snow, and ice, and quiet. No fuss. None of the world's celebrating." She added, ironically, "Up here one gets to know the real meaning of Christmas." At the darkest, loneliest part of the winter, all the Christmas trappings were removed from a box of cherished memories. Memories of happy childhood holidays were resurrected with no need for rationalization beyond the knowledge that Christmas meant food, fun, parties, paper hats, and gifts, all tied up with some basic Christian theology. The activity salved the home-sickness of the women, and provided some gaiety to counteract the more solemn daily lessons of a Christian-based education. For those charged with teaching the children, Christmas offered the opportunity to introduce different themes and to exercise the choirs with some purpose. Christmas added an element of excitement and expectation, which revitalized bored students and staff, and it explains the curious mix of religious and worldly symbolism at the Anglican mission school at Christmastime.

Miss Shepherd brightened up the quarters at Shingle Point that Christmas with bells and red ribbon, and the children anticipated Santa's arrival after a very short trip from the north Pole. The party included Inuit who had arrived for the occasion and who enjoyed native dances while feasting on caribou stew, raisins, mince pie, layer cake, bread and butter, candy, and nuts.[60] The following year, Reita Latham and the children decorated an artificial tree with ornaments, which made the schoolroom resemble "home." A choir consisting of boys and girls who could read English sang Christmas carols for the residents and native visitors. Santa Claus arrived with "a big red sack on his back. Santa's red outfit was very striking indeed," wrote Miss Latham in *Living Message*. And the children were delighted with their gifts. Although Christmas Eve was reserved for parties and fun at Shingle Point, Christmas Day was slightly more dignified. Church services and Holy Communion for visitors and staff were followed by a formal dinner. There, behaviour not normally encouraged was still evident.

There was a card at each child's place and candles were lighted when they came for breakfast. The dining-room looked so warm and cosy and they were all so jolly and happy – singing, playing mouth-organs, blowing horns, beating drums, etc. It was much like Christmas morning in any home, only we had a somewhat larger family than most. Christmas dinner was at the usual hour. The tables looked pretty with red crepe paper down the centre and a candle on a little card at each place. One candle was lit and then the others one after the other. The grown-ups were just as tickled with the procedure of lighting them as were the children.[61]

Addie Butler was at Shingle Point for Christmas of 1933. Her frank letters reveal holiday tensions between the staff, as well as difficulties apparently not encountered by the previous revellers.

All our Christmas presents for the children were those we had left over from last year, as the bales with this year's supply were on that boat that tried to get to Herschel Island in the summer, and hit the ice. We planned to have a Christmas concert on the Saturday evening, to get it over, but OLA (Our light affliction – the Principal!) could not find time to get the toys out of the warehouse for them to be allotted to the different children. At tea time on Saturday I was informed that the concert could not take place, but by dint of combined pressure, we made him get the box, and three of us went into the school and sorted toys, decorated and trimmed the tree, such as it was. It looked very nice, and almost like a real tree.

Mr Crowley, the man in charge of the reindeer drive, took the part of Santa Claus, the younger [children] could scarcely restrain themselves they were so excited. Outside the Mission House is a very high snowbank, and with his pack, Santa had much difficulty in getting along, in fact he fell down once, and when he got to our snow porch, which has become so filled in that it is not much wider than a tunnel, poor Santa stuck, and had to be rescued.[62]

The ironies in this tale are wonderful. Santa's reindeer obviously did not run with Mr Crowley's herd, and it is a pity the chimney was in use to keep everyone warm. The children at the school had been told to hang up stockings for the very first time and questioned how and why Santa Claus was coming back. "We had to play up to them," confessed Mrs Butler, "and make up some tale. For support, and local colour, we had the reindeer herd here, so they almost believed us – but not quite." The children had recognized Mr Crowley's jewelry and boots.[63]

A special caribou dinner was followed by gelatin desserts, which, noted Addie Butler, the children loved. This may have been because of the coolness; certainly the sweetness and jelly would have had the consistency and texture of the gelatinous substance found in bone marrow, with which the children were familiar. Candies, nuts, and fruit were left in the stockings, but because there was little to spare, the menu featured no extra goodies. By 1935, supplies must have been more plentiful. Ethel Hewer listed Christmas dinner items such as Christmas pudding and crackers with paper hats. The school was now better organized, which may account for these additions to the usual carols and Holy Communion. The Christmas Eve concert included a tableau of the Nativity – imagine Inuit children dressed in everything from long flannel trousers, woollen scarves, striped towels, dressing gowns, flowered chintz, and gold-covered cardboard. "A laundry basket filled with straw and hay, and a large gold and tinsel star completed" what Miss Hewer called an impressive little scene; she characterized it as quite an achievement for those Inuit children, who had "not seen acting of any kind beyond their own Native dances."[64] Of course, they had never seen a manger, shepherds' crooks, or golden crowns either, and probably had some difficulty with kings "from afar" (one of them being black). The program included recitations, songs and carols, and the arrival of Santa Claus with gifts for all.

Whether the Grey Nuns celebrated Christmas in their communities in the same way is difficult to ascertain. The first Christmas Eve Mass at Aklavik, celebrated in 1925, stands as the most detailed entry about Christmas made by the Sisters in any of the northern chronicles. The faithful were called to worship by a small chapel bell. Some "Protestants" from Fort McPherson attended, including the manager of the wireless office who sang the *Minuit Chretien* at the Mass. But the sisters were disappointed because no Inuit arrived, although many Dene came from Arctic Red River. During Holy Communion, about forty Inuit finally did join the group, but stayed only long enough to examine the crib; they left because the Anglican priest offered a service at midnight. On the surface, this description suggests a very ecumenical Christmas at Aklavik. However, the chronicles hint at the constant rivalry maintained by the two denominations, which festered even during the season of goodwill. The chronicler recorded that two (Anglican) ministers came to visit the Grey Nuns, but she decided it was more from curiosity than love. The Anglican missionaries presented the nuns with a box of chocolate and asked to see the decorated chapel.[65] Even if this was an olive branch extended for the traditional Christian reasons, the sisters were suspicious. It was in a later memoir that the real spirit of Christmas in the Roman Catholic hospital was revealed. When Isobel Hutchison passed through the settlement some years later, she noted that the nuns had decorated the hospital and the patients had received "wonderful breakfast trays and gifts."[66]

There is a footnote to Miss Hutchison's Christmas at Aklavik in 1933. She was invited to the home of Mary Rivett-Carnac for dinner. According to Isobel Hutchison, Inspector Rivett-Carnac and the

Mounties were dressed in their scarlet tunics, "so the absence of holly berries went quite unnoticed." Because the men were attired in dress uniform, Mrs Rivett-Carnac decided to wear an evening gown. As her husband recorded in his memoirs, the dress had been hanging in a cupboard in the lean-to where it had frozen to the wall. Undaunted by the peculiar northern complication, the hostess pried it loose from the wall and used a hot iron to restore it to its original condition.[67]

Evening gowns were not a useful item of clothing in the north; there were few gatherings where such garments were even remotely appropriate. So when an opportunity arose to wear their finery, some women seized it in an attempt to relieve the monotony and brighten up their lives. Archbishop Fleming was astonished, for example, to meet one trader's wife at a remote outpost wearing what he described as a dazzling pair of beach pyjamas.[68] The archbishop probably thought Mrs Douglas had dressed for his visit, but of course she had dressed for herself.

Acting as a hostess to visitors passing through represented the principal social obligation of white women residing in the north. Their homes operated as makeshift hostels to those in transit, delivering the mail, or making official journeys. This meant northern hospitality was personal and individual and strongly tied to a sense of responsibility. Being hostess at the government agency at Fort Simpson where her husband was in charge was a full-time job wrote Annie Card; there were many visitors who travelled along the river from settlement to settlement.[69] When oil was discovered at Fort Norman in 1921, Mrs Vale noted that Hay River had become a lively place: travellers had been arriving all winter by dog team, and during most of the winter strangers had passed through for meals. Accommodating the travellers took a great deal of time, but she noted that the residents were pleased to do so. Visitors, no matter how important or insignificant, were always welcome to sleep on a kitchen floor and share a meal.[70]

Restricted access to the region meant that growth of the white population was controlled, limited, and slow. It was not until Yellowknife was established as a mining community in the late 1930s that a social pecking order of some significance emerged in the NWT. This mining settlement with its transient population distinguished the Yellowknife of the 1930s from that of earlier settlements; the influx of white families changed the pattern of previous immigration. Richard Finnie explained that mine official's wives were at the top of the social ladder, they hobnobbed with no one else. Aviator's wives came next, then an intermediate class composed of businessmen's wives. In response to men's fraternal groups, these women formed an organization that called itself the Order of the DMS. Curious men were deliberately misled to believe the acronym meant Death, Murder, and Suicide, although, in truth, it meant Daughters of the Midnight Sun. At the bottom of the Yellowknife social ladder were the women who called themselves laundresses and seamstresses, and Finnie concluded that some of them were really just that.[71]

The northern equivalents of social rituals were shaped by necessity, the environment, and isolation, and the women were happy just to have congenial companions and news from outside their own settlement. An excess of socializing occurred in the northern settlements when the supply ship arrived. There were visitors to greet and supplies enough for a feast. When the ship moved on, supplies were more limited and guests were few so the scale of entertaining was humble. The one notable exception to this pattern was among the whalers out of San Francisco and can be explained by the nature of the social group itself. Not only were the whaling ships and their crews largely independent of any Canadian intrusion into the region, they had a hierarchy all their own. Within the fleet, parties and dances were held on the whaling ships wintered at Herschel Island. In the log of the steam bark *Jesse H Freeman*, Sophie Porter recorded a number of gatherings. Staged on any excuse, they featured "old fogies" playing whist, while the wives and families of ship's captains square danced, entertained by minstrel troupes formed from among the crews.

Mrs Porter described how at one party held in 1895, the deckhouse of the ship was decorated with lights and bunting, and the room was partitioned with flags. The icebound ships provided a captive audience as well as participants. During one winter, there were at least six or seven American families on board the whalers. Instead of serving as the means by which the American women played out cultural games to establish a social hierarchy, these events took place more to keep every one busy when work was not possible.[72]

Generally though, Arctic society was dull. Some elements of entertaining may still have been *de riguer*, but truly, in the north no one really cared. While Beatrice Mason wrote that no social function in the north was complete without a "quota of red-coated Mounties," she also admitted that at Rampart House "there was no society for the Mounties to adorn."[73]

CHAPTER THREE

"Speaking of Me and Franklin": Women Travellers in the Arctic

Victorian and Edwardian women who explored the north were members of a unique sisterhood, privileged because they could afford the journey to see parts of the world about which most could only dream. Women travellers published works describing their journeys into the jungles, mountains, and deserts of the world. They may have had the same purpose as their male counterparts, but what they saw and recorded was often different. On her journey north in 1908, Agnes Deans Cameron explained the difference in attitude, by suggesting that "a man who goes North to see rocks, sees little else; the bug hunter looks for bugs, and the oil prospector keeps his eye on the ground for cosy exuditions. But a person who goes as Kipling went through his slice of the empire, just a greedily impressionable bit of blotting paper, will surely soak up impressions that passed the others by."[1]

There has been renewed interest in the enormous body of work produced by Victorian and Edwardian women travellers – Jane Robinson's *Wayward Women: A Guide to Women Travellers*, for example, introduces hundreds of these travellers and their remarkable stories to those who might doubt the extent of the genre. For historians, these travel writings offer a valuable resource for salient detail and for understanding social relations and change over time.[2] Agnes Deans Cameron, Elizabeth Taylor, Emma Shaw Colcleugh, and Lady Clara Rogers all travelled in the Western Arctic, but they have remained relatively anonymous to historians who have studied the region. The account that follows seeks primarily to place these women into the recorded history of Canada's north.

In 1908, Agnes Deans Cameron, a forty-four-year-old spinster from Victoria, set off on an adventure down the Mackenzie River to Aklavik. She was accompanied by her niece Jessie Cameron Brown.

They had planned their trip along a "route unspoiled by Cook's"[3]; that is, one defined by the absence of a resort destination or package tour. In their minds, it was the adventure that separated them from the mere tourists out to enjoy the sights, although the sights were an integral part of the adventure. Miss Cameron was intent upon discovering the magic of the world she entered, as well as the tragedies and hardships endured by its residents.

Despite their stated desire for an unorganized plan, the women approached the Chicago office of Thos Cook's & Sons to arrange a trip to the Northwest Territories. Cook's, not surprisingly, was unable to help and could only refer the women to the HBC at Winnipeg, which according to Agnes Cameron had been "the Foster-Mother to Canada's Northland for 239 years." She might well have added that without the HBC, it is unlikely that any traveller, female or male, could have made the journey. The Company planned the journey, gave the women introductions to post factors, and sold them an outfit. The HBC also supplied a letter of credit, which could be "transmuted into bacon, beans and blankets, sturgeon head boats, guides' services, and succulent sow belly at any point between Fort Chimo and Hudson's Hope-on-the-Peace, between Winnipeg and Herschel."[4]

Agnes Cameron and Jessie Brown were not the first female travellers in the region. Sixteen years earlier, Elizabeth Taylor had undertaken a similar journey into the north, although as she pointed out in 1892, "as a rule, one didn't 'go in'. One most emphatically stayed out,"[5] particularly if one was a white middle-class woman, even one with connections. Elizabeth Taylor was the last of five daughters of James Wickes Taylor, an American expansionist and United States Consul in Winnipeg. As an art student in Paris in the early 1890s, she had been encouraged to make a northern journey by the young Ernest Thompson Seton, who himself planned an Arctic expedition. Originally, Miss Taylor had envisioned a trip to the Peace River area; but after those plans collapsed, she prepared to make her voyage down the Mackenzie in a "queer little steamboat"[6] that plied the river for the HBC. She had high expectations for her tour and wrote to a friend in St Paul, Minnesota: "Helen, I am going to be an Arctic explorer. If I carry out my plans I can next year be able [sic] to speak of Me and Franklin – for I am going to the Arctic Ocean. Think of it Helen, going to the land of the midnight sun within the Arctic Circle."[7]

Two years later, another American woman made the trip north. Emma Shaw Colcleugh's trip included parts of the Peace River journey denied to Elizabeth Taylor, although the *Manitoba Free Press* apparently had forgotten the first "intrepid traveller" with Winnipeg connections and erroneously reported that Mrs Colcleugh was the first white woman to go "summering and sight-seeing in unfrequented districts, so far from civilization."[8] The forty-eight-year-old Mrs Colcleugh was a Rhode Island schoolteacher and journalist who had married Manitoba politician Frederick Colcleugh in 1893.[9] The marriage gained Emma Colcleugh entry into Winnipeg society, which included the officers of the HBC, and as she later explained, passage was arranged as a personal favour of C.C. Chipman, chief officer of the Company. She was to travel with the annual supply expedition. Already an experienced traveller by 1894, Emma Colcleugh had braved Lake Superior and the Saskatchewan River. But like Elizabeth Taylor before her, she only began to understand the sheer enormity of what lay ahead as she proceeded north on the first leg of the tour. She later reported that at the first camp she "felt so remote from civilization, so much as if I had cut loose from all my former world; before me long leagues of untrodden lands, 'Into the North' had, in those few lonely moments, a power of meaning I had never dreamed."[10]

In 1926, Clara Rogers[11] and her friend Gwen Dorrien Smith travelled with the HBC down the Mackenzie, and then further on a harrowing journey by canoe along the Rat and Porcupine rivers to the Yukon and Alaska. Travel conditions in the region had not changed significantly since Agnes Cameron's trip in 1908. By 1926, the steamer was a little larger and the facilities along the way were less primitive. But Miss Rogers was later to describe it as "the most formidable enterprise," yet "the high peak of her life."[12]

Clara Rogers's plans to travel in the NWT were made more difficult by a cynical and decidedly negative family. At the same time, the trip was made easier through the intervention of a friendly neighbour who, by happy circumstance, was a director of the HBC. Leonard Cunliffe encouraged the women and acted as intermediary between them and the HBC carriers, whose officers eventually proposed $675 as the cost of a trip to Fort Yukon via Peel River and La Pierre House. Travel time was estimated at fifty days.[13] The eventual route was decided partly because La Pierre House and the Rat and Porcupine rivers could be found on maps in Clara Rogers's atlas, creating the illusion of a settlement and supply post; in truth there was but one deserted cabin.

The journeys all had the co-operation of the HBC, the only viable transportation authority in the area. More importantly, all four eventually published accounts of their adventures, with the specific intent of informing armchair travellers fascinated by the remoteness and romance of the north.[14] Since Mrs Colcleugh, Miss Taylor, and Miss Rogers also published works about other travel, their northern accounts were part of their expanding world view.[15] But the northern stories stand alone as observations about the region in various stages of immigration and development. They also act as benchmarks, mapping the changes and, significantly, the lack of change, in the north.

Elizabeth Taylor's narrative, which appeared in a four-part series in *Outing* in 1894–95 entitled "A Woman Explorer in the Mackenzie Delta," was illustrated with her own pen-and-ink drawings.[16] An item in *Travel* of 1899 was a shorter version of that piece. Some of the correspondence relating to the plans for Elizabeth Taylor's trip has survived, in addition to her published work; these letters suggest some of the obstacles she had to overcome in order to make the journey.

Miss Taylor expected her father to approve the expedition because the trip had been proposed by one of his friends in place of the Peace River course. Although a Mackenzie trip was apparently cheaper, easier, and more pleasant, Miss Taylor chose to interpret the trip as described by the HBC as the more trifling of the two. Despite her optimism, James Taylor was not entirely happy about this excursion; he expressed his doubts to Donald Smith in Montreal, suggesting that any aid that the Governor of the Company or the Commissioner in Winnipeg could extend would be appreciated. Between the lines, he intimated that outright rejection would be welcome.[17] Smith had reservations even though he offered every assistance. The proposed expedition "would greatly tax the endurance of a lady," he wrote, "and notwithstanding all the efforts the HBC officers and employees would make, it could be an undertaking of great hazard to her health."[18] How much control James Taylor had over his thirty-six-year-old daughter is unclear. Whatever reins he held, financial or otherwise, he failed to discourage her. She continued to make plans from Paris, and then London, in the spring of 1892.[19]

Miss Taylor's plans included the collection of scientific specimens – for some future consideration and with an eye to turning herself into a "far-seeing woman of business." Wise friends advised Taylor to take along a revolver and insisted that she knew how to use it, even though she confessed to one correspondent that she was more afraid of a handgun than she was of "Indians and Grizzly Bears." Her friends had told her that the "moral suasion of a revolver was wonderful" and that just the knowledge she had one would bolster her confidence,[20] a not inconsequential piece of advice after queries such as the one she recalled from a London scientist, who asked her what enemies she expected to encounter. He told her about savage tribes and drew a "touching picture" of her being murdered in her sleep "for the whiskey needed to preserve her specimens."[21]

Miss Taylor assured her father that she would employ a female companion when she began the northern leg of the trip. She told him that although she felt she would be safe enough on the boat, she might be far less independent without someone to perform light duties such as laundry, to carry her sketching materials, or to provide comfort and possibly act as a nurse if required. "Another lady wouldn't do" she told him; and she would prefer a "half-breed" who knew something of camp life – and presumably would not be afraid, or become a hindrance along the route. She would hire the woman at Edmonton or at some point along the way north she proposed, so she would not have to pay her expenses from Winnipeg.[22] If Elizabeth Taylor secured the services of a female companion, her diary and subsequent publications make no mention of one, although it is significant that to explore the Arctic like Franklin, she needed someone to help her with her laundry. This betrays not so much a weakness, as an understanding of her position as a lady and the proprieties of the age: that even in the rugged and primitive conditions of the north, she herself, her father, and everyone else, expected her to act as such. As she departed from Edmonton, Miss Taylor wrote to her friend Helen Carver that people who knew the region had tried to be encouraging about what lay ahead. Nevertheless, well wishers supposed that while her summer might be interesting, it would also be unpleasant. Supplied with bottled and personal spirits, and despite everyone's concerns, Elizabeth Taylor set off from Edmonton at the end of May.

Miss Taylor took pains to describe the scenery to her readers, as well as the perils of travel in freight canoes and on supply barges. She was fascinated with the men of the boat brigades who, for her, were "always a diversion. They would make some great exertion such as lowering the boat through the rapids and then they would fall down in picturesque attitudes and smoke and look off at the water in a dreamy way, while one of them would tell an anecdote with great dramatic fervour, and wild gesticulation."[23]

Scattered throughout the *Outing* articles are drawings depicting many of these men who manned the sturgeon-head boats, which she described as something between a scow and a York boat. At the time of Elizabeth Taylor's trip, sturgeon-head boats operated on that segment of the trip north along the Sturgeon River. The boats had blunt, rounded bows and were built to withstand the shock of the Grand Rapids. Carrying ten tons of goods, they were manned by eight rowers and a steersman who guided the vessel by a long sweep fastened to the stern post by an iron ring. Passengers sat in a clear space on either side of the sweep. Having ferried passengers and freight as far as Fort McMurray, the sturgeon-head boats gave way to the HBC steamer *Grahame*, which navigated the Athabasca River to Smith Landing. At Smith Landing, wagons pulled by oxen carried the *Grahame's* load across a difficult sixteen-mile portage, and Miss Taylor recalled how on the day she travelled across the portage "the road lay through alternating stretches of marshy and sandy pine-land. There were deep, patchy holes, roughly bridged over by loose saplings, over and between which the oxen slipped and plunged, scattering the black mud over us, while the rough carts swayed and creaked, and the half-breeds shouted. The air was heavy with the fragrance of wild flowers; but the mud-holes and submerged parts of the road made it impossible for [me] to follow on foot."[24]

The HBC supply ship *Wrigley* left on its journey down north from Fort Smith with all the cargo piled on deck, leaving little room for passengers. The *Wrigley*, first and foremost a supply vessel for the HBC, was not designed for sightseers or officials on tour. Six diners seated at the table in the boxlike, windowless dining room filled the room. At night, one missionary slept on top of the table, while another bunked underneath. Miss Taylor's room was furnished with a sack of hay.[25] Launched in 1885, the *Wrigley* enjoyed the distinction of being the first steam-propelled vessel ever to cross the Arctic Circle.

The Arctic Circle, one of the northern features that captured everyone's imagination, was the object of fascinating illusions, probably because travelling across it was so far beyond the reach of all but a lucky few. When Elizabeth Taylor crossed the Arctic Circle in 1892, her childhood image was shattered. She had "always imagined a large shining wire, about three times the size of a telegraph wire, suspended in the air, without visible support, perhaps five feet from the ground and disappearing across a barren waste, with musk oxen and reindeer in the dim distance rubbing their ears against it. When the place where that shining circle should have been was pointed out, [she] was disappointed."[26] One aspect of the journey was not a disappointment, however. The treasures she found in the woods were "enough to repay one for the effort." At Peel River, the delighted collector found "cranberries and cloudberries, Andromeda, and lychnis, the pretty yellow flowers of the lousewort, the large white buckbean by the edge of a pond, large northern yellow lilies in the water, shrubby cinque-foil, marsh ragwort, and Siberian asters, two kinds of orchids, the marsh marigold in seed, the fragrant pink and white flowers of the valerian, and the lady smock, all silver white. Dainty pink and white vetches and the bishop's cap were here too, growing high and rank."[27] And this was only one of many flower-picking expeditions. Previous walks had produced up to twenty-five specimens at a time. But there was a downside to the natural history of the north Miss Taylor discovered, for "an enemy lurked" in most areas along the riverbank, the "permanent camp from which the blood-thirsty mosquito regiments ferociously sallied forth."[28]

Elizabeth Taylor interrupted her observations about the flora of the Mackenzie Valley to comment on certain societal conventions that seemed strange to her, but which, she felt, were dictated by the uniqueness of northern conditions. In a description of the Sunday service at the camp at Fort Smith where she awaited the *Wrigley*, she revealed: "I am not quite clear in my mind as to the etiquette of a camp church. It is allowable, it seems, on breezy days to chase hats and fly-away hymn books; also to flap at mosquitoes, if it is done without too much emphasis and with no exclamations. But – may a natural history student grab at a butterfly fluttering close by or tie up a beetle in the corner of a handkerchief? Then as to shying sticks at Indian dogs – well that seems to be without objection, if only those at a certain distance from the clergyman indulge in it. The people within five or six feet of him must keep quiet, even if the dog is sniffing at the bacon box."[29] She added that one northern missionary had told her that during a service he had snatched up his gun in the middle of prayers to shoot at a flock of geese overhead. He defended this as an instinctive action, his wife and children being literally without food at the time.[30]

In "A Woman Explorer in the Mackenzie Delta," snippets of northern history – usually relating to individual settlements, or to explorations and tales of white man's heroism in opening up the north for the fur trade – are sprinkled among commentaries detailing scenery and plant life. While these episodes provided context for Miss Taylor's readers, it is her characterizations of the Dene people that are the most valuable of her remarks. With the exception of a few letters from missionaries, Elizabeth Taylor was the first white woman to publish her observations about the Dene and Inuit who inhabited the region. Her portrayals demonstrate a curiosity, reflecting her artistic eye as well as the scrutiny of an anthropological explorer (one of the many roles she had assigned herself). She noted how the coastal Loucheux[31] had a peculiar habit of gradually raising their voices until the sound reached an ear-splitting shout. Apparently the more important the matter discussed, the louder the howl. Consequently, appeals for tobacco and tea, which the Loucheux considered a necessity, were conducted at the top of their voices.[32] Also described and illustrated was an Inuit dance Miss Taylor enjoyed at Peel River, where, in honour of the occasion, the men wore their best clothes and the women had their dresses turned inside out to reveal the cleanest side. Her comments failed to explore the implication that the men had "best" clothes, while the women made do with the inside of their everyday garments. Such observations are interesting if only because it was the women who sewed the skins for the men in the first place.

Miss Taylor noted that the singing that accompanied the dance, patterned after the "usual Indian chant," was in fact, more musical and varied. Five or six flat drums made of sealskin were beaten with a flat stick. "First one man leaped into the middle of the circle, then a woman followed him, and they went through a pantomime, advancing and retreating, waving one another away with scorn and horror, and then becoming appeased, then friendly; at last they retired and others took their places, while all those remaining beat upon the drums and sang at the top of their voices."[33] Although the description suggests that the dance had sexual undertones, Miss Taylor made no attempt at interpretation. Perhaps *Outing* was not the place to comment on Inuit mating rituals, or perhaps Miss Taylor felt uncomfortable divulging her observations. It could also be that she was not a woman of the world and had failed to notice the significance of the dancer's actions.

Elizabeth Taylor decided that the Mackenzie River Inuit she encountered at Peel River were more warlike, suspicious, and treacherous than those from east and west of the Delta. They came only once a year to the post to trade, she explained, so their dress and customs were less affected than other Aboriginals by the white man's intrusions. While she found them to be agreeable in nature, their method of preparing skins for clothing caused what she characterized as an intolerable odour, which clung to everything they possessed.[34]

Despite the ferocious appearance of the local men, it was the land itself that eventually frightened Elizabeth Taylor. The stillness of summer days, the constant light, the sleepless nights – these only intensified the physical strains of travelling and the steady diet of dried meat. On one of her specimen-collecting walks she was overcome by loneliness. With the exception of a few moths, there was no other sign of life. Seized with panic, she hurried back to the mission.

The same vastness and the emptiness of the region overwhelmed Emma Shaw Colcleugh as well on her 1894 trip down the Mackenzie and along the Peace rivers. Mrs Colcleugh's northern travelogue, less extensive than those of the other travellers, makes up just one part of a nineteen-segment series entitled "I Saw These Things," published in the Rhode Island *Evening Bulletin* in 1932.[35] Shortly after her trip, Mrs Colcleugh also wrote an item for the *Catholic World* depicting the missionaries and nuns she had met along the Mackenzie River route.[36] Emma Colcleugh was not the only white woman on her voyage north. Sarah Camsell, the mixed-blood wife of the Chief Factor of the HBC who enjoyed some social status, joined her husband on one part of the trip, as did Miss Thompson travelling to an Anglican mission school. For another stretch, the daughter of Captain Segers of the *Wrigley* was a pleasant companion, although Mrs Colcleugh was considered the sole passenger. The company was appreciated, especially as she had to learn the northern lesson that "hurry up and wait" was often the order of the day. Interminable waits did allow time for real outdoor adventure, however. At Smith Landing, where she had time to explore, she decided the Dene camped there were the "nastiest savages" she had ever seen. These observations only added to the stereotype, of course, reflecting Mrs Colcleugh's inability to see that rough exteriors resulted from a coarse life and the crude existence provided by local conditions. She was able to stay relatively clear of the locals, and was more horrified at the "monstrous louse" found on Miss Seger's clothing upon their return to the steamer. She wrote "I have felt itchy ever since and have retired into seclusion and instituted several vigorous searches but with no result."[37]

At Peel River, she and Mrs Camsell visited some Inuit. Mrs Colcleugh noted the unusual opportunity the two white women had of seeing themselves as others saw them, and realized that they were the ones who were unique in that environment. Mention of the Dene at Fort Smith was rare in her published accounts, although northern Aboriginals did not go unnoticed in her letters. She wrote from the Peace River region that within three hundred miles not a single inhabited house or teepee had been sighted, and only three deserted ones had been seen. Her conclusion was that the Aboriginals of the north were "vanishing off the face of the earth,"[38] although the empty camps may simply have been a reflection of a nomadic existence. While she was more concerned with ethnographic collections, Emma Colcleugh, like Elizabeth Taylor, collected samples of vegetation. She admitted that the variety and luxuriance of the flowers along the banks drew her attention more than the Inuit she encountered. She had little to say about the premier pest of the north – the mosquito – except in a letter home where she commented on the question of an acquaintance "who knew a little of the locality" and had wondered whether she preferred to eat seal flippers in a snow house or smoke a peace pipe in a teepee. The intrepid explorer was firm in her reply: the skin teepee was the best bet, and she envied the "gentlemen their smoke to drive away the mosquitoes." At one point, she recalled, she thought she might "go frantic" from the insect attacks.[39]

Of her travels on the *Wrigley*, Emma Colcleugh had little to say except that the eighty-three-foot vessel rode the mountainous waves of the Great Slave Lake with courage, and sailed bravely through the rapids of the Mackenzie. She noted that every available space was taken up by cargo, which caused her to reflect on how "much depended on the safety of that boat and its cargo, including as it did the year's supplies for all those far away posts." At the time, her experience at Grand Rapids on the sturgeon-head boat was the high-light of her journey, but she subsequently characterized her anticipa-tion of the excitement as inexcusable stupidity, for she recognized the danger of the rapids that "rushed, whirled, shot and defiled, while about us curled and twisted the smooth green hollowing curves of great whirlpools, dashing chutes, foaming cascades, dangerous eddies – every kind of angry vagary in which water could possibly indulge."[40]

Mrs Colcleugh had told the Edmonton *Bulletin* that the object of her journey was to visit unknown and wild regions so she could delight the stay-at-homes who would read her descriptions.[41] On her return to Winnipeg, Emma Colcleugh told a *Manitoba Free Press* reporter that she had only one regret: she could not spend the winter at Fort McPherson.[42] If she had, her view of the north and its splen-dours might have changed. Her memory of the "hot sun and contin-uous daylight of the summer" might have been cooled by the cold wind and desolation of winter.

Just like Elizabeth Taylor before her, Emma Shaw Colcleugh simply faded from public memory and the recorded history of the north,[43] which accounts for Agnes Deans Cameron's announcement to the Royal Geographical Society in February of 1910 that her journey "between ice and ice" was the first time the distance had been traversed in any one season by any one traveller.[44] Cameron's expedition in 1908 was more extensive than Emma Colcleugh's because it included the Lesser Slave Lake region of Alberta. Except for this extension, however, her route was much the same as that of Emma Colcleugh.

Miss Cameron had been a school teacher and principal in Victoria, British Columbia, before she lost her job because of a number of issues relating to her controversial views on education policy and procedures. She turned to journalism as a means of support,[45] leaving Victoria to live in Chicago, where she worked with the Western Canadian Immigration Association. At that time she was also a vice-president of the Canadian Women's Press Club.[46] Although she claimed to have made the journey just for fun, Agnes Cameron's northern expedition was undertaken as a fact-finding tour designed to increase interest in expansion into the Canadian northwest. Unlike the previous travellers, Miss Cameron was as concerned with education, agricultural potential, government issues, and treaty entitlements as she was with the Dene, the Inuit, and the vegetation.

In some ways, *The New North*, the published account of Agnes Deans Cameron's trip, poses a challenge to the modern reader.[47] The Victorian style, which makes it difficult to separate bombast from useful fact, makes her seem a little more eccentric than she probably was. This may account for an Anglican missionary's comment in a letter from Fort McPherson that portrayed Cameron as a "vigorous romanticist, gathering data for a vivid volume, an intricate compound of fact and fiction, a most interesting and readable romance of travel to be sure, but hardly a reliable book for reference."[48] These comments may have been a reaction to the outspoken and independent female outsider, and in *The New North* Miss Cameron did not spare the mission schools. She wondered, for instance, why the missionary at Smith Landing was teaching "present worth and compound interest to bare-footed, half-Cree urchins."[49] In photographs, Agnes Cameron appears sturdy (almost dauntless), although she felt two years of life in Chicago had made her soft. Yet on this trip she was to trudge through the muck on the Athabasca Trail and attempt to match giant steps with a Northwest Mounted Policeman in order to hear his stirring tales.

Like Miss Taylor and Mrs Colcleugh before her, Agnes Cameron spent some time camped out along the route waiting for various conveyances to take her the next leg of the trip. The familiar tale of waiting for the boat had not changed, even though a new HBC Fur Trade Commissioner had tried to impose an orderly schedule on the northward traffic. The Cree boatmen knew otherwise, for as Miss Cameron explained: "the river was the boss." The keynote of the boatmen's character derived from this knowledge; their attitude was *Kee-am,* meaning "never mind, don't get excited, there's plenty of time, it will all come out in the wash."[50] Either Agnes Cameron was patient from the outset, or she had begun to adopt the same attitude as the boatmen by the time she and Miss Brown reached Fort Smith. Her acceptance is evident in her description of their room in the evening when it rained: it became "a living illustration of the new word [they had] just learned – 'muskeg.' Putting precious cameras on top of the bureau," Cameron "let the rest of the things swim at their pleasure."[51]

At Fort Smith, Jessie Brown and Agnes Cameron were assigned a double cabin on the newly launched *Mackenzie River*. The vessel was half again the size of the *Wrigley* and able to travel at up to ten miles an hour. The boat's unique feature was a steel-reinforced hull designed to withstand ice and floating timber. In addition, the *Mackenzie River* had five watertight compartments to make travel safer for both cargo and the passengers who occupied the twenty-two staterooms.

While they waited for the *Mackenzie River* to take them north, the women were struck by the abundant flora. As they brought in their "daily treasure trove of flowers," recalled Miss Cameron, "we [could] scarcely realize that at Fort Smith, we were in latitude sixty degrees North." As she put it: "One day we gathered careopsis, pretty painted-cups, the dandelion in seed, shinleaf yarrow and golden-rod. Another day brought to the blotting pads great bunches of golden-rod, pink anenome, harebells of a more delicate blue than we have ever seen before, wolf-berry, fireweed and ladies tresses. We identi-fied bear-berry or kinnikini tobacco with its astringent leaves, and pink lady-slippers."[52] The lush vegetation at latitude sixty degrees north, however, did not impress Miss Cameron as much as that momentous point at Fort Good Hope which was located at "the Arctic Circle! When we used to sit on uneasy school-benches and say our 'joggafy' lesson, what did it say for us? Icebergs, polar bears, and the snows of eternal winter. Nine-tenths of the people in America today share the same idea, think of it as a forbidding place, a frozen silence where human beings seldom penetrate."[53] What astonished the women was not so much the concept of the Arctic Circle, but that they crossed the latitude at midnight, and saw on the horizon "the Midnight Sun!" whose "supreme marvel" was "not what we see but what we feel."[54]

Further north at Fort McPherson, Miss Cameron was piqued by the first Inuit she encountered aboard the *Mackenzie River*. She wrote with some passion about the integrity, versatility, and intelligence of these people, suggesting that the Inuit were worthwhile although the world had conspired to libel them; but she concluded that within a decade or two, the Inuit would have "passed utterly off the map."[55] The observations reflect such tremendous ethnocentrism it is difficult to separate fact, fantasy, and Agnes Cameron's expansionist propa-ganda. Having asked herself where the Eskimo gets his versatile ability, she replied "only the walrus knows"[56] and after a lengthy treatise about religious customs in which she decided Inuit were not heathen, she cautioned that "we arrogate to ourselves the term of 'white race' but if these Eskimo were to wash themselves daily (which they do not do yearly) they would be as white as we are." She observed that the Inuit were neither rude, nor unthinking and believed that they had a well-formed conception of a Great Spirit as well as an Evil One.[57] Although Agnes Cameron may have been trying to convince *herself* that the Inuit were not as bad as she had feared, her argument was directed towards those who saw the Inuit and their reputation for savagery as a deterrent to expansion in the north.

Miss Cameron examined all aspects of Inuit life, but she wrote extensively about the Inuit women. She judged them to be "neither petulant or morose," which was interesting considering the women's circumstances. The feminist side of Agnes Cameron knew that the lot of native women in the north was not promising and that in their society, they were fated to play a secondary role in the family. Miss Cameron questioned what pleasure life could hold for these women; even from infancy she contended, "boy babies, even the dogs," had the choicest places to sleep and the best pieces of meat to eat. Conversely, little girls were made to feel that they had come into a world where there was no welcome for them, and their whole life seemed to be an apology.[58] Agnes Cameron faced a conundrum when her personal ideology came face to face with the reality of northern existence. While on the one hand she knew that women were unequal participants in that society, on the other, she demonstrated an understanding of the reasons. "The fact that the women prefer a vulgar-fraction of a man, an Eskimo equity in connubial bliss, to spearing walrus on their own account is a significant factor in the problem of Eskimo men taking more than one wife," acknowledged Miss Cameron.[59] She then explained in terms her southern readers could understand that there were no "want columns North of sixty-eight degrees where unappropriated spinsters may become self-support-ing wage-earners as chaste school-teachers, Marcel-wavers or mani-curists, [and] economically an [Eskimo] woman must herself hunt or have a man or part of a man hunt for her. Ethically, it works out beau-tifully, for each partner to the hymeneal bargain is fat and full of content, happiness fairly oozing out of every pore."[60] Agnes Cameron did conclude that she would not like to picture the Inuit woman as being always content with "a circulating decimal of a husband instead of a whole unit." But for the young second wife, she judged "no suffragette need break a lance for her, demanding a ballot, dower rights, and the rest of it, because she is happy and busy. She plays deference to her co-wife" and "expands like an anemone under the ardent smile of her lord."[61] Given her descriptions of the Inuit as intelligent and remarkably adaptable, it is unclear whether Agnes Cameron had simply dismissed the problem of inequity, based on what she saw as a "primitive" culture yet to evolve to the stage where suffragism and equal rights would improve conditions for women. It would be more appropriate, and considerate, to conclude that the ardent feminist explorer was intelligent enough to realize that the imposition of her southern, gender-based ideals was unjustified.

Her concern for what she called "ice-widows" in the region was an attempt to understand both sides of the cultural issues. She reported that these women who married whalers for a single hunting season were not outcasts amongst their own people, offering by way of explanation that the matrimonial standards of Pall Mall and Washington, DC, could not be applied in the north. She defended those Inuit women who had cohabited with white men because the latter were revered by their Inuit families. These women gained knowledge useful for trading, which was of some financial value to an Inuit husband. More importantly, the tent, the cooking equipment, and the other utensils she often acquired from the whaler were valuable as a dowry. Just because she could rationalize this practice does not mean Agnes Cameron accepted it, however, and she confessed "this state of things startles one, as all miscegenation does."[62]

While she was disturbed by what she saw as strange customs at odds with her own values, Agnes Cameron was able to grasp that situations in the north were different. She acknowledged, for example, that "if a white woman were to be shipwrecked and thrown upon an Eskimo foreshore and presenting herself at a Husky employment bureau, many surprises would await her. Instead of asking for references from her last employer, the general proprietor would first ask to inspect her teeth."[63] She also questioned the "intrusion of whites," which had "changed the whole horizon" in the north. This was not so much the coming of civilization, she commented astutely but rather the coming of commerce. Seeing agricultural development and settlement as more 'civilizing' than trading and whaling, Miss Cameron adopted the accepted notion that farms and families were a stabilizing influence. She was convinced that the possibilities for agrarian pursuits were extensive. This may have been wishful thinking.

On a lecture tour of Britain, Miss Cameron proudly showed slides of wild flax in bloom well inside the Arctic Circle; she also told of potatoes, turnips, carrots, and parsnips cultivated at Fort Good Hope. What she missed by not being an agricultural specialist and at that, only a one-time visitor, was the unreliability of crops as recorded in annual accounts of those resident in the region. If there is a single failing of the traveller's accounts as documentary evidence, it is that in the north, the realities of the harsh environment cannot be judged by a three-month summer journey when the beauty of the landscape can be seen at its best. Of course, some people believed that summer trips allowed them to see the north at its worst – but there were only two seasons: winter and mosquito.

Dealing with mosquitoes required a constant effort, and the Misses Cameron and Brown maintained the pest was worse along the first part of the northern journey, that is, before reaching the Mackenzie River. At this stage the women tried all manner of ways to gain some relief. At Grand Rapids, for example, Agnes Cameron and Jessie Brown went to bed fully clothed and covered. But to no avail. Miss Cameron posited that mosquitoes were Presbyterian, each determined to taste blood. Nighttime became the "first serious trial to good humour, when each of your four million pores is an irritation-channel of mosquito virus. But, the sun and smiles come out at the same time, and having bled together, we cement bonds of friendship."[64]

Because Clara Rogers and Gwen Dorrien Smith travelled more in the bush than the other women, their descriptions of constant encounters with mosquitoes are more detailed, even frightening. Clara Rogers saw the mosquitoes as devilish; at "times, the whole world seemed to be buzzing blackness." The women confessed they had to struggle to prevent being seized by panic, and admitted to the "incredible delusion that perpetual movement meant escape." To get dressed under a mosquito net was difficult but not impossible. Although the women slept in their clothes, "it required a gymnastic effort, and as for doing one's hair, it gave one a frightful crick in the neck." At dinnertime, their mosquito veils were lifelines, as they "munched on bacon scraping away with forks [those] that had settled on the fat and [become] embedded in it." The pests came at them "one wave after another, like Napoleon's inexhaustible attacking armies."[65]

Arctic Adventure was published in 1961,[66] written from notes in a diary kept during the 1926 journey made by Clara Rogers and her companion. Reflection after a long period of time may account for her eloquent descriptions, and of all the women's writing, Miss Rogers's memoir is the most introspective. *Arctic Adventure* offers what one author has called "the wonder of the shrubbery, and less about the actual trees."[67] It is difficult to imagine Elizabeth Taylor or Emma Colcleugh confessing that at camps along the way they stashed their "brandy flask furtively into a rucksack," and "strolled off into the willows while the men who accompanied them laid the fire." In due course, wrote Miss Rogers, she and Miss Smith would return from their imbibing, "ostentatiously carrying bunches of wild flowers." It was, she continued, "a strange tippling place, that thicket of willows, but never did any tavern hunter enjoy his liquor more." It became an evening habit. "If there were no willows, there would be dense alders or secretive firs," and there would always be the wild flowers to justify their absence.[68] Miss Rogers admitted that the liquor kept their spirits up and provided some quiet confidence, which, while false, was entirely necessary.

The women had been warned by the HBC that beyond the steamboat at Aklavik, they could expect considerable physical discomfort. But travelling was the passion of Clara Rogers's life, and she therefore accepted the challenge. In her letters to the HBC she does not waver from her intentions, despite an obviously negative attitude in Winnipeg. The daughter of Cornish gentry, she described herself as neither rich nor poor. She had had a good education and a pleasant family life, free of monetary concerns. As she travelled across the country to Edmonton she decided, not without some irony, that Canadians were tremendously proud of their achievements and had altogether too much optimism. She judged that this was a little too much like tropical sunshine. "It made one long for the coolness of humble shade."[69] As the trip got underway, she was to realize the difference between daydreams and reality. The first shock came on the railway out of Edmonton when after bundling their outfit (which included 252 pounds of food and 175 pounds of luggage) onto the train, they chugged leisurely north. Here was the first lesson for northern travellers: there was no need to hurry. The north began to take on its own "personality, at once alluring, compelling, and sometimes cruel."[70]

On the Mackenzie steamer, all the passengers travelled under the same spell; "it was a peculiar elation as if a Light were shining there,"[71] Clara Rogers recorded. The women made the journey from Fort Smith to Aklavik aboard the *Distributor III*, launched in 1920 to supplement the *Mackenzie River*. By this time, the steamers of the Mackenzie River Transport division of the HBC offered roomy, well-ventilated dining rooms, equipped with linen, china, and silverware. There was a comfortable lounge, a library, and bathrooms with unlimited hot water. Stewards and stewardesses were available to serve passengers, who were housed in cabins with windows and berths that had "soft mattresses, comfortable feather pillows, and gleaming white sheets" covered by HBC Point blankets.[72] This description was the one offered in the travel brochure produced by the Company. It was the first time true passenger service had been available for tourists aboard the HBC steamers.

Native guides were hired for the canoe trip beyond Aklavik, so it might be expected that Clara Rogers would comment on the relationship. Forewarned by her HBC supplier about native guides who took no orders from anyone, and who insisted that the guides be treated on a friendly and equal footing, Miss Rogers always deferred to the guides, or so she claimed. This did not mean that she and Miss Smith were not beneath deceiving the guides with their frequent tipples in the bush. But they did recognize their personal limitations and were prepared to do what they were told when paddling the dangerous Rat and Porcupine rivers. Except for everyday comments about the skills and knowledge of her guides, though, *Arctic Adventure* lacks the type of anthropological comments evident in the other three narratives. Perhaps the Dene and Inuit of the north seemed less exotic by 1961. Or perhaps Miss Rogers decided not to publish her observations made at the time. She did recall the Inuit women at Aklavik with their entrancing smiles. She remembered, too, that attempted exchanges consisted of smiles, more smiles, and still more smiles. She concluded that Inuit babies must have been born wearing smiles. Likely the descriptions of smiles and Inuit friendliness that recur in all four accounts are simply a reaction to meeting happy and amicable people when hostility was expected. Everyone had heard tales of infanticide and cannibalism. As the travellers progressed further north away from the fur trade settlements established to serve the aboriginal population, expectations changed. The travellers became ambivalent about what they might find and unsure about confronting cultural differences.

Miss Rogers, however, was sure of how she felt about what she called the perennial problem of the north: mixed marriages. In her mind there was no excuse for mixed marriages. To her, they were a sign of weakness in white men in the north. But these were not the mixed liaisons or marriages between white women and black men so abhorred by travellers in Africa and India. These unions were between white men and native women, and in some ways were commonplace. Clara Rogers realized that loneliness broke down racial barriers, but judged it could also drive a "temperate man to become a drunkard, or a sane man to madness."[73] (Agnes Cameron also mentions mixed marriages, but her sentiment displayed a peculiarly English-Canadian prejudice. "When a Frenchman marries an Indian woman he reverts to her scale of civilization; when a Scot takes a native wife, he draws her up to his."[74])

Clara Rogers described an Inuit dance performed at Aklavik, noting the fascination it held for her as well as the participants. A celebration dance, it was held after a murder trial in which the defendant was exonerated. The steps and sequences were not rehearsed; they were improvised, mimetic, and spontaneous. "During the execution of that primitive sole seal-dance," she wrote, "I was transported back through the ages into a cave-man mentality becoming unconscious of the crowd about me." Despite her claim that she was unable to describe the experience in words, Clara Rogers remembered that the dancer began by beating a one-sided drum with a flat stick, and then "in a few moments he was no longer Ikegana nor even a human being, he had become a seal, bending forward and shuffling sideways, with every muscle rippling in an almost fluid movement; he seemed to be endowed with flippers and encased in blubber. Curious groans and roars and hisses of encouragement rose from the audience, but however uncouth were those sounds they were obviously used for expressing delight in this scene, wherein a man became a mammal before their very eyes."[75]

As a painter, Gwen Dorrien Smith, Clara Rogers's companion, sketched and recorded the vegetation along the route. The two women collected two hundred and sixty-seven kinds of pressed flowers for the Kew herbarium in London. Like all the women travellers, they appeared to be knowledgeable about botanical species, although it is unclear if this familiarity was acquired before undertaking the journey, or after the fact. Elizabeth Taylor was allowed little baggage on her trip but considered her botany book essential, for example. Fortunately, colourful reports about the botanical species in their narratives allowed the women to contest the image of a cold and barren north; they also permitted a little hyperbole in terms readers could understand. Yet collecting botanical specimens was a legitimate pursuit, which retained a feminine air and provided a cloak of gentility to cover the masculine aspect of exploration. Gathering wild flowers could hardly be seen as a threat to male fact finders. It set women apart from serious scientists while at the same time serving as an intellectual pursuit. Neither was it exploitive.[76] Collecting also served to veil any suggestion of northern travel as frivolous diversion; there was some purpose, after all, if the Kew herbarium was interested.

At Aklavik, Clara Rogers bemoaned the scarcity of species and identified only bog-bean, marsh marigold, bearberry, pyrola, wild rose, yellow anemone, small gypsophila, pink Rubra, and dwarf grass of Parnassus. Silver willow, alder, and stunted spruce were identified as well. Later, along the Rat River, Miss Rogers described the less attractive foliage known as nigger-heads. Nigger-heads were a curse to northern travellers, for, as she explained, they were a "nightmare form of vegetation, bullet-headed tufts of grass, not wide enough to support the length of a human foot, with thigh deep spaces between each tuft. When you step lightly as a ballet dancer on a head, trying to balance on your toes or to grip with your heels, then the head will wobble and you will fall into the space between your tuft and the next one."[77] Along the swamps and riverbanks of the north, nigger-heads posed a real danger to the two women who spent as much time outside their canoe as in it.

Of all the adventures, that of Clara Rogers and Gwen Smith was the most physically taxing. It presented unique physical and mental challenges; at one point on the Rat River they endured the "worst experience of the whole journey, when they stood alone on the muskeg, for the most part in silence, on a ten foot cliff above the river." They were "face to face with naked fear," separated from their guides, and beginning to contemplate the prospects of survival without them. Later, Miss Rogers recalled how the sense "of [the] vastness of the country overcame us, like a threat that might destroy us at any moment."[78] Clara Rogers's readers learned that the north had inspired contemplation, tested their ingenuity, and defined personal physical limits in the two middle-aged English women. They also learned Aklavik consisted of a single line of houses strung out along a twenty-foot mud bank, as well as a beach where crowds of Inuit camped with their noisy dogs. To Miss Rogers, Aklavik seemed to be a comparatively prosperous place, but she added that her "standards of prosperity had been lowered during the last few weeks of association with people living in wooden shacks on muddy river banks with only a dirt track for a main street."[79]

Descriptions of settlements are uneven and inconsistent in the accounts of all four women. Usually they are impressionistic rather than illustrative, so it is not profitable to attempt any comparisons. What can be said is that few changes were noted. Some sort of trading post, mission, and attempt at agriculture were always present, even on a small scale. There were always lots of friendly people and often white women eager to share conversation and tea with the visitors. The neat and functional buildings were set in pretty surroundings, but along muddy riverbanks exposing two classes of inhabitants: native and non-native.

That the northern travellers were of one class and the majority of the people they encountered of another is not lost on anyone reading these accounts. The result is Eurocentric commentary and noticeable biases. Neither should come as a surprise, and they must be accepted for what they are. Accepting what these women saw and felt does not deny their prejudices; it simply adds depth to the kaleidoscopic portrayals already spun by explorers and indigenous people. The north was a curiosity waiting to be examined.

It is dangerous to conclude that these women were travellers because they were feminists. It is more likely that they were travellers, some of whom may coincidentally have been feminists who extended to their personal lives some of the momentum created by the outburst of feminine energy that surrounded them; a feminist perspective would have provided the impetus to overcome objections and obstacles from men in a position to frustrate and otherwise impede their plans. The question of travellers and feminism has held some interest for scholars, who have adopted the hopeful stance that there is a common thread and a feminist link to women's travel writing. The underlying assumption is that because women chose to pursue what was usually a male undertaking, they were attempting some political statement. Perhaps feminist scholars hope that female travellers would be kinder and gentler towards other women, or that they subscribed to the same values as modern feminists. But this was not the case for the northern travellers. Even Agnes Cameron's attempt to understand the position of female Inuit was done within the context of an entire community.

Agnes Cameron was the true feminist among this group of women. She actively supported female suffrage and equal rights, and her outspoken nature and willingness to make personal sacrifices were hallmarks of her feminism. Emma Shaw Colcleugh, also associated with feminist groups, had contact with women's organizations throughout New England in her capacity as Clubs Editor of the Providence *Journal*. Mrs Colcleugh was on intimate terms with the political forces of a developing Canada, but on their travels neither she, nor Miss Cameron, planted a suffragist flag or campaigned for women's rights, whether for aboriginal or white women.

Although Agnes Cameron was an acknowledged expansionist, her settlement vision was a fantasy of internal expansion as insurance for the Canada of the future. Canada was in the position to construct, she explained, where other nations had to reconstruct.[80] Elizabeth Taylor was the daughter of an American annexationist. It is unclear if her travelogue in *Outing* served her father's purpose, although she did comment on the potential for development and settlement in the north. As for Clara Rogers, her record has a distinctive "travelling in the colonies" perspective and she imbued her travels with a strong desire for personal challenge.

Whatever their individual impetus, the principal objective of these women was to exploit their travels for personal profit through lectures and publications. The women were also travelling for travel's sake. The north was romantic and distant, a place few Europeans had seen or could hope to see. It made sense to capitalize on the curiosity of readers in the south. What these women wrote about was what they knew they could sell to publishers and readers. They understood that those parameters acted as a check on what was published.

It is notable that there is little evidence of the travels of these women in the northern mythology. This exclusion begs the suggestion that sex makes a difference to a writer's credibility. The likes of British naval explorers in the Northwest Passage, of eccentric American anthropologists attempting to live off the land, or of strident government and police officials on fact-finding missions were usually quasi-official and had political purpose. Elizabeth Taylor, Emma Colcleugh, Agnes Cameron, and Clara Rogers were not taken as seriously: they were just women out on a jaunt. Without a complex comparison with similar works of men over time, it is difficult to ascertain whether their observations differed because female eyes had viewed the scene. Since the purpose of this study is to place women in the foreground, such an undertaking would be counter-productive. To speak of these women in the same breath as Franklin might seem audacious to those who revere the great white explorers of the Arctic, yet the women's writings are serious comment. Because they stopped to delight at the wild roses and paused to describe the people they met should not diminish their pursuits. Moreover, it might be argued that the women were intelligent enough to push themselves beyond the physical expectations of women of their time without foolishly overextending their respective limits.

CHAPTER FOUR

Travels With the "More Realistic" Sex in the 1920s and 1930s

When professional women travelled into the NWT during the 1920s and '30s, they encountered the same institutions as their Victorian and Edwardian predecessors. Time had effected little change to the structures of male-dominated and male-defined administration in the north, and these men became even more firmly entrenched when challenged by women with some measure of personal confidence. Professional women were still few in number in Canada in the 1920s – their number too small to make an effective attack on the patriarchal structures of religion, business, or science. Individual women developed ways of coping with resistance, strengthening their personal resolve to achieve recognition and respect. However, professional women who went to the NWT in the 1920s and '30s did not necessarily encounter resistance from within their own professional communities as much as from the bureaucracies that administered the region.

Artist Kathleen Shackleton, journalist Marion Grange, and amateur botanist Isobel Hutchison encountered barriers that support the contention that men in the government, at HBC headquarters, and at Anglican and RC missionary societies administered the NWT like personal fiefdoms.[1] Unlike their Victorian and Edwardian predecessors, these women travelled in the NWT for some purpose other than a travelogue production, yet like the observations recorded by Miss Taylor, Mrs Colcleugh, Miss Cameron, and Clara Rogers, their stories add dimensions to northern history. They also allow a gender-based view – one hitherto ignored – that counters the male-dominated focus of the descriptions of other explorations in the region during that era. Since experience combines the personal observation of, or involvement with, fact and the knowledge or skill based on that involvement, women's experience becomes more than simply relevant: it becomes essential to an understanding of the social conditions of the time. How Miss Shackleton portrayed northern residents and herself reacted to the administrators; how Mrs Grange reported on the government patrol; and how Miss Hutchison traipsed through the wilds of the Arctic all provide a focal point for comparison with the earlier works described in the previous chapter.

This focus means peering through a grimy window to see how the male bureaucrats associated with the north actually worked.[2] Obviously such a window needs cleaning. Since it has been long been painted shut, some muscle must be exerted to open the window and view how these men related to those distant from the positions of power, while still exercising the politics of exclusion against those considered marginal to their purpose. Aboriginals represent one such group, women another.[3] The nature of the barriers placed before women and the attitudes of the men they encountered suggest the inconsequential place of a woman's professional and personal status when encountered by men who disagreed with their assessments.

Such was the case of British artist Kathleen Shackleton when she applied to the HBC in 1937 for a commission to produce three dozen portraits. Her purpose was to reflect the Company's interests in the north; controversy was not her intention. Although she was the sister of a famous Antarctic explorer, it is unclear if her brother's exploits figured in her suggestion to the HBC that she produce a series to record "all types of Indians, Eskimos and trappers associated with the Company, and members of the staff, dressed in picturesque or strictly working costume."[4] The HBC and Miss Shackleton had high hopes for her work; they were convinced of the publicity value of any show of work in the USA or Britain that would depict "His Majesty's Most Northerly Subjects."[5] There were prospects for slide and lecture talks, illustrations for articles in periodicals, and perhaps even the incorporation of northern designs in "modern misses" styles. The ways of commercializing the work of Kathleen Shackleton were endless, including quality advertising in conjunction with the Company and general publicity. In short, this was to be a profitable enterprise for both Miss Shackleton and the Company.

Kathleen Shackleton initially asked for remuneration of three thousand dollars in her proposal, excluding expenses. After some bargaining she settled for two thousand dollars. That included an advance and travel expenses from London to Winnipeg, with first-class rail tickets and ten dollars per day while travelling within the range of railway communication lines, with subsequent transportation expenses absorbed by the HBC along its own system.[6] Miss Shackleton's journey to the north was undertaken in three stages.

During the summer of 1937 she toured the Mackenzie-Athabasca Region; she visited northern Quebec in the autumn, returning to Coppermine for Christmas.[7] The artistic project proved successful. Kathleen Shackleton wrote to J. Chadwick Brooks, her Winnipeg contact, saying how "it had all been absolutely *wonderful*. I nearly get *bushed* as I am in love with the 'North' and the people."[8] By the end of her first trip down the Mackenzie River she had already completed two-thirds of her commission and believed the portraits to be the best work she had done in years.

Encouraged and excited by her adventure, like most Arctic travellers of the time, Kathleen Shackleton gave interviews to the press. The Canadian newspapers reported that she was filled with a sense of outrage at the arrogant treatment of the Natives of the north and was "critical of the way the government cared for its wards and the way in which the church was seeking to bring Christianity to them." She contended that there was no need to break down the habits of generations, habits that were fundamental to successful living in the country.[9] Some accounts suggested that Kathleen Shackleton came away from the north "with the feeling that missionary groups were confusing 'anglicization' with Christianizing." The *Globe*, interpreting this to mean "English customs aren't necessarily Christian custom," reported Miss Shackleton as denouncing the construction of the Anglican residential school at Aklavik, and as saying that the Anglican Church could better serve the northern Natives if it would carry its message into native camps and not take children from their traditional surroundings.[10] This view, contrary to the accepted one, was at odds with the practice of both Anglicans and Roman Catholics that had children taken away from their homes and placed into residential schools and settlements. Miss Shackleton was quoted as saying that at Aklavik, "the church, which is used once or twice a week has an electric lighting plant, while the school where the Eskimo and Indian children are living and which is in use daily, is lighted with oil lamps. The teachers are in constant fear of fire."[11]

It was not long before headlines reading "Flying Bishop Resents Criticism from Artist," appeared in these same papers. "Any tourist who goes into the North and elects to criticize what they find should at least give constructive, not destructive criticisms," declared the Right Reverend Archibald Fleming, who argued that Miss Shackleton had never actually seen the church at Aklavik in operation. As for the power plant, he explained that it had been installed for the use of the hospital. There was insufficient electricity left for the use of the school, and "in any event," he noted, "the school plant [was] not under our jurisdiction but the government's."[12] Fleming defended the church on the grounds that "we are only trying to prepare [the Aboriginals] for the kind of life being forced on them by the white man's invasion," apparently unwilling to recognize a significant element of that invasion was from the church itself.[13]

The newspaper accounts generated correspondence behind the scenes that further indicated just how sensitive an issue had been raised by Kathleen Shackleton's purported comments. Fleming wrote to Ralph Parsons of the HBC, asking what his mission had done to warrant such an undeserved attack. He speculated about Miss Shackleton's motives, suggesting that her actions might have been for publicity or stemmed from a grudge against the Church of England. More important, Fleming noted that Miss Shackleton was under contract to the HBC, and he reminded Parsons that "since I first came into touch with you and the Company in 1911 I have not ceased to try and play fair." The implication was that playing fair enjoyed precedence over native welfare. The bishop suggested that since the Church of England and the HBC were in this northern enterprise together, the Company should do its part to clear the reputation of those who worked in the north.

Bishop Fleming's lengthy letter countered the untruths that he claimed were being printed in the newspapers, and he concluded by suggesting that "it would be a good thing if [Kathleen Shackleton] could be persuaded to attend to her Missawing and let other people attend to their business. She has [been] only a short time in the North and has not earned the right to express opinions as against those who have been there [for] many years." [14] He said he was awaiting a reply with an explanation of Miss Shackleton's offensive and untrue remarks. Did it not occur to Fleming that there might have been some truth in Kathleen Shackleton's observations?

"I suppose when Bishop Fleming referred to tourists he meant me," Kathleen Shackleton wrote in rebuttal. She added, "I have never been a tourist, and I was on my job in the North as a hard-working artist, and my criticism I did not consider in the least destructive." With some foresight, Miss Shackleton recognized that "unless the whole face of Nature changes in the Aklavik district, the Natives will have to earn their livelihood by trapping, hunting and fishing." She also pointed out that these were skills the young people of the region were being denied.[15] At first glance, this observation contradicts what Mark Dickerson claims was the government policy for educating the native population, and that the church curriculum was at odds with the NWT Council. What Miss Shackleton was referring to was the education of young children in the absolute basics. They would be back on the land soon enough.

As for the HBC, Brooks wrote to Miss Shackleton on 1 April to tell her he had been "horrified" to read the press reports – copies of which he enclosed. "The publication of such dogmatic criticisms of the Church of England activities is greatly to be deplored and it is unfortunate that they should be expressed and published following your visit to the Arctic on behalf of the HBC," he told her. He noted that there were considerations of which she was probably unaware, and that it might have been prudent to express her opinions in private rather than to the press. The Company's trading operations had always been carried out with careful consideration for the welfare of the native population, explained Brooks, and "the most cordial relations had always existed between the HBC, the government, and all denominations." It was clearly noted in the letter that Fleming was a personal friend of the Governor and that Fleming's protests would be dealt with by the HBC Board of Governors in London, who had been placed in a difficult position by her comments.[16]

"I thought I was a free individual when my contract expired," replied Kathleen Shackleton. Because the views were expressed before the HBC finalized her expense payments, she admitted it might mean she was "retrospectively in [their] employ" but she added that since the contract had expired, "so much for my obligations to your Company." Miss Shackleton proceeded to explain to Brooks that the newspaper accounts were inaccurate and that she had been misquoted. She pointed out that she had spent a "marvellous month" at the residential school at Aklavik with very sincere Christian workers who, nevertheless, questioned the economic value of their work. "They have a splendid staff at the school, living examples of Christianity, who will be remembered by the children long after the Church is forgotten" she said, adding that "they were making the best of a bad job."[17] After her visit, she had decided that the value of the curriculum was probably useless, "but as those [teachers] were so much in earnest, I not only kept my views to myself, I arranged a show of my work to get funds to help them with their little concerts and other purely 'British' affairs and in various other ways tried to make things easier for them."[18]

Kathleen Shackleton admitted she may have gone too far for this cause. She conceded that "a good deal of what I said to the newspapers might have been privately communicated to officials of the MSCC, but you see, the poor dears had so often applied for things and only been told 'we are bearing the matter in mind' that I said 'when I go out and the newspapers ask me questions, I won't talk about my sketches, I will talk about the school needs instead, and above all the electric light plant.' I was burning with the injustice done to the living workers by 'the powers that be' among the Missionary headquarters in concentrating so much on the idea of a "Pro-Cathedral Dream" in the North."[19] Bishop Fleming, Kathleen Shackleton maintained, had "passed the buck" by saying that the school was under government jurisdiction. He had also said "all sorts of unpleasant personal" things against her during a lecture at Montreal, comments for which one vice-president of the Woman's Auxiliary felt compelled to apologize. It had become a personal issue for Fleming, who was known to campaign tirelessly for support for his vast diocese and its missions. Kathleen Shackleton told Brooks that she was convinced that the bishop had made up his mind she was entirely wrong, and that only he was right.[20] What she had really done was question the bishop's policies and challenge his personal hegemony in the Arctic.

Miss Shackleton decided that a return to the "Good Old Days" when the Company reigned in the north would serve the local population better. She told the HBC official: "It would be much better if the Natives could be assisted, not to become half-British (which is not necessarily Christian) but healthy, productive Natives ... you must know how serious are the drawbacks from the point of view of health and general efficiency when they are allowed or encouraged to hang about white settlements. It is bad for the Company's finances to say the least of it."[21] She wondered if it would be more logical if the church concentrated on the attitudes of the traders before they came into contact with native northerners, rather than preparing children so they would not be preyed upon (which was how one missionary justified the northern mission). She was concerned about the values that the female teachers imposed through the religious nature of the curriculum at Aklavik, telling Brooks that boys and girls were not allowed to play together "for moral reasons," even in the snow. Explanations such as that did not enlighten her at all, she commented. Yet she clarified the situation more than she realized.

It would be speculative to conclude that Kathleen Shackleton's statements and the ensuing debate would have been different if she had not been a woman, although it can be confirmed that no male "tourist" of her stature had ever made similar comments to the press. For that matter, there is no evidence that any male visitor without government or Company sanction concerned himself with the issues in question. It is difficult to ascertain if Miss Shackleton was correcting an injustice or had consciously chosen to challenge what she called the "powers that be" and their policies. She may have been unaware of the rules; it may have been her choice not to play by them. As a woman, she identified with the hardships the female missionaries dealt with in the day-to-day running of the Aklavik school. She recognized the practical and domestic problems of feeding, clothing, and housing children. Administrators, on the other hand, worried about the political and economic issues. She understood that the women were in a relatively helpless situation, and that they were meeting the challenges of the moment while unable to effect changes in policy because as women they occupied an inferior position within the hierarchy. They were also situated on the Arctic coast without immediate access to those who might champion their cause in the south, like the WA of the MSCC.

Addie Butler wrote candid letters that included comments about some of the men she encountered as a teacher at Shingle Point. She spares neither the male missionaries nor Fleming. In fact, Addie Butler's experience with Fleming only affirmed Miss Shackleton's commentary. Mrs Butler looked forward to Bishop Fleming's visit to Shingle Point as an opportunity to outline the problems she faced as a teacher at the residential school. However, she later recalled that when His Lordship visited, she did not get much satisfaction from her personal interview. "He wanted to do all the talking," she wrote. "He was too much taken up with the big things that loom up in the front of his vision and the little everyday things that make up our life here, and which help keep the wheels go[ing] smoothly or otherwise, were too small for him to see." Not without some irony, she suggested that the bishop should "come up here and live for a week or two."[22]

Kathleen Shackleton's opinions, which are recorded in personal letters as well as in the newspaper reports, differ only marginally from the press interpretations. She may have been misquoted, but the intention remained the same. Miss Shackleton admitted to Brooks that although she empathized with the women who worked at Aklavik, she reckoned that this was probably due to her own missionary calling. Despite understanding their condition, she concluded that the women missionaries were charming, sincere, but mistaken as teachers – an opinion formed because she had lived with them, not simply because she had visited the school. In the end, Kathleen Shackleton announced to Brooks that she was making plans to pursue her career in Canada, independently of the HBC. She felt it was better to avoid official associations and reaffirmed that since the newspaper accounts had appeared several weeks after her contract had expired, she felt answerable to no one. She added that the HBC should feel free to "disown" her to Bishop Fleming.

Fleming's attitude was a common one. "If you had only lived in the Arctic" was a familiar response to those who questioned how and why things were done differently in the north. Similar reasoning was used to defend criticism about how the north was administered, or how non-native residents made decisions. No one, and certainly no woman who had only made one summer's journey into the region, was apparently entitled to question conditions until they had earned the privilege through some kind of Arctic endurance test, the requirements of which were known only to Arctic veterans.[23] Decision makers were able to deflect criticism by confusing experience with expertise, the assumption being that the north was some kind of special enclave and observations from outsiders were not to be entertained. They were also able to censor reports from the region that were not flattering to the administration. Mark Dickerson cites an example of how the RCMP member of the NWT Council was able to order his men not to include any remarks critical to the administration in their reports published in the Canada Sessional Papers. The order was in response to a report about native consumption of wood alcohol. The *Ottawa Citizen* picked up the story from an official report and published what the NWT Council considered to be a sensationalized and inaccurate version. That may be why Marion Grange from that same newspaper encountered such resistance when she was invited to join the Eastern Arctic Patrol (EAP) in 1938.

Roy Gibson, Deputy Commissioner for the Northwest Territories, wrote to Mrs Marion Grange on 29 June 1938 to inform her that provision was being made for her accommodation on board the HBC supply ship, the *RMS Nascopie*. A movie and entertainment reporter for the *Citizen*, Mrs Grange was to act as the official historian attached to the Dominion government's annual EAP. Gibson enclosed a map and general information about weather and conditions, and pointed out that it was customary for the press representative to comply with certain guidelines.[24] As a reporter for the *Ottawa Citizen* and as a Southam News representative, she would be expected to submit all material written about the journey to Major David L. McKeand, officer-in-charge of the EAP. Gibson explained that McKeand had extensive experience in the Eastern Arctic and knew the full significance of various features of life and conditions in the region. Moreover, McKeand was fully aware of departmental regulations.[25]

McKeand, Secretary of the Northwest Territories Council and superintendent of the EAP, was not overjoyed with Gibson's decision to allow Mrs Grange to act as the historian on the 1938 expedition. In a memorandum written in March, McKeand told Gibson that although the appointment of a Canadian Press reporter as historian the previous year had been an improvement on past efforts, he would urge Gibson to consider four points before confirming Mrs Grange's appointment. McKeand argued, first, that whereas the Southam newspapers were privately owned and articles might be syndicated outside of Canada, the Canadian Press was a co-operative organization composed of daily and weekly newspapers. A charitable interpretation might view McKeand's concerns as security related, but Canadian Press reports could be relayed to other wire services, so the point is lost. McKeand also suggested that problems would arise because articles by a Southam reporter would appear in English only: this too is debatable as the Canadian Press news was in English and French. In addition, he contended that a Canadian Press representative was probably more familiar with departmental practice and government procedure. Why that should be so for a Canadian Press writer and not a Southam reporter, particularly one based in Ottawa, McKeand did not explain, except to add that *he* could be relied on in confidential matters.

The true protest was more evident in Major McKeand's assertion that "generally, newspaper women wrote good copy, but are limited by their assignments." He did not elaborate on what he thought were the limitations, nor did he notice the irony of his remarks. This was his opportunity to expand the narrow horizons of at least one female reporter. Instead he backed up his argument with the observation that "women tourists on the *Nascopie* never seemed to understand the native women or their family life." Although he did not elaborate on this claim, it is likely he was disturbed by the possibility a woman might be less sympathetic toward white European men when she encountered mixed-blood children along the EAP route. McKeand was confident of a male reporter's discretion and nervous about a woman's reactions: even if he, as the officer-in-charge, could initially monitor articles despatched from the north, he knew he would have no control over articles published after the EAP returned to the south. He ended his memorandum by suggesting that there were "a number of other reasons for the appointment of a man instead of a woman to the EAP, which could be advanced, if necessary."[26] Incidentally, by 1938, women travelled routinely as passengers on the *Nascopie* – to join men as wives or housekeepers at Arctic posts, or to take up service as missionaries throughout the Eastern Arctic, northern Quebec, and Labrador; the ship was equipped for female passengers.

Although Gibson overruled him – and there is no indication as to why – McKeand exerted pressure on Mrs Grange in other ways. A memorandum of 7 June reminded Gibson that as far as the HBC was concerned, she was not just another passenger. Mrs Grange, like officers and members of the government party, were guests of the minister and under government control. All messages of a public nature sent by them from the *Nascopie* were therefore subject to scrutiny by the officer-in- charge, who requested that Mrs Grange remember that even as an official member of the EAP, she would not be permitted to attend all the on-board meetings because of their confidential nature. "Newspaper people are not members of any departmental committees in Ottawa, and it could not be expected that a newspaper woman would enjoy the same privileges aboard the *Nascopie*," he reasoned. Clearly, Mrs Grange was only a member of the EAP when it suited McKeand's purpose.

After the EAP's return in September, McKeand reported to Gibson that despite the exclusion of Mrs Grange from meetings, those who attended were less than candid during discussions because of Marion Grange's presence on board as historian. He suggested that this was because the EAP included public servants, or those accustomed to authority and loyalty to their respective institutions. No doubt it was also because they were all men who were suspicious of a woman holding anything other than a tourist's interest in the Arctic. Consequently, the RCMP, the doctor, and the other scientists were "very reticent in discussing the results of their observations and future plans." McKeand added that the same "could be said for employees of the HBC who "flatly declined to co-operate with Mrs Grange."²⁷ Even within the context of the time, McKeand's attitude leaves a lingering suspicion about what was being said at those on-board meetings that the men in attendance could not trust to a woman, but could share with a man. These were meetings of an exclusive fraternity, and the annual trip reaffirmed the nature and exclusivity of that club, defined as it was by male prowess and the ability to withstand isolation and hardship. The meetings on the *Nascopie* and along its route symbolized the traditional bastions of paternalism that ruled the north.

Gibson's memorandum to McKeand on 8 March mentioned that Mrs Grange had written some excellent human interest articles about a northern Ontario mining community, and hoped that she could "write up the Eastern Arctic from an altogether new standpoint." This was what McKeand feared, of course, and to some degree his fears were well founded. Marion Grange did write as much about native women and their families as she did about the scenery, the RCMP, and the workings of the EAP. Whether she misunderstood the issues is open to interpretation, however.

In one article entitled "The Women of Pangnirtung," Marion Grange named the five white women at the settlement and recorded the presentation of Coronation medals to Flossie Hirst and the Inuit wife of a well-known Arctic trapper and explorer. Mrs Duval, she explained, was the "only female Eskimo to be honoured by her King." From the *Nascopie*, Marion Grange wrote as well about an Inuit woman named Napatchie. Napatchie was on board the ship because she and her family were being relocated from Cape Dorset to Arctic Bay, and she had given birth during the voyage. Napatchie's presence on board the *Nascopie* prompted Marion Grange to remark on the lot of Inuit women, who "were able to do two things that her generally considered more sophisticated sister has never been able to accomplish. Never has she been, neither is she now, a slave to the kitchen." This was because the Inuit liked his food raw, so meals were never a problem. Not without some sarcasm, Mrs Grange added in parentheses "whether Christianity with its accompanying civiliza- tion will bring in its wake a female domestic serfdom, it is still rather early to tell." On the surface, this observation appears to be a comment on the primitive domestic arrangements of Inuit women, but as McKeand was a devoted Anglican and lay reader, it is not dif- ficult to imagine this remark being a jibe after she had endured a dinner lecture about the effects of Christianity in the north.[28]

In the same story, Mrs Grange expressed surprise that an Inuit husband would look after his wife's children regardless of who their father was. She decided that this indicated a double standard of morality, "especially if the woman was a good needle-woman, in other words economically independent." From the way Mrs Grange recounted the story, it appears that she was testing the patience of McKeand; in any case, she was certainly offering a different view- point. Male observers had never offered this twist, [29] an omission that hints at some decision-making by Inuit women. Neither had male observers considered whether Inuit women's domestic condi- tions were better than those of their white sisters in the south; the usual assumption was that they were merely beasts of burden to be pitied.

A marginal note on the manuscript copy of Marion Grange's dis- patch indicates that some of her judgments were not included in the *Citizen* articles. She wrote of the practice of interchanging wives, which she noted was a seasonal rather than a permanent arrange- ment. Earlier accounts by travellers in the Arctic intimated that

> this rite was owing to man's variability, that the woman had no say in it. Maybe so. On the other hand many Eskimos show traces of white blood. One authority has stated that there are no full-blooded Eskimos. Blame it on the whaler is a practice of the North. The whalers were on the Eastern Arctic for over a hundred years and left immediately before the Great War,

owing to the almost complete demolition of the whale. In the North, it is deemed unmannerly to suggest that any intermixture may be of a later date. Since whalers all were men, it is to me more obvious that the Eskimo lady had the wandering eye. But then I belong to the realistic rather than the sentimental sex.[30]

Marion Grange's reports describe ship life, shiptime, and amiable Inuit. She recounted the story of Thomas Manning and Ellen Jackson's "secret wedding" aboard the *Nascopie*, as well as the tale of another marriage ceremony when the ship landed at Port Burwell. She recognized that for young white women heading north to get married, theirs was a one-way trip for at least a year. But her description of a scene involving male officials illustrated something more about the expectations of white men acting in an official capacity in the north. It is yet another example of the type of report McKeand was nervous about because Mrs Grange's account makes these men of authority look a little silly. The story began by explaining that many Inuit were machine minded; they only had to be shown how a piece of equipment worked, or how something was made, and they were prepared for the task. But not all Inuit had the opportunity to learn everything, continued Mrs Grange "as the Bishop, the artist, and the ornithologist found out when they cheerfully stepped off the gangplank at Cape Dorset into a motor boat seemingly manned by three Eskimos. The 'crew' and passengers took off, and then discovered all were passengers. None of the Eskimos could run the boat. Neither could the white men. The Bishop was anxious to get to shore to drum up a religious service."[31] For the time being, concluded Mrs Grange, the bishop forgot his real love and admiration for the Inuit. It took the assistance of another Inuk who came alongside to start the engine.

Since there were so few white men and women in the Arctic, any pomposity was immediately noticeable, particularly so to women who were probably already a little cynical about men. For the most part, the men with whom these women came into contact all belonged to the official hierarchy in some way. The men expected to be treated with some respect, in accordance with what they saw as positions of some import. Whereas they envisioned themselves as extraordinary men in a demanding environment, the women probably knew better and often saw the situation in reverse terms.

Marion Grange was not the only woman to make this observation. In one of Addie Butler's letters home, she told how one RCMP inspector arrived at Shingle Point unannounced, only to complain that he was not received with the recognition due a representative of His

Majesty's government. Mrs Butler, after apologizing "for the absence of the red carpet and the brass band and the flag hoisting," told him "that if he would come at school time, he could not expect anything else."[32] Both the inspector and Addie Butler thought of Shingle Point as an outpost of the Empire, but Addie Butler also thought of it as the school where she taught.

While Marion Grange's portrayal shows she was not above poking a little fun at the officials who travelled on the *Nascopie*, she did hold these men in some esteem, while enjoying their predicament. For example, she recounted how the character of the RCMP officers seemed to change when they came into contact with Inuit. "With the majority of white people they were taciturn, almost curt," she reported, "but with the Inuit they were garrulous and often burst into gales of laughter. "Why not?" she asked, for they were "brothers in arms," with experiences of Arctic travels, frozen caribou, and seal meat. "They love the Natives, know their failing, and they appreciate their virtues."[33]

Marion Grange was unable to successfully convince Major McKeand that a woman was up to the task. He wrote to Roy Gibson, reporting smugly that Mrs Grange's first item was so full of inaccuracies that he had suggested she rewrite it. He claimed that although he had been careful to avoid editorial criticism there were errors in "dates, numbers and nautical terms, etc. While some corrections were made others were evidently not thought necessary with the result that the material, style, etc. of the articles" would be the responsibility of the *Citizen*, and not of the government party. He finally conceded he had no objection to the articles.[34]

McKeand had one further opportunity to make his point to Gibson, in his letter of 22 November informing the Deputy Commissioner about a CBC Radio broadcast that Marion Grange was to make the next day. The topic was "The Northern Trek of Eskimos." "It might do well for some of us to hear what Mrs Grange has to say," he declared, and indicated his intention to listen. After the broadcast, he offered that "while Mrs Grange has a pleasing radio personality her voice is not very clear. The material was good," he admitted, but in his opinion it lacked continuity. More significantly, McKeand assigned Marion Grange to her rightful place by concluding "I feel certain that it was enjoyed by many women listeners over the Canadian network."[35]

His memoranda show McKeand doing his best not to be exasperated by having had to take a woman on "his" inspection tour. But he also makes it clear that as he was the single official charged to deal with the Dominion government's business on the EAP, Marion

Grange had to put up with any bureaucratic barriers he decided to erect. The unknown is why Gibson did not bend to McKeand's objections. Why did he insist on Marion Grange's presence on the EAP of 1938? It is curious that McKeand never offered what had to be the best argument against the employment of an individual woman in an official capacity: the remote possibility the *Nascopie* might be stranded in the Arctic. The HBC had used that very reason to initially refuse passage to Mhairi Fenton and her aunt the previous year. The Fur Trade Commissioner wrote Mhairi Fenton's uncle to explain that "in navigating these northern waters we have at the back of our minds always the possibility of the ship being caught and being obliged to winter."[36]

Although eventually seven women were to travel aboard the *Nascopie* in 1937, the potential problems posed by stranded females were enough to make officials balk at taking women along. There was a legal responsibility for the physical well-being of the women, and in the Arctic this included food, warm clothing, and medical attention. This responsibility was clouded by sexual anxieties and fears for the reputations of single, unattached white females, although there never was any apparent need in the north for regulations against what in other colonial settings was called "the black peril."[37] Native men in the north were never portrayed as sexual beasts intent upon violating white women, as they may have been in warmer climes; the obvious conclusion is that Europeans in the north supposed that cold decreased sexual aggressiveness. But as that would contradict the notion that northern Aboriginals were promiscuous and immoral, the reasons are probably more linked to European demographics.

First of all, there was the presence of the RNWMP/RCMP officers, who were an integral part of white communities. Their presence reassured white men and women, who understood the almost omnipotent role of the Mounties. Moreover, the white community was so scattered, that no group was ever large enough to rise up and legislate against imagined dangers. The dispersion of the white population also meant that any threat was individual and not seen in a cultural sense. Of course, no fears are ever openly expressed in the sources about sexual attacks by native men. Official documents only record assaults and alleged rapes against native and mixed-blood women. That white women in the north were unsafe or subject to sexual assault is never mentioned. Admittedly there is little chance that women would record such events themselves and, undoubtedly, official records would have been limited in order to protect the reputation of the few white women in the community. While Mounties could often dispense justice without interference, they could use their discretion to support the women. If there were any danger, it more likely stemmed from lonely white men looking for companionship, or from those who had imbibed too much at shiptime. The prospect of grievous deeds – along with the possibility of a little philandering – had to be in the back of the minds of the men making decisions about allowing women into the farthest regions of the Arctic. It is possible that those in command were as worried about their own reputations as they were about their female charges. At any rate, the *Nascopie* did not get stranded in any ice floes in 1938, and despite her anticipated limitations, Marion Grange was able to offer her "feminine standpoint" and still convey the government's desired message.

Unlike Kathleen Shackleton and Marion Grange, Isobel Hutchison[38] did get stranded in the high Arctic, although she had had few difficulties with bureaucracies when she *planned* her trip north. That was because she chose to ignore the regulations about entering the region, thereby flaunting the rules that were in place to protect travellers. Her adventure, while it proved to be the very sort of trip officials wanted outsiders to avoid, was still worthy of note.[39] It is hard to imagine that Isobel Hutchison did not know the protocols when she started out from Scotland on her trip across the Atlantic, through the Panama Canal, and north to Vancouver. She intended to travel by sea up the coast of British Columbia, around Alaska through the Bering Sea, and along the Arctic coast to Herschel Island and Aklavik.

When she arrived at Vancouver, Miss Hutchison met ethnologist Diamond Jenness of the National Museum of Canada. Jenness told her of the need to obtain a Scientific and Exploration Licence before she entered the north, primarily because she intended to collect specimens for the Kew Gardens and ethnographic artifacts for the Cambridge Museum. From on-board the *Princess Nora* at Vancouver just before she sailed north, Isobel Hutchison wrote to the secretary of the NWT, requesting that a licence be sent to her in care of the HBC Post at Aklavik or Herschel. She said that she hoped to be at one of those posts by August. Considering the circumstances – she was going anyway – the letter was perfunctory. Who was going to prevent her collecting specimens along the Arctic coast in wintertime?[40] Some time in August of 1933, Jenness told a Department of the Interior official about his meeting with Isobel Hutchison and recommended that the appropriate permits be issued; he pointed out, too, that because he had not heard from her since June, he believed she perhaps had not carried out her plans. Apparently Jenness had expected Miss Hutchison to have waited patiently in Vancouver for the department's permission.[41]

The NWT Commissioner was duly notified that licence number twenty-two was to be issued to Isobel Hutchison upon the recommendation of W.A. Collins, acting director of the National Museum of Canada. He, in turn, wrote to H.E. Hume, Secretary of the NWT Council, that Jenness regarded Isobel Hutchison as a woman of intelligence who was collecting specimens for reputable institutions. Since this was usually the only criteria for male explorers, she was not being singled out. The difference though, was that the men often received government backing. Commissioner Rowatt signed the permit but suggested, somewhat belatedly, that Isobel Hutchison should be fully advised of the conditions in the north, operating on the assumption that Isobel Hutchison actually cared.

Hume's letter to Isobel Hutchison outlined the strict regulations to be observed. Her work was to be limited to Herschel Island and the Mackenzie River Delta. Any skeletal remains that she collected had to be turned over to the federal officials in the region, all duly identified. She was to abide by the regulations of the Scientists and Explorer's Ordinance of the NWT.[42] This ordinance stated that no person could enter the NWT for scientific or exploration purposes without first obtaining a licence; without one, the individual could be summarily ejected from the Territories. These were empty words in this case. By this time, Isobel Hutchison was stranded on the coast near the border between Alaska and Canada, no doubt wishing she could be ejected from the middle of nowhere with government assistance so she could carry on with her adventure.

Isobel Hutchison's trip to Herschel Island was eventful. Severe ice conditions in the Beaufort Sea curtailed her journey, forcing her to spend almost two months on the Arctic Coast with an "Alaskan-Estonian Digger" named August Masik. She wrote: "My situation was highly romantic if highly unconventional. I was a prisoner upon a solitary Arctic sandspit – a strip of snow-covered shingle about a mile long and scarcely any part 200 yards wide, washed on all sides by the sea (until it froze).[43] Masik provided her with a wooden bunk in a cubicle separated from the main part of his cabin by a curtain. "With this privacy Propriety and Mrs Grundy had to be satisfied for seven weeks," wrote Miss Hutchison.

While Isobel Hutchison was safe and cozy in Masik's cabin, the RCMP were holding Hume's letter and permit. By October, the Mounties at Aklavik were concerned enough about her whereabouts to inform "G" Division Headquarters in Edmonton that they would try and find her. This meant two men had to travel to Herschel, where they knew one white trapper lived in a primitive state.[44] The necessary trip was doubly disturbing for Inspector Rivett-Carnac, the officer-in-charge at Aklavik. Having just returned from Herschel Island, he now had to go back at a time when hazardous ice ridges were forming on the ocean. While troubled by her fate, he was, at the same time, exasperated by her independence, and annoyed because he had to leave his wife in Aklavik when she was about to give birth. He later recorded that he received a wireless message about a lady botanist who, unaware of the commotion she had caused, "was not to be deterred from her purpose by any impediment."[45]

When Miss Hutchison showed up at Aklavik at the end of November, the RCMP were not as impressed by her adventure as she was. Later, the published account of her journey was to casually note that she had been informed by the constable that she was wanted by the police and had long "been given up as a bad job."[46] The RCMP, albeit vexed, were relieved. Isobel Hutchison should have considered herself lucky that they did not charge her for the expenses of their rescue attempt, as provided for in the Scientific and Exploration Ordinance. After being shown a copy of the letter that had been attached to her licence, she wrote back to Ottawa, saying with some understatement that she had had some difficulty on the trip and that she had risked getting caught by freeze-up because she was determined to complete her task. She then stayed two months in Aklavik planning the next stage of her journey, which included a visit to Cambridge Bay via Coppermine. Probably to the relief of all officials concerned, the aeroplane she hired broke down. Isobel Hutchison found herself on her way home to Scotland. Although she anticipated a return the next summer, Isobel Hutchison never did go back to the Canadian north, saving the authorities from instituting those provisions of the Scientific and Exploration Ordinance that allowed them to refuse permission to individuals who had abused the privilege.

Because Isobel Hutchison had collected ethnographic specimens only in Alaska, they were none of Ottawa's concern. However, those objects and her botany specimens were of some interest in Britain. They also captured the attention of Gordon Sinclair, a Canadian reporter who irreverently referred to her as a "Scottish geranium and petunia Hunter."[47] Gordon Sinclair riddled his article with salacious remarks, managing to belittle Miss Hutchison by assessing the value of the expedition in monetary terms. He advised his readers that just in case they had any ideas about "hunting arctic asters" as a profitable pastime, Miss Hutchison had paid her own expenses and received no salary during the eighteen-month trip, intimating that no one could take her seriously since she had had to pay for the trip herself and there were no sponsors. These sarcastic comments

are significant if only because Sinclair's column had wide distribu-
tion in Canada. He represented Isobel Hutchison as a crackpot lady
gardener on an extended house and gardens tour. While she may
have been cavalier about planning and regulations, Isobel Hutchison
was also a serious amateur botanist and that aspect of her work did
not merit insults. But Sinclair insinuated still more. Having noted
how Isobel Hutchison was "the only woman for the well known
miles and miles and miles," he posited "that's where a woman
prowler gets the big edge." The edge was only indicated when Sinclair concluded the article by explaining that he too had been in far-
flung places, but had "yet to see the place where I'm the only man.
That might be fun."[48]

The British press were kinder to Isobel Hutchison, leaving lewd
remarks to the colonial newspapers. Impressed by the botanical
specimens she had sent home and intrigued by the trip she had
made, the papers offered praise. They also noted the staunch heart
and dogged determination[49] attributed to her by the pilot who had
flown her out of the Arctic. No mention was made of her stay with
August Masik.

These accounts suggest that men believed they had some special
aptitude that not only allowed them to measure the capabilities and
competence of women, but also influenced their decisions. That
should come as no surprise. There was almost a universal assumption that women could not endure the inconveniences of Arctic
travel, the loneliness of isolation from other white women, and the
complications of the climate – and this despite the living examples
already in the north to dispute this view. Men's conception of what
women were able to withstand physically – based upon their male
prejudices and misunderstandings of what inconveniences a
woman had to put up with – also affected their judgement. Overall,
men in the Arctic assumed women to be weaker than they were,
especially when it involved travel. But this was a myopic view,
further hampered by restricted peripheral vision about women's
ability to survive the Arctic with the same regularity as men. Why
the men did not learn from the examples around them is a mystery.
It was as if the continued impression of women as delicate and men
as robust allowed them the delusion of superiority even when
proved inaccurate.[50]

What men really thought women could do is relatively unimportant. What is significant is what happened when the men were challenged. There was an informal "Northern Compact" among the men
who had braved the wastes, or at least those who had done so in a
cerebral sense from their desks in Ottawa and Winnipeg. Women

entering the region found that administration of the north involved a series of personal empires, which could be expanded and managed on a broader scale or contracted to defend one another's interests. While the elasticity of officialdom had its merits when budgets were tight, employees spread thinly, and communications stretched, individuals often got caught when the tension was allowed to relax.

Men who have written about their life and experiences in the NWT shared the same community, and their projected view has never questioned the "old boys network" as women did – as outsiders. The men's assessments rarely made use of records concerning women, because to them, women were of no concern. How men saw women was unimportant to their overview. As women were never considered important enough for membership in the Wide World Club, it should come as no surprise that they were not invited to become associates of the Northern Club either. It may be that Kathleen Shackleton, Marion Grange, and Isobel Hutchison represented a new breed of women about to start up their own branch membership. Or it may simply have been a sign of the times that they received the press coverage which made it seem so. Nevertheless, they transgressed the frontiers of their own professions as well as those of the north and northern administrations.

CHAPTER FIVE

"Standing in the Gap:" Anglican Women and the Northern Mission

Christian missionaries deliberately sought to place themselves in close relation to the indigenous population so as to proselytize European culture along with the Christian Gospel. There was nothing subtle about the missionary message. Both Roman Catholic (RC) and Anglican missionaries in northern Canada were instruments of change if only because of their vocation. They were also children of their time: included with their message was the idea that aboriginal peoples could only survive contact by adopting Christianity and its concepts. In time, this became a fundamental postulate of all missionaries.

The missionary's concern with religious beliefs and the saving of souls intruded into the very roots of native heritage and culture. The imposition of such ideas as sin, thrift, and work – tied closely to the Christian ideal and its European views, and coupled with attempts to teach the English language – together with the introduction of European healing practices, promised a kind of dominion over the Inuit and Dene that went well beyond those promised by government agents or encroaching settlement. Of course, while missionary efforts are now viewed as paternalistic, they themselves would have viewed their work as humanitarian.

Since the first goal of both Anglican and RC missionaries in the region was spiritual conversion, social change was only a by-product, initially accomplished through these humanitarian services. The morality of that cultural imposition raises difficult questions and historians must be alert to parallel transgressions. It is unfortunate that academic scrutiny means humanitarian efforts are submitted to judgmental enquiry which is in itself fraught with bias and prejudice of some kind, but at least that approach counterbalances to some extent the hagiographic accounts that constitute the literature authored by northern missionaries. Because these stories are part of the masculine history of the north, they are in some ways doubly damned. In fairness, however, it should be pointed out that many male missionaries at least noted the presence of women, or remarked on the difficulties women encountered.[1]

Most general studies about Christian missionaries are geographically specific; the basis for comparison with other mission fields is often shaky. That there tends to be two approaches to the study of missionaries adds to the complexity of the problem. First their virtues are extolled within the structure of the religious institution itself. Second, in one of those "unquestioned orthodoxies of general historical knowledge," they are condemned because of what Brian Stanley identifies in *The Bible and the Flag* as the notion that Western expansion and Christian mission go hand in hand, and also because "readers who do not themselves possess a strong religious commitment are likely to find alien and unattractive the confidence in their own rectitude displayed by most of the missionaries who will be discussed."[2] In addition, anyone apprehensive about the missionaries and unable to cope with intense religious faith might well choose to interpret the women's mission in the north as feminine religious zeal manipulated by male-dominated church hierarchies.

It was believed that missionary women were more adept at dealing with native culture than other white women because they specifically sought contact, essentially breaking down barriers instead of working to maintain them. Missionary wives were expected to be helpmeets, in both the domestic environment and the mission itself, meaning that they often had to subordinate their personal problems to God's work. The northern experience indicates how difficult that was to do because their own personal dilemmas were so intricately laced with their sense of duty. A close examination of the women's work in the mission shows that their role was often more personal and direct than that of the men, particularly in relation to women and families. While an analysis of women's work at the mission deflects attention away from policy and policy-makers (a constant theme in the official histories and memoirs left by the men), the female missionary remains an easy target for blame because of her religious goals and because Christian mission was irrevocably tied to the concepts of racial superiority. Complicating the issue is the knowledge that indigenous women were being sexually exploited by white men, while simultaneously serving as the subject of white women's sincerity.

The policies of the Church of England in Canada and its missionary societies in the north played a fundamental role in the way women carried out personal missions in the region. But it is obvious, too, that the environment in which they lived often functioned as a balance to the policies of this, one of the most patriarchal of churches. This does not mean that faith was an unimportant factor in the women's lives, or that their practice of religion was insignificant, only that the structures of their church had less effect than might initially be expected. The simple truth was that rules were broken and decisions made because it was more expedient to ignore advice in instances of less than perfect living conditions and drawn-out communication lines. The environment set the tone for this mission field, just like any other.

Wives of Anglican clergy had been in the north since 1862, although it appears the earliest wives were local women of mixed-blood or native heritage.[3] By 1876, Selina Bompas had arrived at Fort Simpson with her husband William, Bishop of Athabasca, joining the Reverend and Mrs W.D. Reeve, who opened an Indian residential school at Fort Rae the same year. Reeve had been at Fort Simpson since 1865; Bompas had been in the north since 1872. Augusta Morris and Rose (Gadsby) Spendlove arrived at Fort Norman in 1881. Miss Gadsby married clergyman William Spendlove at Fort Norman, while Miss Morris acted as secretary and companion to Mrs Bompas at the Fort Simpson mission.

By the time Sadie Stringer arrived as a new bride at Peel River and Herschel Island in 1896, precedents had been established for wives as well as single women. By 1890, teachers had begun to arrive at the Indian residential school at Hay River. The first residential school for Inuit children was established at Shingle Point in 1928, two years after the hospital and school at Aklavik were built. And in 1930, the mission hospital at Pangnirtung was constructed. Single female missionaries were employed at the schools and hospitals; the wives of missionaries were more often at smaller local missions such as Bernard Harbour, Coppermine, Fort Resolution, and Herschel Island where their husbands were in charge of the missions.

The married women were in the north initially because the clergymen who were there saw the value of having a wife beside them. William Bompas preferred married men for his missions, or men engaged to be married whose brides would accompany them north. He claimed married men were more reliable and settled,[4] which was one way of saying that the Church Missionary Society (CMS) wanted its missionaries to preach the Gospel with diligence and fervour but without distractions.[5] Writing to his superiors in London, William Spendlove argued that wives were a real necessity at lonely stations.[6] Charles Whittaker felt so in need of a wife that when his fiancée in

Toronto died, he proposed to Emma Harvey, whom he had met while travelling north two years previously. Whittaker wrote that the bishop had intimated to him that he liked his missionaries to be married because they were more likely to remain in the field. After their marriage, Miss Harvey, who was already in service at Fort Chipewyan, was described by Whittaker as "an immaculate housekeeper, an excellent cook, and a congenial companion, a very great pleasure indeed."[7]

A cynic might suggest that what the men really needed was a woman to look after them and to share their beds; or that if the Church of England did encourage its missionaries to have wives, it might have been because there was an unwritten rule against miscegenation. Not unexpectedly, none of the men was candid enough to confirm those assumptions, and it was probably a combination of factors that influenced wives to accompany their missionary husbands to the north. William Fry, for example, wrote that his wife Christina was a "great help to me in the work" and "a good wife and a true missionary. There are some things that only a woman can do," he wrote, and "when our people need help she realizes their need long before I do and has been of great service where I should have failed utterly."[8] Women were socialized to be sensitive and nurturing, but this does not mean that men could not share those qualities. Whether there were things only a woman could do in the missionary field is open to debate – what is important is that the men professed that this was the case. More important still was that the men recognized that the task required more than they as individuals could manage.

That does not mean that the same sensibilities about marriage applied to single women already in the field. Unlike Emma Harvey Whittaker, Gladys Fosterjohn's efforts to marry a lay worker at Hay River met with an unenthusiastic response from Bishop Lucas. Miss Fosterjohn was employed as matron at St Peter's Mission when she wrote of her plans to Lucas in November 1921. She told the Bishop that she had every intention of fulfilling her contract, leaving him to inform the WA (who had sponsored her employment) at his discretion. Bishop Lucas advised her that she and her fiancé Mr Grant should "realize the importance of absolutely discreet behaviour around the Mission." He cautioned that the "lynx eyed children will detect the least sign of 'courting' and they will not be slow to comment upon what they see, 'with sundry additions.'"[9]

Gladys Fosterjohn wrote back to explain that she fully realized "the need of being very cautious," for the children were "quick to notice." But she added: "I am here to represent as far as lies in my power, my

Master to these children. I will always endeavour to behave seemly before them and not be a stumbling block to one of the least of Christ's brethren."[10] These intentions were based, however, upon her assumption that she and her fiancé would not marry until her contract had been completed. When they decided to get married later that same year, Lucas announced that her decision would "cause trouble with the WA." He said he was surprised at the lighthearted way in which she looked forward to marriage and the continuance of her work as before. It is difficult to determine from the punctuation in his letter whether he thought the two were incompatible, or if he was just being conservative. While noting that she had conferred with her mother who had advised the marriage, he commented that "surely she cannot be aware of the conditions around you."[11]

Only conjecture can explain why Gladys Fosterjohn's impending nuptials were not expedited with the same dispatch as those of the Whittakers'. Her fiancé Mr Grant was not a clergyman; he was single, and working at a fairly large and well-organized St Peter's mission. Mr Grant had journeyed north at the same time as Miss Fosterjohn. As for the Whittakers, Charles was a veteran northern missionary of some standing and Emma Harvey, who had ceased to be a single, female mission worker when she became the missionary's wife, did not insist on maintaining her paid position.

Gladys Fosterjohn's file is the only one extant which deals with the issues of single women missionaries marrying while in the field. She certainly was not unique – the problem may have been simply her unwillingness to be patient. Of necessity, the Missionary Society of the Church of England in Canada (MSCC) had to make plans well in advance for their northern missions, and any threat to those plans upset the general order. Field staff were difficult to recruit and replace.

In 1904, the first head of the MSCC declared that "owing to the great lack of men for the ministry and the unlimited field for workers in the territories and western provinces, it is necessary that trained, efficient, God-fearing women should stand in the gap."[12] Single women were already at Hay River and Fort Simpson when this decision was made, and the directive did not mean the north would be overrun by female Anglican missionaries after 1904. This was just a more concerted effort to recruit women for the north who were trained in Anglican theology, as teachers, and as nurses.

Enlisting for Service, a recruiting pamphlet produced by the WA of the MSCC , was quite specific about the Church's requirements.[13] They needed nurses – well-trained, devoted Christian nurses for residential schools and hospitals. Each mission school had to have at least one qualified teacher, until a change in government regulations in the 1920s required that all teachers be certified. Matrons (housekeepers), to take charge of the girls and boys and kitchens, were always in demand. To work as the matron, a woman needed a knowledge of sewing, plain cooking, and laundry work; a love of children; and some skill at managing them. The recruitment booklet offered the following incentive to the missionary who would put up with this drudgery: "she has endless opportunities in her association with [the children] to show what is true, Christian, everyday living." Everyone, regardless of occupation, was required to have "an ability to find one's pleasure and social recreation among the few [with] which one may be associated, and varying gifts of personality, executive ability, common sense, cheerfulness and the ability to make friends rapidly and to get on with people of varying temperaments."[14] While these may not have been the most demanding of qualifications to meet, in the north they were often the most challenging to maintain.

Addie Butler, whose candid letters often depicted the spats between the women she worked with and included her grumps about the male principals, had cause to reflect on how hard it was to be a model missionary in a northern community. In one letter, she wrote, "I don't want to be [a model missionary] if some folks are here," and added "if they go to heaven, I don't want to go there, and I am sure the children don't either." She had some zeal when she arrived, she noted, although her enthusiasm had vanished at that point in the winter when everyone was getting on each other's nerves.[15]

Inasmuch as the same few people were always present at social gatherings at small missions like Shingle Point, where the close quarters only served to magnify the foibles and imperfect traits of some, it is most significant that some missionary women actually committed such thoughts to paper. Of course, writing out frustrations undoubtedly provided some catharsis. As the mail boat sailed away carrying with it the year's reflections on fellow workers, some of that frustration must have travelled with it through the ice floes.

Complaints about individuals and grievances arising from personality conflicts often arose because of a mission pecking order that had only one person at each step of the employment ladder. Just about everybody was in a position overseeing someone else. For most of the year, there was no escape from petty tyrants. Susan (Bessie) Quirt, who commented on how frustrating it was to work with the deaconess at Shingle Point, recorded in her diary that she "is indeed most aggravating and drives us to despair." The "us" included Flossie Hirst, who would later be assigned to Pangnirtung. Miss Quirt noted that the two of them got "so peeved, for it seems to us that we get no thought or consideration whatever." Those in charge "have no idea of overcoming difficulties – they just let the difficulties do the overcoming."[16] The complaints referred to an individual whose brother was the resident principal and Anglican priest. It seems that the deaconess was "very conscious of her superior intellectuality" and had "a busy time pointing out the obvious things that anyone without a degree can see," explained Addie Butler, adding that her own powers of concentration were quite as good, but that she gave "other people credit for having a few brains.[17]

In a published address, Helen Sowden described the two special qualifications she felt were needed for service in the northern mission. Not without some irony, she maintained that loyalty and adaptability were needed for harmonious well-being.[18] Only four years earlier at the hospital at Aklavik where Miss Sowden had been employed as matron, the missionary-in-charge had written to his bishop about the mission staff not working together in the way they should. An exasperated William Geddes remarked how he had expected difficulties to arise, but to his annoyance they kept arising over the merest of petty details. He wrote: "One very often can find Miss Catt in the nurses' sitting room at one end of the building and Miss Hackett in a room at the far end of the building. They have divided the building between them and certain things are the property of one that the other may not touch. Miss Catt has her stove that she looks after as well as her own wood box which Miss Hackett must not touch and vice versa."[19]

Geddes decided the problem was due to Miss Hackett's inexperience. As she was a graduate nurse, Miss Hackett had been put in charge of two older women, one of whom was a veteran missionary. He thought that if Miss Hackett could exchange places with a nurse at Hay River, the problem might be solved. He signed off by apologizing for the added burden of this problem, explaining that he did not see any prospect of the two women ever getting along together. The isolation of the northern missions meant that such situations impeded progress and development through training and experience. The MSCC recruiting pamphlet stated that the Society's goal was potential missionaries, not perfected ones. That may be why the bishop and the MSCC ignored the missionary's appeal, and why a frustrated Geddes wrote again to the bishop protesting that he doubted the hospital would ever be able to do its intended work as long as Miss Hackett was the nurse-in-charge.[20]

Occasionally an open conflict of some proportion would develop between staff members as a result of the isolation and structure of the mission communities. One recalcitrant missionary could upset the entire mission, as illustrated by the case of Miss Donnelly (Christian name unknown), who was the nurse at Hay River in 1923. Some of the surviving correspondence indicates that Miss Donnelly upset the staff at St Peter's over a number of issues, and the administration was not at all sure how to deal with the situation. From the letters of the principal, the Reverend W.A.B. Stoddart, and the bishop at Fort Chipewyan,[21] it appears that the men were unable to deal with Miss Donnelly's behaviour and concluded that she would have to be "out of her mind" to "possibly do such a thing so insistently." That sounds more like a smokescreen than an assessment based on fact. More importantly, perhaps, was the notation that this was "a serious matter and altogether subversive to discipline."[22] Of course, keeping the troops in line was one way to stop them baiting one another.

Both the letters and the subsequent report are full of allegations that would be damaging to individuals, and revealing their contents would serve no purpose – the controversy was over what can best be described as a whispering campaign, which had the staff "in a state of excitement" and which followed a number of spiteful incidents. For example, the nurse had removed a child from the playground without the matron's permission. The principal reported she had "coolly told [him] she did so for no other purpose than to annoy" the matron. That Miss Donnelly had also committed the sin of "unburdening herself" to everyone who would listen meant that the situation was beyond any form of damage control. Whatever her misdeeds at the mission itself, however, Miss Donnelly was doomed to exile because she danced "in attendance at every boat that came." As Stoddart put it: "Her profuse and evident admiration for men was certainly uncalled for, and un-wise (sic). Her conduct one evening when we were entertaining some officers of the Liard River was certainly uncalled for and savoured more of the fast and loose set of a large city than of an institution caring for the moral and spiritual welfare of the children."[23] Other, less specific offences, had annoyed the staff. Miss Donnelly apparently walked around the kitchen while scantily clad (no further description) and used water already boiled for breakfast for her personal tea. There were even a number of minor physical assaults which might indicate the woman was a trifle unhinged. What she was eventually chastised for, however, was her unsuitability as a missionary. Under the circumstances, perhaps this was warranted.

The principal was concerned because there was some "imputation" that Miss Donnelly was a Roman Catholic. She was seen at the presbytery when visiting the RC mission, ostensibly for medicines.

She had secured rosary beads from the RC mission and was indiscreet enough to offer them to the Anglican mission staff. "Considerable comment had been made among the Roman Catholic of the village as to whether Miss Donnelly was working for the Anglican mission or the Roman Catholic, and had she remained, it was likely to lead to some difficulty,"[24] wrote Stoddart. For missionaries in the north, it was a grievous act to present such difficulties.

The Anglican hierarchy was concerned about the effect of Miss Donnelly's behaviour on the historical rivalry between the Anglican and RC missions. Church leaders worried that the Dene and Inuit were confused enough by the competition between the two faiths. One contemporary observer described the enmity as "a savage game in which the Natives [were] bewildered pawns."[25] It was a game of power, prestige, and money, involving the evangelical beliefs of the CMS and MSCC missionaries, whose opposition to the Roman Church was firmly entrenched.[26] Certainly, the more pupils in the schools and patients in the hospitals, the more cash would come from the government. But a tally was kept as well: the greater the number of Aboriginals converted and baptized, the more points won. Just who was keeping score besides the missionary societies themselves was never recorded. It was a game in which church*men* had set out the playing field; the women were part of the team, and the women make continual references to the competition – with some notable twists. It cannot be denied that this rivalry may have been used by the CMS and MSCC men on the scene to boost morale and generate excitement among women missionaries, much as some present-day cults motivate their followers. Such action would have capitalized on the contemporary understanding of religion as a legitimate activity for women within the accepted norms of feminine behaviour.[27]

Without definitive records it is impossible to categorically list which Aboriginals belonged to which religious faith.[28] It can be assumed that generally the Dene in the Mackenzie River valley were ministered to by the Oblates of Mary Immaculate. The Oblate Fathers were assisted by the Grey Nuns, who acted as nurses and teachers. The Church of England served some native families at small missions in the area, although the Anglican influence was most evident among the Inuit of the Arctic coast. Not unexpectedly, each side endeavoured to change the denominational loyalties of the Inuit and Dene. In fact, the contest for souls resulted in a duplication of services offered in almost all settlements of some size. This is the context in which the following women's remarks should be placed.

Miss Tims wrote from Hay River in 1898 about two Dene coming to the mission of their own accord and asking the missionaries to look after their children. "It shows their growing confidence in us, as they are professedly Roman Catholic," she decided. She was also elated by the prospect of Mrs Nagle staying at St Peter's over the winter while her husband went to Edmonton. Because the Nagles were Roman Catholics, Miss Tims believed that the mission work would be affected and would allow the Anglicans to make inroads into the RC community, which was, she declared "our great enemy."[29]

Bessie Quirt convinced herself that the Aboriginals at Arctic Red River were "so friendly and happy looking" because they were "all Protestant here, and one cannot but help noticing the difference in their faces."[30] Mrs Jane Clarke informed the *Letter Leaflet* that although the Roman Catholics "have most of the Indians," at Fort Norman "those who belong to us are very loyal and attend worship very regularly."[31] And Mrs Harcourt, referring to mission work, reminded the loyal mission followers in the south about the school work at Aklavik that "crowded out other important duties." She added "that in view of the keen opposition from the very efficient RC school in Aklavik, that at all costs our school [has] to [be] maintained." Mrs Harcourt seemed to be aware that nominal Anglicans who sent their children to RC schools would be identified as having changed their allegiance.

Mrs Harcourt made clear her views about "the RC aggression in the Mackenzie Delta," but it is her final statement that provides a clue to the real purpose of her appeal. "They are making so determined an effort to take the Eskimo away from our Church," she lamented, "and they seem to possess an unlimited supply of money and workers to further their ends, while we are so pitifully handicapped for the lack of both."[32] The "missionary mind," fired by the intense desire to reform, and the rancour generated by denominational loyalties no doubt explains some of the sense of quiet desperation behind these appeals. Without funds, the mission could not withstand the competition. But something else is going on here as well. For the Anglican women in the region, the most visible competition at their level came from the Grey Nuns living in community, whose vocation and lifestyles represented the antithesis of the evangelical tradition to which most of the Anglicans ascribed. Female Church of England missionaries were not just competing with Roman Catholic ideology, but with other women, for prospective female converts. In other words, some of the missionaries were jealous, partly because they saw the sisters as having the benefits of support from a strong Mother Church obsessed with the desire to save heathen souls. The women were probably unaware of this manifestation and would have likely dismissed any such charge.

If the Anglican women were disheartened by this phalanx of women who wore grey habits and epitomized fortitude, it is difficult to tell because the sisters are seldom mentioned in the primary documents surveyed. The absence of the Grey Nuns from the chatty letters and diaries of the Anglican missionaries is notable even though the order had been in the region in some numbers since 1867. Remembering that communication between the two groups was hampered because of language provides some explanation. The nuns were, for the most part, francophone, while the Anglicans were, of course, anglophone. This division itself provides a unique Canadian twist because it implies some social order as well – at least it would have to the British and English Canadian missionaries, given that church affiliations, language, and ethnic origins often defined social distinctions in Canada.[33]

The silence would be less significant if the other women who were not missionaries had not mentioned the Grey Nuns. Isobel Hutchison, Luta Munday, Agnes Cameron, Clara Vyvyan, Emma Colcleugh, and even Ann Lindbergh all had something to say about the brave sisters, while the Anglican missionary women remained mum. Dr Isobel Greenwood was the one exception. It was her visit to the RC school at Fort Smith while en route north that elicited one of the few observations about the sisters from an Anglican missionary woman that may explain the chasm between the two groups of women. Dr Greenwood, who reported that the sisters were most kind and showed devotion and a very real interest in their work, then added, "I feel we could learn something from them on the score of making the most of one's opportunities, and the least of one's difficulties."[34]

Anglican women were more often in a position to complain than the sisters, whose vocation required a degree of devotion, obedience, and sacrifice. There is evidence that some of these Anglican women effectively pressured the prevailing bureaucracies to make practical changes at northern missions. Their attempts were probably more a measure of the Anglican women's social class, however, than their level of compliance with missionary doctrine. For example, in 1926, Bishop Westgate at the MSCC in Winnipeg wrote to Canon Vale at St Peter's Mission. Westgate had received a letter from Miss Howie, the kitchen matron at St Peter's, about a native employee who was creating difficulties. Miss Howie had complained to Canon Vale but receiving no satisfaction, took the opportunity to petition Westgate. "I do not know the [native] girl" involved, wrote Westgate, admonishing Vale to do something about the situation because he knew "Miss Howie very well and [was] satisfied that the conduct of [the native girl] must have been well-nigh unbearable otherwise it would not have been reported."[35] Miss Howie apparently knew Westgate well enough to send her complaints over the head of the principal. How Canon Vale interpreted her action is not indicated.

Single and married women were required to have the knowledge and training more likely available to a middle-class woman, or at least someone of respectable background. Whatever their status, these women were likely accustomed to taking some level of initiative based on privilege. That presents an interesting question. According to Ken Coates, William Bompas was concerned about the social background of his missionaries, insisting that "gentlefolks" had had to "come down a peg in their position which [was] most painful to themselves and those about them. Those of an inferior grade ... generally rise a peg which is most pleasant to themselves and their neighbours."[36] Bompas indicates this attitude pertained to both men and women and Coates concludes that the clergymen and lay missionaries hired for the north were less than first-class candidates. There is no indication, however, that this holds true for the women; in fact, the reverse is more probable.

A decade later, Bompas was still vacillating about what kind of women the northern mission field required. When Isaac Stringer wrote to Bompas about bringing women workers into the north in 1906, Bompas suggested that he should engage what Stringer had described as a "lady helper as teacher or Matron, or something else," Stringer still being "rather perplexed as to what to do about women workers." Bompas said he would be happy to send a "treasure"; but Stringer countered by pointing out how hard it was to get "a real treasure," and added, "I do not find them without much searching."[37]

What might a northern missionary look for when recruiting a woman for the north? More to the point, "Who are those who should not venture upon life in the Far North?" asked Selina Bompas, an Arctic veteran who surely knew what the wife of an Anglican clergymen could expect in the north. She was speaking particularly to women, but her advice could apply to any northern missionary. She wrote: "The nervous and hysterical should not do so; there are too many surprises in the North, too many startling incidents and unlooked for events for any who have not acquired the art of self-control and absolute composure under trial of provocation. Those who have been subject to rheumatism should not come, nor should the very delicate or the consumptive come. Those who suffer from weak eyes should not come for the glare of sunshine on our vast fields of snow is apt to produce snow blindness. These are [a] few of the physical causes which should make one hesitate."[38] Mrs Bompas's postscript contained the most important bit of advice. A missionary, she said, should "start with a fair prospect of clinging to the life [she] has chosen, and not [think] of coming back at the end of a year or so, having discovered a little too late [she] had made a mistake." The vague reference to a year or so carries a subtle message – would-be missionaries had to be prepared to stay there for at least a year. Winters made it almost impossible to serve a shorter term.

There is little concrete evidence regarding employment contracts for that early period when the CMS was in charge of Anglican missions in the north, but there is information about the expected length of missionary duty for women engaged somewhat later by the MSCC. In general, the MSCC correspondence provides some insight into the conditions under which women were employed by the society. In reply to a request about employment conditions in 1938, Bishop Fleming noted women were required to serve not less than four years and not more than five; six years, he said, was inadvisable.[39] It appears that this rule was inflexible. Witness Fleming's remarks in the *Arctic News* in 1931 that Prudence Hockin had requested a fifth year at Pangnirtung instead of taking the mandatory furlough. Fleming sought the approval of the nurse's mother before he allowed Miss Hockin the extra year. When she applied for a sixth year, Fleming refused. He felt that a five-year stay in the Arctic was the limit for even a healthy person.[40]

Fleming may have considered five years a long time, but as early as 1921, J.R. Lucas reminded one correspondent that Mrs Reeve had stayed thirty years, Mrs Spendlove twenty, Mrs Whittaker twenty-three, and Mrs Lucas twenty-eight – and all under "conditions which were far worse than those which exist today." Of course, Bishop Lucas was remembering married women with husbands, if not families, to provide them with moral support for their service, so it was a little unfair of him to conclude "that the younger, present generation of men and women lack something of the true missionary spirit which actuated the older workers in the Far North – sacrifice makes no appeal to the newer, it seems like foolishness to them."[41] By the time Lucas wrote this in 1921, it had become easier to move in or out of the Arctic, and so "newer" missionaries were more readily able to take advantage of the transportation system.

The "true missionary spirit" required personal economic sacrifice as well as physical discomforts. Naturally, wives of missionaries were unpaid, even if they performed professional duties as nurses and teachers. Single women, though, were actually employed. Salaries and terms of employment changed over time, although there was one financial condition that remained constant. The missionaries' pay was usually deposited in an Edmonton bank on their behalf because cash was "of little use to missionaries on arctic service," suggested the secretary of the MSCC.[42] This means that many of the women would have had some financial security when they left the north after four or five years. There is little evidence, however, to suggest any financial motive for mission work, with the possible exception of Addie Butler who "was tired of not having a regular job and a regular income instead of outgo."[43]

The range of salaries for single women was wide, depending on the service and, of course, the era. In 1913, Miss Leroy and Miss Page at Hay River were paid a quarterly sum of $57.00 with $5.50 deducted for superannuation. The WA forwarded cheques to the mission for their room and board.[44] To provide some context for this amount, in 1915 Miss Jackson claimed $47.80 for her fare, meals, and the war tax paid for her journey to Hay River from Smith's Landing.[45] Compare these salaries with those of 1924. The male principal at Hay River was paid a salary of $80.00 per month; he was also a clergyman. The farm instructor at the school received $60.00. The general male assistant was paid $55.00 per month and the fisherman employed at the mission received $50.00 for work in December. Women "agents" included a matron-in-charge, whose salary was $45.00 a month; a laundress, who was paid $30.00; and two supervisors, who each received that same amount.[46]

In 1933, the MSCC informed then Archdeacon Fleming of the following salary schedule: head matrons who were qualified nurses would receive $50.00 per month, including room and board. Teachers were to be paid $35.00 per month the first year and, in subsequent years, $40.00 per month. Kitchen matrons would receive $35.00 monthly; supervisors and assistant matrons were paid $30.00 per month. In comparison, engineers and farming instructors in larger schools might receive $50.00 per month, although if the schools were smaller, the instructors received $40.00 per month. Night watchmen received $30 to $35.00 per month, depending upon the size of the institution. Free board and accommodation were provided.[47] A furlough allowance of one month's salary for each year of service was paid at the appropriate time, although this policy seemed to be more flexible, depending on the contract and the circumstances. Women sometimes had difficulty collecting out-of-pocket expenses, but this appears to be due to communication problems. Either communication was lacking – which caused confusion – or the process of getting letters back and forth impeded that communication.

Contractual obligations for health care varied according to the times as well. The employment contracts of Marion Harvey in 1928 and Winifred Neville in 1929[48] indicate that employees were expected to accept full financial responsibility for all necessary medical treatment. By 1938, this policy had changed; a charge of one dollar per day was instituted to cover all health care services.[49] This change coincided with the building of Anglican hospitals in the north. As health care became available in the NWT, it became more accessible and relatively less expensive. There was some concern about the health of potential candidates, and the report form supplied to the medical examiner by the MSCC had specific references for women. Along with gender-neutral health questions was question number ten: "If the applicant is a woman, is she now suffering or has she ever suffered from uterine or menstrual disorder?" This query, a usual question on all regular medical examinations, had a significant rider. "It is desirable that particular attention be given to this enquiry, as the climate of all our mission fields bears heavily on those thus affected."[50] What climate has to do with gynecological disorders is unclear – isolated locations can account for difficulties, but no more than might arise for men with kidney stones or appendicitis. By reflecting the views of the day about how women's reproductive system affected their lives, and how their biological functions affected what they could, or could not do, the question confirmed that the north was really no place for a woman.

After the MSCC undertook to maintain the northern missions in 1920, candidates were required to fill out a number of "preliminary papers," which included an application form as well as the medical questionnaire. Female candidates were screened by a candidate's committee for women, which operated under the auspices of the WA of the MSCC. This organization was responsible for the work done by the MSCC among women and children abroad and within the Dominion. Its mandate was to support all women missionaries, exclusive of wives of missionaries, and all female native agents, whether evangelical, educational, or medical. That included the financial support of children in orphanages and the expenses incurred by women missionaries travelling to their posts.[51] The WA of the MSCC raised money, sent bales of supplies to northern missions, helped fund hospitals and schools, and eventually selected and sponsored candidates for the field.

The Candidate's Committee of the MSCC asked all sorts of questions about religion, dependents, musical ability, and education. Male candidates were queried about their spouses' religious affiliation and asked if their wives were in sympathy with their plans. The form also asked how the applicant's parents felt about the mission. These questions were used for all mission fields, although qualifications for the Canadian posting were less stringent than those for the "foreign" posts, and may reveal as much about the lure of the location as about the mission itself. Above all, explained the missionary guide, the Christian missionary "had not only to be able to describe Him to them, she must be able to *reflect* Him." Women were required to have a working knowledge of the Bible and to understand the doctrines and teaching of the Church of England, although some training was provided before they departed for the field.

Candidates for overseas work had to be at least twenty-three of age and no older than thirty-two, primarily because the MSCC believed the learning of oriental languages was too difficult for anyone older. For the Canadian mission, concern about a candidate's age was more related to health than language, especially problems caused by the harsh climate and isolation, as the Aboriginals were being taught to read and speak English anyway. The assumed difference between missionaries proceeding to the Orient and those in the Canadian field was also evident in the required educational qualifications. Arts matriculation was the minimum standard for the Orient because, in the words of the pamphlet, women missionaries would be in touch with "highly intellectual and well-educated" non-Christians; this explains the pressing need for women with college degrees noted in the pamphlet. Standards were not fixed for women acting as missionaries in the Canadian field; obviously prestige was less important there.[52]

The enlistment guide did note that nurses were needed for Indian residential schools, although it was specific about "devoted well-trained Christian nurses." The guide indicated that graduate nurses were preferred; others would be considered for more menial tasks and as nursing assistants. Whatever their qualifications, the women worked within the confines of a Christian mission. That vocation prompted D.L. McKeand to write to the NWT Commissioner in 1940 saying that he "had yet to meet the nurse [in the north] who did not feel she was first a missionary and second a nurse,"[53] and the MSCC certainly desired that orientation from its nurses. McKeand's comment was related to the complications that arose at hospitals where the federal government paid for only one single nurse, whether she was a Grey Nun or an Anglican worker. The Candidates and Furlough Committee of the MSCC turned down one nurse in 1926, for example, because "it was evident from her papers that Miss Yonge's ideal was purely as a nurse and [did] not [stem] from Missionary motives."[54]

In some ways, the correspondence generated by the bureaucracy over payment of nurses is an aside to this particular chapter, yet it must be pointed out that no other issue concerning women generated as much bureaucratic palaver as did the payment of these nurses. Two reasons account for this. The first was that the missionary societies chose the nurses, who were then nominally members of the civil service. They were, fortunately, exempt from Civil Service competition.[55] The Civil Service Commission had nothing to do with the hiring. Some of the nurses were already in service in the north, replacing someone on furlough or someone who had left the northern mission service altogether (there was often overlap because of the transportation system). Both the Roman Catholics and the Anglicans moved their nurses around within the region at their pleasure, a practice that gave some pause to bureaucratic minds. One letter from the Diocese of the Arctic to Ottawa illustrates why officials in the Ministry of the Interior got so frustrated with the whole issue. The letter, dated 24 September 1934, informs the department that the Bishop of the Arctic had recently sailed for England, leaving the honorary secretary to explain.

> We had planned to send Nurse Brown to Shingle Point School and Miss Somers to Aklavik Hospital and the Bishop requested that Nurse Somers be substituted for Nurse Rundle at Aklavik and Nurse Brown for Nurse Tomalin at Shingle Point. At Aklavik, however, in discussing things with the Rev T. Murray, the Bishop decided that if on the arrival of the nurses, Dr Urquhart and Nurse Bradford approved of having Nurse Brown at Aklavik and Nurse Somers sent to Shingle Point, they could be switched. Rev T. Murray now advises that this arrangement had been adopted.[56]

The government stance was no forms, no appointment, no pay. In 1936, Deputy Minister J.M. Wardle decided that

> Evidently the Church authorities are unfamiliar with the Civil Service Regulations and they have taken it for granted that, as long as a Nurse was on the job, it did not matter to the Department what Nurse it was. The Church authorities have certain ground for this belief as the Department and the Civil Service Commission invariably accept the Church's recommendation in the filling of these positions. However, this does not satisfy the regulations, as the Certificate issued by the Commission must name the person employed. It will have to be explained that the failure of the Church authorities to report this case makes it necessary for the Department to call for a refund in order that the new appointment may be authorized from the date that the former incumbent of the position ceased duty.
>
> The Civil Service Commission states that there is no way of authorizing the employment of a Nurse without specifically designating the particular individual and to satisfy the Auditor General, a refund must be made.[57]

All this may seem insignificant until it is remembered that nurses so employed had to fill out and sign civil service forms. This was not always possible, and it certainly meant that most nurses who were already there were working at the job long before the form arrived.[58]

The federal government paid the nurse more than the missionary society had contracted with the women,[59] but there were differences in the maintenance payments. A letter from the MSCC to Miss E. Goddard about her appointment as a nurse at Hay River in 1935 indicates she was to be paid $85.00 per month by the federal government, but that $25.00 per month would be deducted for room and board. In addition, she had to pay all her travel expenses as far as Waterways. She was also responsible for any medical expenses incurred.[60] Another problem arose because the Civil Service Commission was not empowered to pay funds directly to the church on behalf of the nurses. Eventually, all the bureaucrats in all the affected bureaucracies worked everything out. Much of the paperwork – they wrote many letters and memos – still remains in the National Archives. But the bureaucratic nonsense had little or no effect on the women themselves: they just went about their business, unhampered by the transmissions between Ottawa, Winnipeg, and Edmonton.

Confusing these same paper trails were the regional medical officers, who thought that if nurses were not placed under the auspices of some federal government department such as the Department of the Interior or the Department of Indian Affairs, "it would be difficult, if not impossible, to get nurses to follow the doctors orders and particularly to treat out-patients."[61] The nurses were all women, so by definition this is a gender issue. As in other colonial situations, the role of nurses reinforced the established cultural order by perpetuating the masculine role of doctors and administrators. In the north, the structure appeared even more patriarchal because the government made it a practice to hire medical doctors as Indian Agents. It would be wrong, however, to assume that the sex of the staff had any deeper meaning than was already evident in the south. These missionary nurses did not aid military and expansionist activity, nor did they contribute to rigid racial divisions. In fact, the evidence is to the contrary. They were hired primarily to look after the native population at the hospitals. White residents were welcome at these hospitals, but the facilities were built in response to mission needs, and nominally designed to eliminate barriers, not reinforce them.

McKeand rightly considered the northern health system as cumbersome and costly; he determined it would be more efficient if the government just paid the missionary societies for a nursing service in their hospitals.[62] His concern had nothing to do with the nurses themselves, just the finances. In 1922, the Privy Council itself debated the issue of supplying nurses to northern posts. That auspicious body decided the proper course was to approach the Victorian Order of Nurses (VON) to work in northern hospitals. After all, the VON was "an organized and disciplined body, the workers of which are imbued with an *esprit de corps* and loyalty to the general purpose of the Order. They also wear a special uniform, which would be an important feature of the work on an Indian Reserve, as Indians are always impressed by a uniform."[63]

A uniform meant that women would always maintain a sense of being properly and adequately robed, said Bishop Fleming writing to Arctic workers about their use. The uniforms have been described in an earlier chapter, although it was not mentioned that women married to missionaries were issued one as well. They were not required to wear the uniform when travelling or even when "functioning as wives of missionaries," whatever that meant. The shoulder straps were partly red and partly blue, "making a very nice combination and indicating that the missionary wives were associated with both branches of the service," explained Fleming.[64] It might also be argued that it indicated that the MSCC was not awfully sure what kind of authority the women held, although the uniform was most definitely part of the trappings of authority. When (and if) the wives wore them is not recorded.

The uniform may have been significant because of the association the Aboriginals made between religious leaders and healers of the sick. Missionary women (and nuns) wearing any uniform that bespoke authority could evoke a certain aura of power. It may have been a case of presenting a specific image to native observers, for gaining the confidence of local people was the first goal of any of the nursing staff. This was not an easy task, and often providence had to lend a hand. "At first the medical work" at Aklavik "was not popular, for the Native thought his own remedies were as good as anything white man could provide," wrote Mildred McCabe in 1932, but she added that "the influenza epidemic of 1928 proved to be a blessing in disguise."[65]

Bessie Quirt outlined the kind of medical work being done in the hospital at Aklavik on her way out on furlough from Shingle Point in 1933. Accidents were common among both white and native populations, she reported, but there was also the "dread scourge of tuberculosis," which she believed attacked the Dene more often than the Inuit. Miss Quirt also thought that digestive ailments were common due to the overconsumption of meat, especially in children, and commented that although the number of maternity cases was increasing, the native women were still reluctant to use the obstetrical facilities available. Miss Quirt decided that the women considered the five-days of bed rest that the hospital required of maternity patients to be a waste of time.[66]

At times, this unwillingness of native women to take advantage of the hospital was probably fortunate, because the nurses worked long hours without much relief. When Ann Lindbergh and her husband flew across the Arctic in 1931, she wrote in her diary at Point Barrow about the send-off they had received at Aklavik: "One of the nurses had to stay at the hospital, everyone else was at the dock. The Anglican hospital has two nurses who do everything. One girl I talked to was so discouraged and tired and hadn't had more than five hours sleep for a month."[67] Mrs Lindbergh was probably not exaggerating, for the nurses' schedule at Aklavik was incredibly demanding. A guide to duties explains that

The two nurses on the hospital staff shall divide their work as follows:
One nurse shall be in charge of the hospital for one month, and during that time the other nurse shall be the assistant or relieving nurse.
The nurse in charge of the hospital shall have full charge of the patients during her period of duty, and shall arrange all matters concerning their treatment, diet, etc. always in accordance with the directions of the Medical Officer.
The assistant or relieving nurse shall be responsible for the cleanliness of the hospital building, and the hospital laundry, and shall supervise the work of the kitchen and the residence, and shall be ready to assist and relieve the nurse in charge of the hospital whenever required to do so.
HOURS:
Under ordinary conditions, when there are no patients in hospital that require constant attention during the night, the nurse in charge of the hospital shall be on duty in the hospital daily from 7 am to 10.30 pm, and on alternate nights shall sleep in the hospital from 10.30 pm to 7 am to answer any and all calls from patients. The relieving nurse shall sleep in hospital for the same purpose on the nights that the nurse in charge does not. It shall be the duty of the nurse sleeping in the residence to call the nurse sleeping in the hospital at 7 am daily if necessary.
When there are patients that require considerable attention during the night, the nurse on duty shall be relieved from 10.30 pm to 4.30 am, and shall be on duty from 4.30 am to 10.30 pm daily, and the relieving nurse from 10.30 pm to 4.30 am daily. It shall be the duty of the nurse on duty to call the nurse who is sleeping in time that the relief may be made promptly and on time.

The nurse on duty in the hospital shall be relieved daily from 3 – 4.30 pm so that she may have opportunity for rest or recreation.
Both nurses shall be on duty in the hospital on the first day of each month at the hour of the visit of the Medical Officer, the nurse who is being relieved for the purpose of reporting to the Medical Officer, and the nurse who is taking over in order to receive the Medical Officer's instructions regarding the patients. The monthly term of duty in the hospital shall begin and end with the visit of the Medical Officer on that day. In the absence of the Medical Officer from Aklavik, the change shall be made at noon on the first day of the month.
It shall be the duty of the Assistant or relieving nurse to answer all calls for and from outside the settlement, subject always to the wishes and directions of the Medical Officer.[68]

With this kind of taxing schedule, the wonder is that nurses such as Deaconess Margaret Solomon were able to carry out the religious instruction and missionary activities as well as the nursing duties. Miss Solomon may have told the loyal mission followers in the south about how she had time for fifteen-minute services in the Aklavik hospital every evening, but she also noted that her arrival meant that the other nurse could finally get some much-needed rest.[69] Despite McKeand's understanding and the intentions of the MSCC, the mission was more likely the avocation; the nursing came first. Unlike teachers whose primary role was to christianize their charges through education, nurses had to heal first and then worry about christianizing.

The establishment of Woman's Auxiliary branches was part of that christianizing and allowed Anglican women to actively pursue mission work among women and children in a more relaxed setting. The WA was an integral part of any Anglican parish and operated with some small sense of autonomy from the men. Although it afforded women an opportunity to exercise executive skills, the WA should never be confused with any body that actually ran parish affairs. The national WA of the MSCC was something else altogether, meaning the WA had a double grasp on women and missions in the north – but a grasp less tenuous than that of the Church of England itself.

The support of missionary women in the North by the WA of the MSCC was vital, which was why the letters published in the *Letter Leaflet* and the *Living Message* convey so much news about individual success, hardships faced, and mission activities. The women in the south wanted to know where their dollars were going and how their gifts were being used. The women in the north wanted the flow of money to continue. In essence, each side was aware how the game had to be played: at the national level, in local parishes, or at northern missions, the WA gave capable women who were second-class members of the church an outlet, without actually interfering with the operation of the church itself. When they arrived in the north, Anglican women considered the creation of the WA the real woman's work at the mission and an important step in the development of the settlement's Anglican community. The women would have been active in their own home parishes as members of the WA, and they probably looked forward to remembered companionship and activities. Uprooted from their traditional activities at home, their eagerness to introduce the WA was probably as much self-serving as it was proselytizing. They had to make some adjustments for the situation, of course, but northern groups were modelled on the same four aims as groups in the south: we pray, we learn, we work, and we give.

From the beginning, the white and mixed-blood wives of traders ran the WA; despite the involvement of Dene and Inuit women in WA branches across the north, this was still a white woman's organization. In the Mackenzie River valley, women in the community were gradually integrated into WA groups as they moved into the settlements. By 1928, the Diocesan Board of the WA had managed to convene three important meetings. The published report of those meetings announced the motto of the Mackenzie River Diocese WA: as "the willingness and the solitary place shall be glad for them." The Hay River branch was formed in 1906, and a year later, Miss Wilgress recorded the names of twenty-seven members. The meetings consisted of business and missionary news, prayer, and educational talks. The Diocesan Board of the WA was organized in 1914. Mrs Vale was elected president and held this post until 1927. It appears from recorded dates that the Diocesan meetings were scheduled to coincide with the supply vessel's trip downriver. The women presumably met, then went home on the return voyage. What a wonderful excuse to visit old friends they had not seen for some time.

In her presidential address at the 1927 Diocesan Board meeting, Sadie Stringer introduced the concept of annual reports. These reports have proved useful for this study because they are printed in one booklet, with information about activities and the financial statements of several branches in the region. In 1927, the total membership in the diocese, which included Fort Chipewyan, was 82. Because there were no missionaries at Fort Smith or Fort Norman, there was no WA.

The first meeting of the Fort McPherson WA was held on Ash Wednesday 1919 under the direction of Mrs Reid. "Amidst many discouragements, the WA forged ahead, described as here a little, there a little." At that first meeting, the six members set to work with needles and thread and three yards of print fabric to make a quilt. By June of the next year, they had completed fourteen quilts and had donated the proceeds of a sale to Bishop Lucas.[70] This group apparently functioned as a sewing group, although prayer and the singing of hymns were part of every meeting.

In 1927, the Aklavik Branch showed a roll of twenty members; most were native women who spent only some part of the year near the settlement. It was impossible to organize a branch of Inuit women, wrote Minnie Hackett in the annual report, but the Dene women attended faithfully when they were in the area. The group made garments for the hospital, as well as moccasins and moose skin gloves which were then embroidered and sold to the white residents of the settlement. With the funds raised, the women donated a hymn board to the church and drew up plans for supplying more furnishings.[71] It is particularly interesting to compare this report with the one that followed five years later. Mrs Murray wrote about their "tiny WA branch" in 1933; there were six members, she reported, including the mission staff and the RCMP corporal's wife. In that small isolated Aklavik branch, the women saw themselves as doing their part "in the weaving of the widespread web of the WA."[72] But why were they suddenly operating with fourteen fewer members? Had the aboriginal women deserted the branch? Or had they never been full members in the first place?

An article about the Arctic in the 1938 *Living Message* explained how Anna Rokeby-Thomas was working to bring knowledge of the WA to that settlement. But it notes that her goal was to enrol every woman as an associate member, "teaching them, little by little, their responsibilities, until in the course of time they may enrol in a full membership."[73] This makes the WA seem a little like a ladies' Girl Guide company where everyone worked her way up through a series of levels. And in some ways it was. Isobel Greenwood recalled how badges were presented to the WA branch at Fort McPherson when she arrived there in 1935.[74] Mrs Rokeby-Thomas wrote that it had been her "ambition and hope" while training at the Deaconess House to organize a WA branch at Cambridge Bay. "It was a big disappointment to learn it would be much harder than I thought it would be." She said that the Inuit at Cambridge Bay were "most primitive, and while the men are capable and a little more progressive," the women were always in the background. Of the first all-woman's meeting, she confessed that "they looked like a flock of unherded sheep" and noted that she had "to fall back on our interpreter as I wanted them to understand fully." Teaching the meaning of the WA was so important to Mrs Rokeby-Thomas that she made an effort to convey the message at every Inuit camp she visited.[75]

At Pangnirtung, the WA was one of Flossie Hirst's chief joys. For her, it was a "means of becoming more intimately acquainted with the mothers and babies" and the large contingent of juniors.[76] The group worked hard at a fundraising project to help rebuild the hospital at Aklavik that had burned to the ground in 1926. The women made sealskin picture scrapbooks, unique as souvenirs. Realizing that supervision of the project took up a lot of her personal time, Miss Hirst flippantly recorded that she might start charging for her time. Upon reflection, however, she decided that Bishop Fleming "will rise in wrath and ask whose time we think we're using!"[77] Sewing groups seemed to be the mainstay of northern WA Branches, especially those with large native memberships. Since Inuit women in particular were extremely adept with a needle, it allowed a cultural compromise to take place. Both groups of women could make the best use of their skills to work towards some common ground.

Even white women who had no such skills could be useful to the WA, or so Mena Orford argued. "Sometimes," she said, "the evenings I went up [to the hospital] they'd have a sort of WA meeting, and Nukinga (her help) and her friends would be there too. Everyone would sit around chattering, or sewing, or knitting. I wasn't much help at the sewing or knitting, though I did come in handy to hold things down when someone else cut a pattern off whatever it was, or [to] hang onto a skein of wool with both wrists while one of the women carded it into balls. I could also baste seams."[78]

Florence Giles, another Anglican missionary at Pangnirtung explained how everyone took part. Each member's work was rolled into a towel and marked with her name so it could be kept separate. Some were making dresses, some were taking them apart. Some were knitting, others were undoing old knitting. (She does not say whether the one activity resulted from the other.) They closed these meetings with a hymn, and everyone went away with a "smile and a *Tabvoutit Kitonamic* (Good-bye, Thank You)," she wrote. She added that she prayed "their dear souls will appreciate the real meaning of the WA, as they do need it."[79] While the Inuit women may have needed some understanding of the WA, they probably did not need to learn about the joy of giving – which in this case meant giving up what they had produced to raise funds for the WA and other missions in Ceylon and Malaya. In the Inuit experience, sharing meant survival. It is interesting how one of their own cultural truths was distorted as part of the WA lesson.

There are many other examples of the activities of WA branches in the north. One entry bears some mention because it hints at how the Inuit viewed this female enterprise. At a WA picnic at Pangnirtung, the sports events featured sack, egg, spoon, and three-legged races. One hundred and fifty women and children were in attendance. Flossie Hirst wrote that "this was one day when it would seem that the men almost wished they could be women."[80] How disappointed the men must have been to be barred from the excitement. Of course to the white women, this was a day when men did not run anything and the women could do what they wanted. As for the Inuit families, they just wanted to have fun.

The extension of WA branches to native women represented the closest thing to feminist reform that the Anglican women could manage. Although they would most adamantly deny it, the message was to take initiative. The other message – sisterhood – was what passed for female bonding in a male-dominated setting. The WA did introduce concepts of sharing with women for the good of other women, an approach radically different from sharing as a community in order to survive. The WA branches also perpetuated the image of women as adjunct to their men, within the church itself and within the community. Inuit and Dene women were already aware of their place in their own cultural order, but that place was not as clearly defined as in the white culture which they were being taught to emulate. Gender roles may have been separate in native culture, although production and occupation were interwoven within those parameters.

The female Church of England missionaries and the wives of Anglican clergymen and lay missionaries have left the most impressive documentary record of the white women who went to northern Canada in the fifty years prior to the Second World War. What is evident from these documents is that their concerns often appear more pragmatic, yet petty, next to those of men involved in the same mission. That should come as no surprise, because even the missionary wife was absorbed by those small practical things that make up any woman's day. If it seems that women missionaries complained more, perhaps it was because they had more to complain about, although it could be that as independent women, they whined because they were less afraid of the consequences. The church was their *raison d'être* but the situation often controlled how things actually worked. Even missionaries can be un-Christian when they are all cooped up, although negative commentary about their mission purpose would probably be met with equanimity. Sometimes, that left them standing in the gap between southern ideals and northern realities – not quite the way the MSCC envisioned.

What is noticeable as well in the sources is that all of these women believed that the object of their life among the Inuit and Dene people was to convey the spiritual message of Christianity and to teach them "the eternal things that matter."[81] This was as much a personal notion as it was a denominational one. Take the young nurse who Ann Lindbergh met at Moose Factory when she flew across the Arctic. The nurse, said Mrs Lindbergh, was on her way north to a settlement where there was only "a missionary, a Mountie, a trading post, and Eskimos. Although she did not say much, it "made me quite sick to think of five years up there, a boat once a year, and no other white woman." Mrs Lindbergh remembered that she "couldn't think of anything encouraging to say except that she would be doing pioneering work." There was "a slight flicker of satisfaction on her face at that."[82]

"Faith Inspires, Distinguishes, and Explains It": The Grey Nuns' Mission in the North

Because of their long service in the north, the Sisters of Charity of Montreal have styled themselves as *Arctic Angels* [1] – their service in the north marked by Christian faith and the heroism inherent in *their* interpretation of the experience. Heroism, a term often used in their literature, is characterized as personal and community sacrifice and privation – hardships concomitant with the arctic climate – and geographical isolation in the service of God. Early epistles from the Roman Catholic missions in the north speak frequently of the torments of hunger, or the fast of correspondence, even though the abnegation was self-inflicted because of vocation. Vocation sanctioned a form of martyrdom by which the Grey Nuns in the north measured their success, even celebrated their suffering. In a comprehensive history of her order, Sister Clementine Drouin notes "that simple, obscure heroism is neither the easiest nor the least noble. Only faith inspires, distinguishes, and explains it."[2] Those two brief sentences convey how the Sisters of Charity of Montreal viewed their mission to *le grand nord-ouest*.

What they sought was a better life for their charges. They simply *knew* that an acceptance of the Roman Catholic form of Christianity was the solution to what *they* saw as the problems of poverty, paganism, and Protestantism. Like any active missionary of their time, they pursued those goals with some zeal, as well as considerable personal sacrifice relative to women of the same class, background, and ethnic origins in the settlements and towns of the south. Those uncomfortable with Christianity will find the sisters' zealousness no less difficult to grasp than the Anglican variety, and the very style of their records with the continual praising of God or His omnipresence might even offend. But the evidence cannot be dismissed out of hand because it rings untrue in a more secular climate. Neither is it necessarily corrupt because there is another version of events. What follows is an attempt to offer the version left behind by the sisters themselves.

An important factor in the execution of the mission design is the Grey Nuns' association with the Oblates of Mary Immaculate (OMI) and their employment as teachers and nurses under the Oblate plan. The Oblate "assault" on the region has been recently documented in works sponsored by the OMI, although unfortunately, though not surprisingly, these studies offer little insight into the personal and daily lives of the women who worked alongside the Oblate fathers.[3] Documents recording these northern missions are scarce; unlike their Anglican counterparts, the Grey Nuns did not operate communication networks with the south that might have retained any of their extant records. In official and sometimes translated *Chroniques*, faith, religious observances, subservience to higher authority, and vocation continually interfere with historical analysis of the daily entries. While the documents confirm both the nature of the community and the missionaries, there is a virtual dearth of personal information about the more than 130 women.[4] This is because the Grey Nuns generally acted communally, not individually. With a few exceptions, they were all sisters sent from Montreal under the auspices of the same Mother House; as such they inhabited a parochial world defined by strict rules. Appreciating that sense of community is essential to understanding this particular mission. The sometimes small, yet solid, company of determined women were conspicuous as a religious community, as well as visibly distinguishable from other white women in the north because of their habit with the distinctive head wear that sported a large bow at the chin.

The Grey Nuns went to Fort Providence after a number of invitations from the OMI to work alongside them in the region, developing schools and hospitals to provide a foundation for evangelizing the Roman Catholic faith in response to Anglican forays into the north. Theirs was the ideal order because their vocation encompassed both education and medicine. Like their Anglican counterparts, the Oblates assumed that the nuns, being women, could insinuate themselves better with women and girls in the native community – who would then pass on the Christian (read Roman Catholic) faith to their families. The nuns, unlike the OMI, could teach domestic skills.[5]

So it was that in April of 1866, Superior-General Jane Slocombe wrote from Montreal to Monseigneur Faraud, Bishop of Athabasca-Mackenzie, about how she had chosen the "cinq Victimes que le bon

Dieu me demandait par votre veix."[6] There had been many requests for missionary nuns, she explained, so only two sisters from the Mother House could be spared. She was able to find volunteers at a sister convent in Sainte Hyacinthe, she continued, and so Sisters Rosalie Brunelle and Emélie Michon were officially transferred to the Montreal community and along with Adèle Lapointe, Elizabeth Ward, and Marie-Louise St Michel made up the number. "Puissent nos chères Soeurs," she added, "conserver parfaitment l'esprit de leur sainte vocation."[7] The sisters embarked west in the fall of 1866 and wintered at St Boniface (in the NWT, now Manitoba); from there they proclaimed eternal optimism for their mission at Fort Providence, reinforced in part by the knowledge that Sr Lapointe was a scrounger and fundraiser of some repute within her community. From a priest in France she had been able to secure funds to pay for shipping personal belongings. For the mission itself and its chapel, she had found blankets, two statues of the Virgin Mary, and a stained glass window.[8]

The five nuns chronicled the trip north in a journal. They left St Boniface on 8 June in torrential rain, encountering overflowing streams and flooded creeks almost before they got started. The first part of what they later described as the "wonderful" trip took them to Lac La Biche (now in Alberta), where they arrived at the end of July for a short but happy stay with the sisters there. Their journey then took them by boat along the Athabasca River, where ironically the water levels were so low that the nuns were required to walk much of the way through the forests and tall grasses along the bank. By then it was obvious to all that faith was not a substitute for strength: at one point the sisters reported that they hitched themselves to collars, two by two, and towed the barges around an obstacle in the Athabasca River. They eventually sailed across Great Slave Lake to their destination, arriving at Fort Providence on 28 August 1867. They carefully noted that their first act was to enter the church and to thank Providence for their safe deliverance.

These five Grey Nuns *trekked* from St Boniface to Fort Providence, because at the time there was no railroad to Edmonton and no HBC steamer. The long account describing the obstacles and difficulties encountered along the route includes a story about the bishop clearing a fresh trail with a hatchet. The nuns built temporary bridges with logs, slogged through mud, and made camp in soggy marshes. At their destination, the nuns immediately discovered the incredible poverty of the people. Expressing their surprise that not a single one was Roman Catholic or religious, they realized that the task ahead was even more formidable than the one just undertaken. The five sisters also had to come to terms with the inescapable finality of their situation. They wrote a farewell to their dear sisters at the Mother House saying that Fort Providence would be their tomb and predicting that they would probably not see the others again in this world.[9] Walking back to St Boniface was clearly not an option.

What was important was their work. They had three specific goals: to relieve what they called the moral misery of infanticide, to educate mixed-blood and native children, and to care for the sick. They firmly believed that the Dene and Inuit frequently killed newborns, particularly baby girls. Both published histories of the Grey Nuns cite examples of barbarous infanticide, which enraged the sisters and mobilized them to eradicate the custom.[10] There were suggestions that mothers who had no means of support abandoned their babies in the bush or buried them in the snow. The sisters even believed that one father had left a small boy hanging in a tree because he was unable to look after him, although, in general, the missionaries interpreted native society as decidedly misogynist – its people believing that sons were the only important offspring. Cannibalism was also suspected. Since the Grey Nuns assumed this barbarity was due partly to paganism and partly to economic conditions, they set about to feed and clothe the Natives, to foster self-esteem through training and teaching, to share their appreciation of Christ, and to show the value of hard work in His name. They rationalized their attack on native tradition by convincing themselves that the "wretched people" would be happy to hand over unwanted children to the nuns rather than kill them, or let them die.

Compassion for orphaned and abandoned children in itself cannot be faulted, but like most Christian missionaries the nuns failed to grasp that the same kind of integral relationship between God and baptism in their faith existed between custom and survival in the native tradition. Infanticide did not just offend the sisters like it did the Anglican women; rather it assaulted the very roots of their belief in the blessing of baptism to provide a better life in the hereafter. More specifically, souls had to be saved before they were given up. Providing a good education for mixed-blood and Indian children was part of that process. An education would allow these children to spread knowledge and the Roman Catholic religion among friends and relatives. Perhaps more important to the competitive missionaries of the region, education in the Roman Catholic tradition would place any converts in "a higher place in the esteem of our separated brethren."[11]

It is unclear what kind of education the Grey Nuns initially hoped to deliver. Sr Ward and Sr St Michel acted as teachers in the first school in the crowded small building prepared for them, but language difficulties, cultural differences, chronic shortages, and constant hunger among the nuns and their charges hampered the curriculum. The other three sisters were nurses. The new convent at Fort Providence was, in fact, named the Sacred Heart Hospital. In some ways the designation was optimistic. The hospital was in the same building as the school, the kitchen, and the living quarters. The beds in the new building were simply wooden frames with no mattresses. Caring for those sick from diseases caused by poverty and poor living conditions such as measles, scarlet fever, diphtheria, and dysentery was part of the hospital's mandate, as was caring for the chronically ill and infirm.

It has already been noted in a previous chapter how medical care was an insidious form of cultural invasion. In native societies, a close association exists between healing and religion; pursuing that route to conversion was therefore a natural one for northern missionaries, despite the inevitable reaction when European medicine failed.[12] The level of medical care provided by the sisters would have been primitive even by turn of the century standards, of course, but its impact was substantial, particularly at a time when no Anglican infirmary was present to serve as an alternative.

Despite the nuns' response to perceived need, this early attempt at establishing a convent/hospital/mission/school in the Mackenzie River valley was not entirely a success, yet the qualified success was not, if the nuns can be believed, due to a lack of response from the aboriginal population. It was more a matter of management of the sparse resources allocated to the enterprise, one deemed foolhardy by Bishop Grouard. Nominally, the early missions were sustained by contributions from the Society for the Propagation of the Faith in Paris and Lyons, the Society of the Holy Childhood, and the Catholic Church Extension Society of Canada. By 1915, the northern missions were also supported by the Province of Quebec and the Dominion government. The Grey Nuns and the Oblates made up the difference in what would now be called "sweat equity," clearing the soil, building shelters, growing food, seeking alms, and living sparingly.

Such sacrifice in the early years, though, was simply not enough. When in 1880 an Assistant-General from Montreal visited her sisters and spent the winter at Fort Providence, it was hard to hide the reality of sparse living. She soon realized that the reports to the Mother House had understated the hardships and suffering and that the nuns were overly optimistic about future improvements. Crops had failed. Constant food shortages and the coarseness of the diet had taxed the health of the sisters. They were overworked and exhausted. Rough canvas habits had replaced worn-out clothing, making daily chores uncomfortable. Even the devout Assistant-General recognized that the convent at Fort Providence could not flourish simply on prayer and faith. She recommended that the Grey Nuns at Fort Providence be recalled.

While prayer may not provide bodily sustenance, the power of prayer is strong to those who believe in it. So the sisters at Fort Providence prayed. The sisters also generated interest and obtained financial support from the young Dominion government and important people such as Bishop Taché at St Boniface. John Camsell of the HBC wrote from Fort Chipewyan to lend his encouragement. He told the Mother Superior in February 1882 that he was "very glad to hear that there [was] a prospect of the Sisters at Providence remaining in the District & anything [he could] do towards attaining such a desirable end shall not be wanting." Camsell added that when he had passed through Fort Providence the sisters there had been preparing to depart in the spring and were a very unhappy lot. He added a note two weeks later to say how pleased he was to hear that the Grey Nuns would stay.[13]

Distance and slow communication lines account for the sisters at Fort Providence being able to hide the conditions at the mission from the Mother House, although the silence cannot be explained simply by the fear of being recalled. The Grey Nuns were unwilling and unable to declare the mission a failure in the midst of desperation and distress: to do so was offensive to their vocation and an assault on the very faith that sustained them. It is curious that it took so long to secure even meagre financial support from the very bishop who had initiated the original invitation to participate in the northern mission; but pride, coupled with optimism and confused with faith, and a stubbornness required by the situation itself discouraged any supplication and the mission's status remained precarious for some time. (Ironically, those same attributes were critical to any southern woman's ability to function in the northern environment.) A letter in 1885 from an OMI priest explained how the sisters were doing the best they could because Sr Ward, now the Mother Superior, was very capable, and the missionaries were devoted to their task. He shared his belief with the Superior-General that they would survive the winter, saying that despite any rumours she might hear, she should not worry about the sisters.[14] And indeed, their hearty and persistent efforts and fanatical enthusiasm were rewarded.

In 1889, the Grey Nuns opened a much larger Sacred Heart Hospital at Fort Providence, and the mission expanded northward along the Mackenzie River. The first satellite mission was established at Fort Resolution in 1903, with the advice of the bishop of the new Diocese of Mackenzie, Gabriel Breynat. Sisters Mary Virginie Boisvert, Mary Délia Magnan-Généreux, and Alice McQuillan, along with auxiliaries Honorine Caron and Ernestine Lemay departed from Montreal at the end of April and arrived in Fort Resolution the following June. According to the record, they were welcomed by the people there with curiosity and affection; and "leur habit serait bien plus beau, s'il était rouge, faisait remarquer une savagesse,"[15] A letter from Sr Boisvert, describes the beginnings of the St. Joseph Mission:

...nous arrivons enfin au cher Résolution, notre terre promise. Notre première visite fut à l'eglise pour rendre nos hommages au Divin Mâitre, et lui offrir nos humbles personnes pour travailler à sa grande gloire et au salut des âmes. Nous avions les plus vives actions de grâces à rendre à Dieu de nous avoir protégées au milieu des nombreuses difficultés contre lesquelles nous avons eu á lutter, pour arriver au terme de notre voyage. Mais les fatigues, le froid surtout et le mauvais temps, loin d'affaiblir les forces, semblaient en donner á celles qui n'en avaient pas et les augmenter á celles qui en avaient déja. La petite Soeur Ernestine, seule, fait exception á cette regle. Elle s'est sentie malade tout le long voyage, ne pouvant même garner un peu de boullion. A Saint-Albert, elle parut se remettre; mais à peine parties une rougeur, que nous avons prises d'abord pour une piqûre de maringouin, lui causa de fortes doleurs. Cette rougeur s'est agrandie et est devenue une plaie. Je fais reposer cette chère soeur et la soigne du mieux que je puis.[16]

Sr Boisvert's letter is typical of those sent to Montreal from the sisters in the north. It was as if all understood that the sisters at the Mother House were interested in the details of their western confreres' lives and work in the mission; that they would want to know that the church was equipped with benches, stations of the cross, a font, and an harmonium, but no sanctuary lamp because the oil used for fuel was too expensive. The mission, Sr Boisvert informed them, was poor, and the inhabitants were going to be hungry because the caribou had not yet appeared. The fishing that summer had been poor as well – only 400 fish for the mission – and despite Sr Ernestine's brave attempts, the kitchen could be stretched to feed only twenty-five children and five sisters. The inclination to dismiss letters such as this as appeals for sympathy is strong, but like the other European women who described the contents of their pantries to friends in the south, the nuns were commenting on situations that the sisters in Montreal could recognize and target in their prayers.

One of the most evocative of the Grey Nun's letters was sent from Fort Resolution in 1915. Sr Antoinette Latremouille had been at the mission only thirty-one days when she wrote to the Superior-General in Montreal. The newcomer's enthusiasm is evident; she told of finding old table linens stored away at the convent and of trying to revive the napkins and cloths that had long since been forgotten. These details were mixed with more serious concerns. Sr Latremouille wrote that she had undertaken her mission with joy and no regret but she was confused by the situation at the convent, partly because one of the sisters was being sent back to Montreal; she was not considered suitable for the north, because she was "old-fashioned" and had asked Sr Latremouille to intervene on her behalf. Sr Latremouille insisted that her colleague had a strong vocation – the sisters, she said, had been reminded over and over again at one of their retreats that they must maintain their vocation and devotion in order for the mission to succeed.[17] She was sure that Sr Pisonneault was faithful and earnest, and clearly wanted to stay at Fort Resolution.

Since Sr Pinsonneault was to spend nearly twenty more years in the north,[18] the suspicion is that something else was afoot at Fort Resolution. Later in Sr Latremouille's letter, there is a hint as to the cause of the general unease. Remember that the Grey Nuns worked under the auspices of the OMI in Oblate missions so the priests were ever present and no doubt demanding, in keeping with the principles of a male-dominated Church. "Ma Mère, j'ai peur de Monseigneur," Sr Latremouille confided. Recognizing that she was in a difficult position over what she was about to write, she couched her words carefully, referring to her vocation. She directed Superior-General Piché to Sr Beaudry, who had returned to Montreal, implying that the sister would have already informed Mother Piché of the situation – which was never actually revealed, but concerned the relationship between the Oblates and the Grey Nuns. Sr Latremouille wrote that she was afraid to go about in the north the same way she did in the east, afraid to go about her work in a manner reflecting a true daughter of Marie d'Youville.[19]

Sr Latremouille's fear was that the Monseigneur had forgotten that Grey Nuns make a profession according to the rules of their own order and not of that of the Oblates; the sister wanted Mother Piché to assure her that she would be a Grey Nun for eternity and not have to change "her congregation." The Monseigneur was not always at the mission, she explained, and *sometimes* he was nice. But at times she was uncomfortable with his presence, or his questions. When he had asked her which of the nuns spoke English to the children, for example, she had told him that it was she, adding that she did not tell him where or when. This suggests a developing power struggle between the Oblates and the Grey Nuns about responsibilities and goals.

Sr Latremouille may well have been the catalyst for change at the mission (she appeared to be the first to openly complain of shortages and personality problems); her few comments certainly heralded the need for some formal acknowledgment of responsibilities. In 1916, the Superior-General took the necessary steps to contract officially with the Mackenzie Diocese. The contract was signed by Bishop Gabriel Breynat and Mother Anne Piché, the Superior-General who had made an inspection tour to the Mackenzie missions in 1912. The inspection tour confirms that Mother Piché had a fair understanding of those conditions before she negotiated the contract, although her *De Montréal à Mackenzie: Notes de Voyage* speaks little of those conditions, concentrating more on the journey, the route, and the religious celebrations along the way.[20] Given the comments in Sr Latremouille's letter from Resolution and that the Grey Nuns were expanding their operations, the contract was undoubtedly long overdue.

It was agreed that the Superior of the Oblates in Fort Providence would be responsible for the mission – providing the necessary supplies – but that the operating authority would be the Rule and Constitution of the Grey Nuns and their Superior-General. This ensured a distinct, although not strictly autonomous, operation. Each sister working in the mission was to be paid $50.00 per annum, and the Oblates would pay room and board and any necessary fares. The sisters remained committed to educating the native children and caring for the poor and sick. The sisters also promised to assist the Oblates in every possible way, while the OMI agreed to meet the mission's spiritual and material needs. The contract could be terminated upon five-years' notice by either party. [21]

In 1915, at about the same time as the Grey Nuns made the formal contract with the OMI, the Mackenzie Diocese was severed administratively from the Athabasca missions. The Rev Duchaussois's book *The Grey Nuns in the Far North* appeared to inform the faithful of the sacrifices made by the Sisters of Charity and to garner financial support for the missions. The consolidation and confirmation of responsibilities marked an aggressive expansion in the Mackenzie River valley as well. St Anne's Hospital and Religious Education Centre at Fort Smith was founded in 1914. At first it was staffed by Sr Marie-Louise Léveillé, then Provincial-Superior of the Province of

Divine Providence and Srs Célina Fortin, Corinne St-Germain (Beaudry), and Adrienne Gadbois. They were joined later that year by Srs Mary Zoëlla Turcotte (Jobin) and Mary Albina Ferland. In addition to the convent's usual educational and religious duties and the care of the Oblates' home, the nuns were given a new role. Sr Gadbois was asked to maintain the meteorological station for the government and to make periodical reports.[22]

In 1911, the Indian Agent at Fort Simpson suggested that a hospital be built on the island near the settlement, and in the spring of 1916 construction began. (Mr Card was an Anglican and the nuns chose to interpret his request as a small religious victory, instead of recognizing it as a government initiative.) The hospital was staffed by Srs Boursier and Latremouille and by Novice Marie, a Native from Fort Good Hope who would later make her profession at Fort Simpson. Sr Girouard was the mission's first Superior. The *Historique* notes that "the erection of such a hospital and school in such a place in those days was surely an act of religious rashness,"[23] although the significant event in the early history of the mission was more likely the arrival of four cows and twelve chickens to provide the much desired milk and eggs.

Sr St Dosithée, the first registered nurse at the hospital, arrived in 1917, which was the same year that St. Margaret's School was opened. By 1920, the government had become involved, paying the teacher a salary of $75.00 per year in return for using a curriculum designated by the Indian Affairs Branch and similar to one followed in the English-speaking provinces. Moreover, under new civil law, St. Margaret's was now designated a private institution, although the church considered it public and open to all children. Government involvement marked a significant change in direction for all northern schools; however, the nuns made some of their own changes over time, including the introduction of English-language religious instruction. Until 1926, French and Slavey were the languages used at Mass and during religious classes.

By 1939, more than fifty Grey Nuns had served at Fort Simpson. Their tenure had not been uneventful. A year after St. Margaret's opened, the resident Grey Nuns found that the Lord continued to challenge them, despite their good intentions. In the fall of 1918, fire broke out in the nursery of the mission, taking the lives of several infants. That disaster followed a summer of floods and poor crops; flooding had ruined the flour supply, one cow died, and there was no feed for Sr Bourcier's chickens. An early freeze had left the fishery in question, and the war in Europe was beginning to have an impact. Sr Girouard wrote that three local métis men were called up for service.[24] But not all was bleak: Mother Superior had reason to be optimistic about the mission because a young protestant boy was deserting his flock of sheep every day to attend class at the RC school, despite the admonitions of the Anglican priest.

In August 1924, three senior members of the order travelled north to Aklavik to scout the town. Their intention was to establish a mission school and hospital. The "Historical Account of the Aklavik Mission" describes Aklavik as a small community with only about twenty families permanently residing there. About half of these residents were Inuit, while the rest were Dene or of mixed-blood. It was no accident that the OMI and Grey Nuns were building a mission at Aklavik; the Anglicans were doing the same, and the competition for souls and government funds was fierce. The two Aklavik hospitals epitomize the ludicrous nature of that religious race. It would have surely been more sensible to expand the hospitals further south so as to provide services to the Dene, but the Inuit proved too much of a temptation and the cause too important for the missionaries to procrastinate. Father Duport wrote to Mother Dugas in 1924, begging her assistance. He explained that the OMI had "declared war" on the Anglicans, attempting to establish a mission in an old cabin in poor condition. The expense of renovations was prohibitive. But they were still eager to fight and had decided to find a new form of attack,[25] which included the Grey Nuns.

Mother Girouard left Fort Resolution for Aklavik in July of 1925. Accompanying her were Sr Alice McQuillan, who had been the Superior at Fort Resolution since 1903; Sr Adelard, a registered nurse from St. Boniface; Sr Obéline Pothier (Firmin) from Fort Simpson; Sr Marguerit Lussier; and Mrs. Lucien Mercier, who was married to one of the carpenters hired to build the convent. The building was called La Mission de l'Immaculée, Chez les Esquimos d'Aklavik et la Delta du Mackenzie, sur les bords de la mer Glaciale, a grand title for a convent that existed only in the sisters' dreams. The *Chroniques* record that instead of building a foundation thirty-five by forty feet they opted for one much bigger at sixty-two by thirty-five feet. Work began immediately, and so did the worries about winter. Since Aklavik is located above the treeline, there was little wood available for winter stoves. The men who had been building the convent began searching for fuel in early July, and the nuns lamented that they could help only with prayers.

The concern was precipitated by a cold spell during the summer, when the nuns recorded the necessity for woolen blankets and socks to keep out the cold during the night. "The great fuel question" was answered when the search party arrived with a scow load of wood, but that the question arose at all among women who had been suffering supply shortages for sixty years in the region speaks of hasty planning in the face of a perceived threat from the Protestant side. The Grey Nuns, undaunted by the prospect of personal suffering during the cold weather, focused entirely on the threat, which had developed into a crusade. Not long after their arrival at Aklavik, the sisters visited the Anglican mission and met the Reverend Hester. "How many 'Sacred Heart of Jesus may thy Kingdom come' we did sow while visiting," the chroniclers wrote, adding "yes Jesu may your Kingdom come in these souls so dear to you and yet so blind."[26]

The original complement of sisters, who had begun to refer to themselves as "the three poor little exiles" waved good-bye to Mother Girouard in August of 1925, then turned their attention to strengthening the mission. They were pleased when the Inuit, arriving in their schooners for winter supplies at Aklavik, dropped in to see the nuns who eschewed their monthly retreat in honour of the visitors. This attention would be short-lived, but the sisters were keen to note *any* apparent conversion or treachery from declared Protestants in the community. Consider the story of "a protestant man by the name of Carrol [who] came to the Frs house and asked Fr Sup. If he would accept his wife at the convent for the winter as he had to go to Edmonton for medical treatment. He then made his will and placed everything he had into the Frs. Hands. What confidence those people have in the catholic missionaries. It must make the protestants reflect seeing the confidence they put in the fathers who are strangers for them."[27] Days later, the chronicles lamented the scarcity of white parishioners in the village and noted how disappointed the sisters had been that none of the visitors from the recently docked SS *Liard River* had appeared at the Catholic mission. But the sisters were comforted by the knowledge that the Aklavik mission might still serve its purpose.

In January 1926, Sister McQuillan wrote to the Mother House to report that the Father Superior of the OMI at Aklavik had registered 30 children from Arctic Red River and Fort Good Hope to attend the school the following summer. This was cause for celebration, and there was hope for more pupils still. She wrote: "I have confidence our Lord will send some Eskimos to complete the decoration. It appears all the protestants here want to put in their children as boarders. Many of them naturally feel sore at our being here, but cannot help admiring our life of sacrifice. Father Superior says he is surprised at their sympathy towards us, it is altogether beyond his expectations as he dreaded the thought of coming among these protestants so bigoted. They are all on friendly terms with us even the two Ministers [Anglican] who sent us a Christmas present and came to us on Christmas Day."[28] The "minister" would prove to be a true nemesis the following summer though, when he stopped the Inuit visiting the nuns. As the *Chroniques* entry for 8 September explains: "Undoubtedly [he] has told them not to come. He takes great care of his sheep walking up and down between their tents and the Catholic Mission. Our Lord in the tabernacle is also a good shepherd and He will one day gather those sheep into His fold, waiting for that we can only pray. We might not have the pleasure of receiving them but we can say we had the honour of planting the first seed.[29]"

Sister McQuillan's letter hints at problems in the "cold, dark country of Aklavik," acknowledging that there were some spirits which could not be rendered happy despite hard work and affection in the religious community. It was, she wrote, "very hard country on certain characters, and one would be obliged to dispense them of one quarter of our Holy Rules to satisfy them," but she added that if those characters could keep the spirit to themselves and not make everyone else "uncontented," the job would be made easier. Sister McQuillan asked the Mother Superior for advice on the matter, making it clear that she was "perfectly happy notwithstanding the little contradictions which [they] must go through with joy for the salvation of souls." This was, after all, what the mission was still about. For example, in keeping with the goals of the first mission at Fort Providence, the Grey Nuns in 1926 petitioned the government for funds to enable them to open a *crèche* or nursery for newborn babies. They were still convinced that baby girls needed protection from being either left in the wilds or crushed to death because they were valued less than boys in the native community. But with the shift of focus to the Inuit of the western Arctic at the Aklavik mission, a different set of "barbaric" customs needing attention were highlighted.

It is not surprising that when the OMI sent out a call for missionaries to tend the hospital and school at Chesterfield Inlet, it was the Grey Nuns at the l'Hotel Dieu de Nicolet who responded. Sisters Marie-Anne Fréchette, Adélard Fafard, St Ignatius of Loyola (Anasthasie Héroux), and Therese de l'Enfant Jesus (Yvonne Désilets) arrived at the mission in August of 1931. The Oblate Bishop Arsène Turquetil had founded the mission 400 miles north of Churchill on Hudson Bay in 1912. The arrival of the Grey Nuns marked a "great missionary adventure among the rocky desert and ice of Hudson

Bay," suggested Sr Yvette Paquin's fiftieth anniversary notes in *Eskimo*. They were quickly christened by the local Inuit as *"Nayas"* meaning sisters, and the Mother Superior was called *"Ananatsiak"* or grandmother. The nuns were convinced that their arrival was welcome and the Inuit saw their medical prowess as a marvel.[30]

Interviewed in 1980, Sister Ignatius, then 80 years old, remembered the Inuit as curious, yet confident and happy with the arrival of the nuns. But she also recalled that "those good people were very primitive and had all kinds of superstitions which they gave up as they became Christians." She was the nurse, and her responsibilities were made more onerous because the doctor was not always present. She confirmed her spirit of faith, saying that God's help made difficulties easier to bear. Sister Désilets's recollections were more chauvinist and paternalistic; she remembered the Inuit in their "primitive state": the children under four were naked and the others were clothed in caribou skins. That the naked little ones were warmer that way in the hoods of their mothers' *atigis,* and that caribou skins were the best nature could provide seems to have escaped the sister's memory. She was clear on one point, however: "They were lovable, those children of the snows."[31]

Neither of these sisters remembered having to learn Inuktitut. However, the *Chroniques* for Chesterfield Inlet record that as soon as they arrived, the nuns began to receive an hourly lesson from one of the Oblates. Learning the local language represented a small shift in attitude to accommodate the times, and the goal of the mission on the shores of Hudson Bay did not differ from those in the west. The Grey Nuns' conviction that they were in the Arctic to assist the OMI to convert the heathen Inuit so that they might find their souls at rest in heaven was as tenable in 1931 as it was in 1867. Perhaps that is the strongest marker of just how blindly driven the Grey Nuns were by their purpose in the north.

In this chapter, no attempt has been made to assess – from the perspective of the native population – the impact of the largest, single, identifiable group of white European women in the Canadian north before the Second World War. Of course, what the sisters thought of as a successful contribution to the development of the region has since been interpreted as something less than positive. And it is unlikely the Grey Nuns would have published derogatory comments from their charges because any such remarks would simply have fallen on deaf ears. Despite any such contentions, the sisters held as strong a perception of their success as they did of their vocation to the northern mission. Success, no matter how small, was such a vital part of their faith and vocation that it became impossible to conceive of failure. Success was measured not by how many boys and girls graduated from their schools, or how many bodies were healed, but by the number of souls saved – an almost unintelligible concept to those not counting, and perhaps even intangible for those who were. The catch is to appreciate that while it may make no difference to those who cannot understand, it was all that mattered to the nuns.

CHAPTER SEVEN

White Women Have Strange Ways: Connections and Distinctions between Cultures

During her first winter at Shingle Point, Addie Butler wrote to her sister about an Inuit wedding she had attended – although she noted that "you would never have known a wedding was about to be solemnized. The bridal couple was sitting amongst the rest of the congregation, not together, and there were no bridesmaids, no confetti, no fuss, no nothing." Mrs Butler thought it remarkable that after the wedding, the married couple went their separate ways. It was 1933. Anglican missionaries had preached their message in the region for more than seventy years. But in the isolated mission church, the Inuit showed that even though they embraced the concept of Christian marriage, the sacrament had an indigenous character. It "seems strange to us," Mrs Butler concluded about the wedding in particular; but her statement, and the wedding itself, may well have represented a more general commentary on the contact between races in the North.[1]

"Strangeness" raises the issue of racism, certain concepts of racial superiority, and the spectre of racial tension – none of which can be ignored in a study of indigenous contact. But how can racial tensions be measured? What behaviour is considered as racist? Does racist behaviour necessarily result from a belief in racial superiority? How can any historical study say with certainty that women were more racist than men – a concern that has become common in studies that focus on white women and indigenous communities? More important, perhaps, is whether it all matters. These questions are particularly vexing when there are no documents to offer parallel evidence from the "other" side. Racism is one of those contemporary terms often used to determine culpability or to explain behaviour now considered abhorrent. It is, in itself, a value-laden term. Perhaps a more valuable approach would be to consider racism as implying a distinction between "the powerful and the powerless, the rich and the poor, or those educated in western culture and those who are not."[2] That description is a useful reminder of how racism not only encompasses class distinctions, national heritage, and the visually obvious, but also introduces the most important dimensions of racism: power and authority. In the case of white women in the Canadian north however, racism provides a limited conceptual framework, partly because the power and authority that these women held because of race was merely intellectual, based on their own concepts of racial superiority.

The term racism belongs with the genre of history that Edward Said has called "the rhetoric of blame";[3] that is, the genre that judges the past through the eyes of the present. Political agendas have long since contaminated the term, and new bigotries have replaced the old. These new ones do not allow for any distinction between levels of outlook, degrees of oppression, historical context, or indeed for the possibility that women can and do change their attitudes over time. More profitable, then, would be an examination of how the women of one race dealt with racial and cultural distinctions. There is more value in understanding the setting created by the white women in the north, and within the context of female culture.

Any evidence used to illustrate the cultural exchange was provided by one side, of course, and because of the resources available to that society, it retains essential control of the information. In this northern case, there is no view from the indigenous cultures, only that presented by the white women. Nevertheless, the focus on female interaction opens up a range of topics that have hitherto not been addressed in this milieu. While the story is incomplete, it cannot be assumed that the white women who left the documents and memoirs necessarily meant to mislead; it is just that their views on the cultural differences of significance to *them* create cultural markers for studying the people who are agents of change. On the whole, white women who emigrated north went with the attitude that, as a race, they were superior to the native population. Their oft-expressed cultural arrogance pervades the sources, along with stereotypical and patronizing remarks. What is also apparent is how the differences between native cultures and customs affected the lives of white women, and how often white women were stymied in imposing their own preferences. Cultural arrogance does not necessarily translate into domination and control. The transition to a *civilized* culture in the north was not a smooth one; and there was a necessary collaboration between cultures, as well as an imposition. Positive as well as imperfect connections occurred, and there were separate realms as well. Like the cliched twain of east and west, the north and south could sometimes never meet.

One element of racism is simply to prefer one's own appearance and customs over that of others. This is not necessarily a benign bias, but in the case of the north, it is advisable to remember that it was not only the white European cultures that held racist beliefs based upon skin colour. Like most other southern women who ventured north, Anna Rokeby-Thomas discovered this for herself. She expected the Inuit to be ignorant of "civilized" ways, and simply *knew* them to be superstitious and un-Christianlike. "We think of the Eskimo as being very unclean," she told the *Living Message* in 1938, noting that they lived in snow houses "exactly like the pictures one sees of an igloo." Yet after an eventful stay at Victoria Island, Anna Rokeby-Thomas discovered enough about herself and her environment to write an almost self-deprecating description of her "northern" persona.

In her imagination, she saw a "tea" party hosted in her honour by some Inuit women at Baffin Island before she returned south. She was still an outsider, and her position unchanged after three years of missionary and medical work. Anna Rokeby-Thomas suggested that the Inuit women were amused by the way she crawled through the snow tunnel and her awkwardness once she was finally inside. She decided that they thought her pallor was an indication of ill-health and that she would be better looking if her skin had been bronze-coloured like theirs. As they all sat together on the snow platform, with Mrs Rokeby-Thomas in the place of honour, she imagined them thinking "it was all we could do from laughing at her white spots." The fictitious Inuit author explained how

the foolish woman took several mugs of tea and pretended to drink them. All the time she was spilling it into the snow blocks. That's because she doesn't like caribou hair mixed with her tea. We have even heard that she turns ill when she gets a piece of blubber in a mug of tea. This proves that white women have strange ways.

When it came time for her to leave, we gave her a new fur outfit, with boots to match. We also gave her a lot of sinew to encourage her to sew on skins. We doubt if she ever uses it! Even so, we invited her to pay more visits. We'll make a party if she does.[4]

The cynic may well see parody and patronage in these words, but Mrs Rokeby-Thomas had learned a valuable lesson. Another northern visitor, Wallace Manning, told those who read her memoirs to "remember that in their own language [the Eskimos] are Innuit, THE People, while you are only a white, whose origin according to eskimo legend is to say the least, uncomplimentary."[5]

It was impossible for white women to effectively dominate the indigenous people they encountered, if only because of limited numbers. It was also quite impossible to impose cultural values and even religious conventions on people who might, and would, up and leave on a moment's notice to follow the seal, the caribou, or the run of Arctic char. In the Mackenzie River valley, missionaries and teachers had to compete with deer herds, ice conditions, and the trapping season. Life simply revolved around these seasonal events, and the advance of "civilization" had to be put on hold while the native population engaged in traditional pursuits. The slower infusion of ideas is another matter – more insidious, even malignant – because over time the new cultural norms replace those of the indigenous culture. Recognizing that insidious changes occur, however, then raises questions about how effective limits can be placed on any societal change. Should these agents of change, for example, have checked their cultural baggage at the Arctic Circle, marked it not wanted on the voyage, or even have stayed at home? Are any of those options realistic?

Sexual jealousies can be indicative of racial tensions between women. The sources do not show evidence of sexual jealousies between white and native women in the north, or at least the women did not reveal their thoughts on the matter. Incidentally, Jean Godsell did note one manifestation, but strangely it was an observation made from the other perspective and contains only a hint of sexual jealousy. It would be naive to assume that sexual jealousies did not exist, but there is some substance to the idea that such a preoccupation is a condition generated by male-defined frameworks. Women were capable of reflecting on perceived and real power within the community, as well as sex. As she settled in the Mackenzie River valley, Mrs Godsell pondered on how she "represented, without realizing it, the very thing that native born members of the old regime viewed with such suspicion – most of the Company's Factors were still intermarried with the tribes, and women of mixed blood dominated the social, and to a large extent the business life of all these forts. Instinct seemed to tell them that once their place was usurped by women of the acquisitive and dominating white race, they would be relegated to a position of more or less obscurity, completely shorn of all their power and glory."[6] To accept Mrs Godsell's assertion that native women thought in terms of power and glory is *unfashionable* in the current academic climate, which tends to view any Eurocentric position as misguided. Yet how can her assessment be dismissed? Women of both races probably did feel somewhat threatened by her arrival in the north as wife of an aggressive and flamboyant HBC Factor. She had an appearance to maintain, and the Dene women were likely interested in at least maintaining the *status quo*. To pretend otherwise gives no credit to the Dene women concerned. Native cultures were not passive, and there is no reason to believe that native women were any more submissive than either the native men or the white women.

As early as the turn of the century, Sophie Porter noted that the Inuit along the Arctic coast – and in particular the women – showed some ambition to adopt white customs.[7] Native women displayed almost excessive curiosity about their white counterparts and were receptive to the ideas so foreign to their own experience.[8] This placed an unusual burden upon white women: while they were prepared and even expected to spread the knowledge of a more "advanced" civilization, they were not equipped to do so on the Native's terms, which was what the circumstances demanded. Luta Munday noted that the Inuit she met "always wanted to know everything, and the hardest thing I ever attempted was to try to explain things to them."[9] White women, and particularly missionary women, thought it their duty to communicate the details of the uniquely female elements of southern society. Unfortunately, Inuit women had no analogous experience with which to compare. The gender roles were completely different.

All their expectations and attitudes of superiority could not shield white women from the scrutiny of the native people. As in other outposts of the Empire, their white skins set *them* apart. Even if they carried some sense of privilege, they were nervous because of their preconceptions of the Aboriginals as savages. They were continually reminded that this was no place for a white woman. Until they learned otherwise, these white women reacted within the limitations of their own customs and experience.[10] They had heard stories of cannibalism, slavery, infanticide, and wife swapping, which no doubt made them apprehensive. What surprised them at first meeting the native population was how much of a curiosity they themselves were, and they commented that the scrutiny came especially from native women. The reasons for that scrutiny are not entirely unclear. The native men may simply have not been interested, dismissing the white women as unsuitable for any native marriage union. They may also have seen the white women as unattractive. White men who accompanied the white women north may well have directed them to native women because they assumed women's interests would be mutual. It may also have been that the white women were naturally drawn to the native women because of their supposed common interests. Any of these factors complicate what was a simple dilemma, easily solved under the circumstances.

Luta Munday's explanation was more rooted in female intuition about men. "No man" she wrote, "either native or white, cares to have white women in the country." Men found women "a nuisance in every way," she noted, because the men were no longer as free to come and go as they pleased. Mrs Munday's remark followed the revelation that Inuit men had certain habits that disturbed her sensibilities, habits that were "most embarrassing to a white woman when out among them, or travelling with them." She insisted that the men had to learn that certain rules must be kept.[11] Of course, this would have necessitated white men explaining those rules, and it was probably easier for them not to do so. Anna Rokeby-Thomas remarked on a similar experience; time had made little difference in changing local customs. She described how when walking through the settlement, she was startled by an Inuit who "came out of his igloo, shook hands and then urinated – while [we] talked (or tried to), then went casually on his way."[12]

Elizabeth Taylor was not the first white woman in the Mackenzie Delta. Yet the scarcity of white women in 1892 was enough for her to remark that "few of the Eskimos had ever seen a white woman, and they evidently found [me] strange and amusing." They all treated her with the greatest of courtesy she claimed, urging her to visit their skin tents. They presented her with gifts of arrows, and trinkets made from walrus ivory. Miss Taylor was sure they expected gifts in return, although since most of their initial contact had been with traders and whalers, it is more likely the Inuit were looking for the usual reciprocation.[13] More perplexing to Elizabeth Taylor was the reaction of one Inuit woman who looked her over, shut her eyes, and then shook her head from side to side as she departed in a fit of laughter. "Evidently, I impressed her as presenting an utterly absurd appearance," wrote Miss Taylor,[14] unable to see herself and her image as anything but the norm.

The Rev Harold Webster recalled that when his wife Edie arrived at Coppermine she was the first white woman the Inuit there had seen. "They wanted to touch her," he wrote, "to touch her clothes, to watch what she did. They followed her everywhere, even into her bedroom." Not surprisingly, Mrs Webster found this irritating, so she shut the door behind her. Eventually, "they got used to her and she got used to them."[15] Compare this welcome to that given Christina Fry at Herschel Island. The local Inuit treated her to a cup of tea.

Later, she wrote that while visiting one family, "many of the Natives called and gazed upon me"; she supposed "it was to see what the Parson's wife looked like."[16] The inquisitive Inuit women, and men, were probably intrigued by the obvious distinctions in dress and demeanour between the sexes of the white race. The Inuit had some difficulty with the Grey Nuns, for instance, and not just because of the strangeness of their habit. Since the Oblates provided for the nuns' spiritual and material needs, it should come as no surprise that the Aboriginals viewed this as some sort of marital relationship.[17] Anything else would have been incomprehensible in their culture.

Being subjected to a "gaze" from visitors often resulted in lengthy, pregnant silences during which the white women were unsure how to react. In their experience, hostesses were obligated to offer some social response. They were unaware that in the Inuit tradition, this was neither expected, nor necessary.[18] Beatrice Mason recounted what happened when natives visited her cabin in the northern Yukon. They just stared, she recalled; "it was very disconcerting to me and at first I felt called upon to try to make conversation, but not speaking the same language, they just stared the harder." Her solution was to "cut my monologue and [go] about my business as if they were not there."[19] Annie Card, who was alone with her young daughter when her first Dene women callers appeared, confessed she "felt a little timid." But she "shook their grimy hands, and asked them to come in." Mrs Card, thinking she knew what was of interest to women, showed them her stove; they were fascinated by her mirror. After making them tea, she took them to see her chickens. That, she recalled, was the most entertaining part of the afternoon for her guests.[20] Inuit women and their families often dropped in on the Anglican missions as well. They were uninvited, but in the north visitors understood they would be welcome.

No doubt the visual differences between white men and women account for Grace O'Kelly's depiction of her first encounter with Inuit women. No doubt, too, that description only hints at how perplexed and frightened she must have felt. She wrote:

The women stood in a group on the shore and when I arrived they rushed towards me in a body completely surrounding me. Some of them fell at my feet, examining my brogues and spats most minutely, others felt and rubbed my beaver coat – for it was fur they had never seen before, and my gloves were taken off and my hands examined with [extra]ordinary interest. They were most desirous to remove all of my clothes but I had this part of the performance stopped by an interpreter whom I called to my assistance. The children who were then brought forward screamed with fright when they saw me and ran away – not particularly complimentary, but a fact nevertheless.[21]

Sadie Stringer reported this same fascination with hands. She remembered the Inuit women taking her hands and stroking them. "They guessed I was tired and a little lonely," she thought, and their ministrations were intended to soothe. Mrs Stringer was impressed by the Inuit women telling the chief that she was frightened and needed their support.[22] To knowing eyes, hands can often tell more about an individual than simple skin colour. The Inuit women would have used those observations to form their own opinion about the white woman in their midst; they would have been looking for indications of Mrs Stringer's capabilities as an Arctic wife and mother, whose primary duty was to provide warm clothing for her family. Because of the hostile climate, the manufacture of suitable clothing was a valuable skill. White women relied heavily on native women to provide the clothing for white families as well, partly because white women did not know how to prepare and chew skins to be sewn, and partly because they could not bring themselves to do it after they learned the procedures. The realization of who was necessary to whose comfort was not lost on either white or native women.

Caring for their families was a role shared by white and native women, although motherhood, a singularly common experience, created one of the most significant gulfs between the two races. Childbirth itself reinforced the cultural differences – there were two sets of practices, each in its own way reflective of the environment and traditions. Only in rare instances did the two cultures meet so that white women aided native women, or native midwives assisted white women. The explanation is more complicated than simply racial distinctions, for the practices were deeply rooted in both cultures.

What if white women just simply preferred to have a trained white attendant because they did not trust what they saw as inferior native procedures for care? In the Arctic, the reasons for anxieties were obvious. Faced with what they viewed as a perilous undertaking, white women were apprehensive, whether because of language difficulties, or what they believed to be unhygienic and "primitive" practices. Why white women would be suspicious can be appreciated when their views about native childbirth are known. Sadie Stringer's narrative, written at Herschel Island in 1898, follows her announcement of a native birth near the community. Remember here that the value of Mrs Stringer's report lies more in the realization that this is how she envisioned the native experience. She wrote:

Whenever an Eskimo child is about to be born, a snow house is always built for the mother and she enters it alone. After the birth of the child, the mother remains in the snow house for a period of five days. No one goes inside the house, and no one goes to see her, only one woman who carries her food to her and passes it in through the low entrance called a door. After the expiration of five days, she is allowed to go back to live with her family in their house. This woman I speak of now did not want the child to live because it was a girl, so immediately [after] it was born she herself carried it about half a mile away to the side of the hill and left it out there in the snow to die.[23]

Emily Craig Romig, who had met Mrs Stringer on a trek to the Klondike that year, remembered Mrs Stringer telling this story. She said that Mrs Stringer had also told her about visiting one Inuit woman when she was alone in her snow house. When the Inuit learned that Mr Stringer had taken ill shortly after, they told her that he would still be well if she had stayed at home. Mrs Romig commented that when Inuit babies were born, the mothers just sat on a box; she added that "this was apparently not too much of a ceremony, and not much thought of as a performance, it just happened."[24] With variations, this view about native childbirth prevailed.

Carolyn Soper was determined to see how Inuit women managed in childbirth; as a trained nurse, she was prepared to offer any assistance she could provide. The first opportunity arose when her own Inuit helper gave birth shortly after the Sopers arrived at Lake Harbour in 1930. When Neve did not arrive at the house one morning, Mrs Soper paid a call at the family's *tupik* and found Neve kneeling on sleeping robes, stitching sealskin boots. The native midwife was present, but Mrs Soper stayed for about an hour. When she returned after lunch, Neve was outside the *tupik*, with the baby safely tucked in her hood, "cozily swathed in skins of the Arctic hare. The umbilical cord had been cut several inches from his body and tied with a piece of string" from a coal sack. Given her training, Carolyn Soper thought immediately of infection. But she reconsidered her hasty desire to help, concluding that these "primitive" women had managed quite well without outside help and her interference might even prove harmful.

Mrs Soper decided that for Inuit women, "childbirth was usually a quick and easy function." This implied to her *Beaver* readers that childbirth for Inuit women was distinctive from that of white women. It was her understanding, she related, that out on the land, dog teams were halted and a few snow blocks were thrown up to provide shelter. When the baby was born, the infant was placed as quickly as possible in the hood of the mother's parka, and for the remainder of the day the mother rode in the sled. Usually by the next day, the mother trudged along on foot beside the sled.[25] To women conditioned to view childbirth as a confinement, an illness attended by nurses and doctors, the "primitiveness" of Inuit birth was pointedly apparent. It must not be assumed, though, that the white women were insensitive to the need for essential adaptations.

Mena Orford described one specific aspect of native practices alluded to by Carolyn Soper. Mrs Orford's medical officer husband, who had noticed the high rate of postpartum hemorrhage and death among Inuit mothers, was unable to get anywhere near an Inuit birth, but his young daughters had occasion to be present in an Inuit tent when a baby was born. Over dinner that evening, their astonished mother heard them explain how the midwife had tied the umbilical cord only once – towards the baby – which, for the doctor, explained the puzzling number of postpartum deaths.[26]

Like Dr Orford and Carolyn Soper, Anna Rokeby-Thomas lamented that the Inuit women at Cambridge Bay would not allow her to attend as a midwife. She had undertaken special training with the Victorian Order of Nurses before she left Guelph to prepare her for "igloo deliveries." "I'm sure [the VON] felt they were making a contribution to mankind," wrote Mrs Rokeby-Thomas. After her first year in the Arctic, she realized that the Inuit women did not want her present at any births. "I was to learn that child-bearing was something they took for granted and was not considered a sickness," she recorded. "But the main reason," she continued, "was that if they should be having a run of girls, it was more than coincidence that some of the girl babies didn't survive. I found the thought of old people and babies freezing in igloos and baby girls being allowed to die revolting."[27] Mrs Rokeby-Thomas, recognizing that the problem was with her own feelings, concluded that "my pride was hurt because of my non-existent role as midwife." She had arrived in the north prepared to provide "civilized" assistance, only to discover that she could simply be ignored.[28]

By the time Mrs Rokeby-Thomas arrived at Cambridge Bay, it was possible for white women to fly south to give birth. It was, however, risky to assume the doctor could fly in when needed. White women in the north viewed childbirth as ominous, for the process of birth was fast developing into a medically supervised condition characterized by artificial intervention. So when the opportunity arose, some women chose to go south, or at least to one of the mission hospitals. Their fears can be attributed partly to the isolation, and partly to the lack of help at hand (except, perhaps, the help of a husband).[29] A case in point is Catherine Hoare's commiseration with Sadie Stringer that she had not known Mrs Merritt was at Fort McPherson when she gave birth to her son at Aklavik in 1921. "If only we had known," she wrote, thinking perhaps that everything would have been easier as both women were trained nurses.[30] No doubt tales such as that of Rose Spendlove at Fort Norman in the late nineteenth century had circulated among the women. Mrs Spendlove had nine children; apparently all were breach presentations. The story is that the only assistance to Rose Spendlove at these births was provided by her husband, a carving knife, and an Indian woman – probably a colourful description meant to impress the point.[31]

Because the Dene in the Mackenzie River valley were not quite as nomadic as the Inuit on the coast, childbirth for these women had other implications. There was no need for them to give birth and then move hastily along the trail, for example. Native women did have midwives of their own, and at least two examples show them attending a white European mother (although it is clear that to the families of the women about to give birth, these attendants were there only to assist the designated midwife). Missionary Charles Whittaker recorded that two native women provided assistance at the birth of his daughter Mabel in June of 1899 at Peel River.[32] Apparently, he had gained some experience when attending complications arising at native births. In an unpublished memoir, Mrs Louisa Mills described how native women in the region managed childbirth. She recalled that they were usually alone and described how one young girl at Fort Simpson went into the bush in the middle of the winter. "About a mile from the Fort she made a little camp for herself, first clearing away the snow with her snow shoes, then cutting down some spruce boughs to sit on. She then built a small fire, and there, all alone in 50 degrees below zero weather, her baby was born. The next day she walked into the Fort with her infant strapped up in a moss bag on her back, neither suffering any ill effects after their trying experience."[33]

Mrs Mill's position was somewhat unique because she was not a temporary resident in the north: her own mother was of mixed blood and had lived there since the 1860s. Her trust of a native attendant may have been more a matter of a personal relationship, and she knew that her mother, Mrs Camsell, and the Bishop's wife were also available. Interviewed in later years, Mrs Mills recalled: "When my first baby was born, I really needed a doctor, but there was none near. After a great deal of consultation between my mother, the Bishop's wife, and my Indian midwife, they decided to call in an old Indian who said he could help me. He gave me some dried up root which he cut up carefully with his jack-knife. He then sat smoking his pipe and after he was finished, got up and said, 'you'll be all right in a little while', and strange to say, I was."[34] Louisa Mills had remained sceptical of the native healing practices for childbirth complications, even though they were a part of her own heritage.

Until mission hospitals were established in the early thirties, or unless women lived in settlements in the company of other white women, the only white midwife available was a husband. It is quite common to find entries such as: "Herschel Noel was born on Christmas morning. As on the previous occasion we were alone,"[35] or "our little son [was] born at 5.30pm. Only myself in attendance upon Mrs Reid."[36] Ironically, this male presence contributed to the notion of birth being a family event, and this during a period when the trend throughout Canada was to consider childbirth as an illness that required medical attendance in a hospital setting. Under the guise of a new field called "obstetrics," the unique female experience became male dominated. In the north, circumstances required parents to adopt almost the opposite approach.

Some feminist scholars have traced the nature of changes in obstetrical practices in Canada, and the subsequent elimination of the traditional midwife.[37] Northern Canada has not been included in these studies (although recently government efforts to send Inuit women south to have their babies away from family networks have been highlighted in the press). Regrettably, there is insufficient material available to seriously address this exclusion, but the northern model could offer some additional insight for studies which, up to now, have focused on developed urban centres or the rural areas of more mature provinces. These studies, unfortunately, do not address the impact of isolation and the frontier or the influences of indigenous customs, all of which are important to the Canadian experience.

The available evidence does suggest that white women's experiences in remote regions demonstrate how otherwise independent and adaptable white women were trapped by their own cultural sensitivities and fears about birth, rather than being influenced by racist tendencies. It was cultural conditioning that prevented them from using the traditional technologies around them. Not only did they lack the necessary facilities and assistance deemed necessary by the medical and paternal institutions of the time, they had to deal with the anxieties those ideologies generated. As a consequence, what might have been a shared experience among women never materialized. Only the biological process remained constant.

White men and women viewed the birth of a child in the north as a momentous occasion, which, of course, it was to the families concerned. The birth of a white child was often presented as a heroic feat, especially if it was the first white child to be born in the region, in a particular settlement, at the farthest north point, or on some particular Arctic island. The immediate reaction to these "records" is how Eurocentric they seem. After all, babies had been born to indigenous mothers in the Canadian Arctic for centuries.[38] Viewed from another perspective, these special claims testify to the absence of a collective memory of safe births in the region for white mothers. These were mothers who had been raised to fear childbirth and its complications, who expected difficulties and were well aware of the consequences should anything go wrong. Their concern was not only for themselves; it extended to any infant left motherless. For one thing, no records attest to the practice of using native wet nurses, and there always loomed the spectre of infanticide associated with native custom. Motherhood may have allowed for closer social intercourse with indigenous women, and through the traditional occupations associated with women's work, white women made attempts to train indigenous women in those mysteries associated with motherhood and marriage in the south. The northern model is somewhat skewed, however, because while white women were teachers and nurses, a considerable number of those women were unmarried; sometimes, therefore, the interchanges operated at a different level.

Only Mena Orford expressed any specific concerns about the Inuit woman who looked after her children. She had difficulty with the differences in child-rearing attitudes and viewed native practices as very lax. That the Inuit allowed their children to do as they pleased and viewed corporal punishment as culturally unacceptable seemed to particularly offend the missionaries, who could not recognize the positive effects of that freedom. "We have so little trouble with our children, they are so well disciplined, if dealt with consistently," recorded Reita Latham."[39] What amazed Bessie Quirt was that the Inuit were willing to leave their children in the care of strangers, with the knowledge that they would not see them for months because the families would be out on the land. But Miss Quirt understood why these children were not disciplined within their families. In a newspaper interview she explained the Inuit superstition that children were born with the spirit of an ancestor, and this was especially the case if there had been a recent death. So the parents thought that "it would be presumptuous on their part to correct the child or force him to do anything he did not want to do, since he was really a reincarnation of the older person. This feeling remains until the child is about fourteen when he is supposed to revert to normal. If you ask an Eskimo father to send his child to school, he replies 'I'll ask him,' and if the child does not want to come to school, he is not made to do so."[40]

Knowing the reason for certain cultural practices did not make acceptance any easier for white women, however. The Inuit practice of infanticide offended their sensibilities so much that they chose to disbelieve, or rationalize the practice in some other way, probably as a defence mechanism against having to deal with the unthinkable. Sophie Porter thought that while Inuit were "liable to leave their female children around anywhere, or trade them off for dogs or rifles to any one disposed to take them," she did not think this was done from "natural unkindness, only habit." As a rule, she noted, the Inuit "treat children well as long as they have food or clothes for them."[41] This sentiment was reiterated by Grace O'Kelly who noted that an Inuit family rarely had more than two or three children. Any more children were adopted by childless couples "or disappear in mysterious ways while young." In the north there was no need for "the advanced ideas of our old friend Malthus" and his theories on eugenics. Nature and culture took care of that. But she observed that the Inuit appeared "to be very fond of those they do bring up" and showed off those children with some pride.[42]

Mrs O'Kelly, who had been so closely inspected by the local women, was intrigued by how women on the Arctic coast carried their children with them. She observed that every woman she saw carried a baby against her bare back under her *artigie*. The parka-like garment was tied around the woman's waist to keep the child from falling through, for the baby travelled in a large hood. As soon as the baby whimpered, the string was untied and the mother leaned forward, shaking her shoulders. Like magic, the baby would appear from beneath her skirt in front. No doubt Mrs O'Kelly could not visualize herself performing the same feat. She was astounded to realize that no matter how damp the ground, babies of only four to six months old were put down and exposed to the icy wind while their mothers nursed them at leisure. Just watching, said Mrs O'Kelly, made her shiver in her tweed suit and heavy beaver coat.[43]

In her memoir, Grace O'Kelly talks about the lack of sexual equality in Inuit society. The women followed her everywhere and wanted to trade sinew and skins for Mrs O'Kelly's clothes. So they would leave her alone she gave them cigarettes and needles. One of the men snatched the cigarettes out of her hand even though she told him they were for the women. His reply was that he had a perfect right to the present because the recipient was his woman. Knowing that women's rights were not an issue in the Arctic and that nothing she could do or say would change the lot of Inuit women, she let it go at that. But she also remarked that in certain ways, these women were held in some esteem. Like Mrs O'Kelly, Luta Munday observed that "woman suffrage" (using this term in the sense of equal rights) had not come to these people. Having explained how Inuit culture did not permit women to eat deer tongues, she astutely pointed out that this was a wise rule for the men because it assured them of always having that delicacy themselves. She also noted that until they had given birth to one child, Inuit women could not eat the eggs of wild birds. The men, concluded Mrs Munday, were clever and artful to impose these customs.[44]

In another telling entry, Grace O'Kelly described an Inuit woman being held at the police barracks with a male and a female accomplice who had aided her in strangling two previous husbands. She was an old woman, remarked Mrs O'Kelly, who had eluded capture by making doglike tracks in the snow. Mrs O'Kelly was impressed by this clever manoeuvre, and intrigued by the third husband who "seemed most devoted and could be found sitting in their tent with his arm around his lady love, or holding her hand as he walked." It is not clear if the Inuit woman had murdered her first two husbands so she could marry the third, although it is apparent that Mrs O'Kelly believed that to be the case and that she was more envious than damning of the woman. She also noted that this behaviour was the only form of lovemaking she had "witnessed among the stolid, and apparently unresponsive natives of these coasts."[45]

Perhaps Grace O'Kelly expected to see more open affection from the Inuit because of the rumours about sexual customs. The Inuit practice of wife swapping was misunderstood as promiscuity by most whites like Luta Munday, who determined that moral conditions among the Eskimos were not good. Of course, evaluation of those moral conditions was based upon Christian and European codes of conduct, and Mrs Munday recognized that the Inuit were *unmoral* rather than *immoral*. For them, the relationships that Europeans considered immoral were not wrong. Not surprisingly, it was feminist Agnes Deans Cameron who put the issue of wife swapping into perspective. She noted that in the "rest of America," the rule was one man, one wife. But she pointed out that there was an "elasticity of the rule in Chicago and elsewhere, so that it may read one man, one wife at a time."[46] Was the Inuit custom, she asked, really much different?

Relations between the sexes in Inuit culture puzzled Anna Rokeby-Thomas. She reported that the "smiles on the faces of Eskimo women were genuine, they were happy and content, they have great respect for their men, even though they get an occasional beating. There were not enough women to go around, so men share women. It seems SAD, but WORSE, women are exchanged like chattels."[47] Anthropologist Diamond Jenness explained the practice of exchanging wives in an account of his two years among the Inuit during the early part of the twentieth century. The "transfer of wedlock was not made indiscriminately but according to definite regulations." He added that a man may have wives and children in many tribes, but this also means that he has kinship ties which allow him to hunt and fish in another family's territory. "A stranger," wrote Jenness, "was a potential enemy who could be killed at sight, but by this system of temporarily exchanging wives the natives could travel from one end of the country to another."[48]

Despite reasonable explanations, the problem of temptations of the flesh perplexed missionary women in the Mackenzie River valley like Margaret Tims, whose concept of morality was too tied up with the religious notions of sin to account for northern experiences. The missionaries likened the frustration of conveying the message about sin and temptation to their native charges as "trying to break down a thick stone wall with a few pebbles." Miss Tims visited the homes of natives at Hay River to tell them Bible stories and show them pictures. But if she talked about sin, the Dene would tell her they never sinned. And, of course, if they never sinned, they never felt need of a Saviour.[49]

The concept of sin was not the only abstract notion that thwarted white women's attempts to change native customs. Wallace Manning found that the notion of time was "not a cut and dried commodity parcelled out into valuable sections each of which must be seized and spent in a manner advantageous to the spender." For the scientist with limited time at her disposal, Mrs Manning found it difficult to accept that time for the Inuit was a "leisurely thing that goes on and on at one's convenience." She decided that "Eskimos on the whole hurry only when they must and [do] not think of tomorrow."[50] What escaped Mrs Manning was that the Inuit did indeed live for the day: their struggle for survival was simply a daily one; and while routines of the day and season were important in their lives, they were not necessarily conspicuous. Besides, where would they get a timepiece? The Inuit had no way of reckoning time, neither for the day, nor for the long term. Only by remembering some incident could they reckon time in the past.[51]

After her lengthy stay in the north, Selina Bompas told readers of the *Imperial Colonist* that women who went into the north should be prepared to deal with the idiosyncrasies of the local population, "to meet them as equals, not inferiors, to deal gently with their failings and above all, show towards them under all circumstances, the summer calm of golden charity."[52] Determining the failings of the native population may have seemed easy enough, but remaining calm was a difficult lesson for the white women to learn. After all, they were the ones who were there to do the teaching. Reita Latham lamented that the Inuit at Shingle Point had not the slightest idea how to use money, for example. The Inuit felt that they had to spend it. Miss Latham viewed it as part of her function to teach them to buy "such things as will be of real use and value to their lives,"[53] not recognizing that their purchase of things which took their fancy was not a reflection of her failure to instruct, but more an indication that they were capable of using the exchange to serve their own needs and desires. Obviously, material wealth accumulated with an eye to the future – like time – was not as much a priority for them as it was for her.

Although white women expressed frustration about their inability to teach the value of southern customs to the Inuit and Dene, *nothing* offended them more than the apparent disregard for cleanliness. Eventually, those who lived among the Inuit for any time recognized why bathing in the Arctic was unrealistic. Anna Rokeby-Thomas, for example, wondered "How many of us under the same circumstance could even endure a weekly bath?"[54] The personal hygiene of aboriginals has already been touched upon in a previous chapter, but for missionaries, dirt interfered with their vocation. Margaret Tims remembered her arrival at Hay River in 1890 because, even while the physical surroundings surprised her, her "heart sank" when she looked at the people. "Would I ever get used to them?" she asked. "They were awful, especially the women." Even though she told herself that "they were my sisters and I must love them if I would do them good," it was no use. She confessed, "I was ashamed to think I felt like that and tried to pretend to myself that I loved the Indians." Gradually, she wrote, that victory was won.[55]

Catherine Hoare believed the Inuit at Herschel Island lived practical Christian lives. They were a joy to work with, she wrote, because they were sincere, kindly, truthful, and so "honest, one cannot help liking them. But oh! they are dirty! Dirty in every way." What was most annoying to her was that "they seem to make slower progress in this respect than in any other."[56] The missionaries saw that the way of dealing with a lack of progress towards cleanliness – and consequently, godliness – was to work through the children. Reita Latham told the *Living Message* that the school at Shingle Point had a neatness contest during the winter of 1931 in an effort "to tidy up the Eskimo race of the future." This was a successful enterprise, she declared, for the Inuit children were eager to learn and were responsive to mission teaching in the short term.

One teacher described how the children's faces were "at all times interested, responsive and happy." She had expected less and revealed that "once one had been among them even for a short time, one almost forgets that they are native children, because they have so many of the same natural traits as white children."[57] Ten years earlier, Mary Samwell had written to her bishop from Hay River saying that she felt Inuit children were intelligent and "can quite readily accomplish what they put their minds to, and have excellent memories." She decided that like other children (meaning white children) her pupils were more interested in concrete work than the abstract. Nevertheless, she added, they "were lacking in the power to apply themselves."[58] View this attitude from the perspective of a teacher, through a window of racial superiority. As teachers, white women felt they were well placed to indoctrinate Inuit children into a "better way of life." Reita Latham wrote from Shingle Point in 1932 that "in every instance where we see the lack of culture and training, we endeavour to work towards the end of so educating and training the children we have with us that they shall develop and choose rather to go by our teaching than to follow after the foolish method and manner in which their parents have trod."[59] She added that this task was made easier by the unlimited opportunities for teaching generated by the children's acceptance of nearly everything.

At Hay River ten years earlier, however, Mary Samwell had expressed concern to Bishop Lucas about doing memory work with her native pupils. She noted that while they had little difficulty memorizing, they did not seem to understand what she was teaching. She would rather they understood, she told Lucas, but there were just too many children to teach. More importantly, she wrote, many in her class were soon going back on the land and this was their last opportunity for lessons.[60] Mary Samwell's problem was not necessarily the size of her class. Her comments reflect the inability of these outside teachers to properly evaluate the impact of their lessons. The northern lifestyle simply did not fit the patterns with which the teachers were familiar. The concerns also indicate the usual northern problem of sporadic attendance and a diversity of ages and levels of achievement in a single class.

When the school at Shingle Point was established in 1930, Priscilla Shepherd reported that there were eight boys and fifteen girls. The youngest boy was six and the oldest thirteen. Four of the girls were still babies, she noted, with the remainder being between the ages of six and fourteen. Only one child knew any English; a few could count and recite the alphabet, which she attributed to mothers who had had some missionary contact.[61] By 1933, Addie Butler was the only teacher for thirty-eight pupils. According to Isobel Hutchison, Mrs Butler taught English, reading, writing, and arithmetic, as well as English folk dancing and recitations. This curriculum caused Isobel Hutchison to ponder on what Robert Louis Stevenson's reaction would have been "if he could have sat with her, listening to a little frosty eskimo glibly reciting his verses."[62]

The course content should come as no surprise. The teachers employed the same style of curriculum as did other Canadian and British schools, which is where they had been trained. But although Priscilla Shepherd proudly reported in 1930 that her prize pupil was able to recite "Our Flag" with competence and relish,[63] it is questionable how much of the content was absorbed by Inuit and native children. Some sources show that the women working with the children were sensitive to the need for some local content in their teaching, although the educational content provided in the northern schools tells more about the teaching than about the spread of cultural concepts. Just because the teachers taught something does not mean it was learned.

Samples of work sent from Shingle Point to the Deputy Minister in 1932 show spelling sentences such as "Do the naughty kittens smell a rat nearby" and "He is crying because he cannot get there out of the turnip field." These would have been difficult if not impossible for Inuit children to comprehend. Rats, kittens, and turnips were well outside their life experience. In fairness to the teachers, the same tests show such sentences as "Mr Smith is at Kittagazuit" and "I did not go to Bernard Harbour."[64] When Flossie Hirst repainted the nursery at Pangnirtung, the scenes depicted Inuit families and northern wildlife,[65] rather than the kittens, sheep in meadows, or windmills that were featured in spelling lessons and might well have appeared on the nursery walls. These small adaptations do not suggest any overwhelming attitudinal changes regarding notions of cultural superiority. They indicate that change was possible, and occasionally attempted.

Some teaching efforts, however, were decidedly unsympathetic to local custom. One example was the formation of Girl Guide companies. Boy Scout troops and Cub packs operated in the north, but Brownie packs and Guide companies were under the exclusive direction of women. There is something bizarre about a white woman from the south teaching native girls in the Mackenzie River valley how to follow a trail in the bush using Baden-Powell's woodcraft signals, or how to light a fire at the end of a day's hike. Yet at mission schools in the north, Guide and Brownie meetings were considered to be a great help in character building; as Helen Sowden wrote from Hay River in 1935, "the outdoor activities called for in the programme afford [the native girls] the pleasures very dear to their former mode of living."[66]

Few documentary sources about pre-war Girl Guide companies in the NWT have survived, but an early log book of the First Hay River Girl Guide Company is still intact.[67] The log runs from 1934 to 1936. Although no signature appears on the handwritten scribbler, it was probably kept by Helen Sowden, who reported on Girl Guide activities to the *Living Message* during those years. Although this group was established in 1934, it had an unsuccessful first year, and an entry for January 1935 declares that "after a lapse of almost six months, due to unsatisfactory behaviour on the part of the Guides, we restarted on probation and had an opening meeting." It is not known if the original members were simply recalcitrant Girl Guides; the leader's disclosure that patrols were not named at this time suggests that that might have been the case. Patrols permitted a system of peer control; older girls earned responsibility as they progressed through the program. Perhaps under the circumstances this was impossible as there were no experienced girls to accept responsibility. Perhaps too, the authority of another girl was not recognized because of cultural considerations.

The company's activities may have been suspended simply because, as a favoured amusement, the withdrawal of activities could be used as a punishment for school infractions. The company was subject to short-term shutdowns for more important activities such as confirmation classes, but the log entries suggest that the program followed closely the ideals and activities of the Girl Guides of Canada. Included in the teaching were the Guide Law and Promise, much of which would make little sense to native girls at Hay River, although those who had already been indoctrinated by the Christian mission would have some idea about duty to God, the King, and their country. The Girl Guide company at Hay River, and later at Aklavik, also provided an appropriate setting for teaching the girls modern views about health and hygiene. Child welfare classes included lessons about baby health and nutrition and the proper way of bathing an infant. Of course, this socialized girls as mothers; but as there was never any serious doubt that their future in this setting held any other promise, it was seen as a useful skill. The Girl Guides also learned first aid, although supplies were often in short supply. The log records that once when smelling salts were unavailable, one of the Guides suggested using hung fish as an equivalent.

By the time the First Hay River Girl Guide Company held their meeting on 24 May 1935, two patrols were in operation: the Pansies and the Bluebirds. During the spring a number of outdoor excursions had taken place, including one in which two Guides had fallen into a slew, but this particular meeting was held indoors because of inclement weather. The company reviewed their lessons on the flags, played Kim's game,[68] and listened to the story of the daisy, which at the time was the floral emblem of the Empire.

As these activities reveal, there was nothing subtle about the cultural impositions of the Girl Guide program in use in the north in the 1920s, although again the question must be asked as to how much of this instruction was absorbed and how much discarded when the children returned home to their families, where there were no regular meetings. There is no way to measure the impact. Guiding may simply have been another weekly chore for some girls. It may well have been just a lark for others – there is no reason to believe that these Girl Guides were any different from adolescent girls elsewhere in Canada. All that can be concluded is that the missionary teachers fostered the paramilitary groups with enthusiasm; they saw the structure as an effective means of teaching the life skills they identified as important, including self-discipline, pride in appearance, self-respect, and respect for authority.[69] Those skills are not damaging in themselves, but when coupled with the assumptions that went along with their teaching, they take on a deeper meaning and show how good intentions can be labelled as racist.

By the time a Guide company at Aklavik was formed in 1937, this was an Empire-wide movement and supposedly adaptable to cultures of all kinds, provided they subscribed to the ideals of duty to God and country. Leaders felt that being a Girl Guide was one way of having girls in the north see themselves as a part of a wider group. Ethel Hewer wrote to *Living Message* readers that while parkas, fur boots, and mitts were the usual uniform for the "most northerly Company in the British Empire," the girls were "very proud to belong to the Great Sisterhood of Guides, even if they were so far away at the top of the world." It may have been that the enthusiasm was Miss Hewer's; she also noted that some girls were a bit bewildered by the whole idea on arrival at the Aklavik school. When Guiding was explained to them they were, she decided, "somewhat amused at the funny things these white people do."[70]

Despite efforts to convey the message offered by Girl Guide and Boy Scout activities, Anglican and Roman Catholic schools in the north were primarily concerned with fostering spiritual change rather than dealing with education. In evangelical denominations (and in this case that included the Anglicans), literacy was crucial to understanding the Scriptures, even though many prayers and hymns had been translated for native use. The mission schools had restricted finances and limited contact with the children, so reality dictated compromise if that goal was to be achieved. Teachers reported that the children learned English quickly despite the strain, but like Flossie Hirst at Pangnirtung, mission workers knew their work would not be truly successful until the Inuit learned to speak English.[71] But before they could do so, the missionaries had to communicate somehow. The result was a curious mix – teachers struggling to teach English while grappling with the strong guttural sounds of the native languages.

Outside the schools white women resolved to make some attempt at meeting the Dene and Inuit halfway. Compromise was to their advantage if they wanted to teach white, southern customs. Not being able to communicate only contributed to their isolation. Helen Merritt, for example, wrote from Bernard Harbour in 1921 about feeling so alone when her husband was away. A native woman came to help lay fires in the morning but they could not converse; Mrs Merritt knew only about thirty words of Inuktitut and could not put them together to make sentences. For Helen Merritt, learning Inuktitut meant that she could teach well-baby clinics, although she recognized that before doing that she "would like to start instructing all in the use of handkerchiefs,"[72] something she thought would be difficult to convey through an interpreter. Undoubtedly, there was no Inuktitut word for handkerchief. More importantly, an attempt to convey the more covert message through an interpreter would probably have proved to be unsatisfactory. Not only the language was foreign.

In a letter from Hay River to the *Letter Leaflet*, Gladys Booy wrote about her attempts to learn the language. "It will take a long time," she said, but "a few words to show willingness are always appreciated by the Natives. It will be such a help to have the knowledge. I can go then without an interpreter."[73] At Chesterfield Inlet, the Grey Nuns recorded in their journal how important it was that they learn Inuktitut – even though it might be difficult for those approaching middle age – and called their daily lesson "une dure entreprise."[74]

A hard undertaking, indeed. Some women, like Winifred Marsh, used the opportunity afforded by long Arctic winters to learn the intricacies of Inuktitut. Louisa Camsell Mills, however, who lived almost her whole life in the Mackenzie River valley, never mastered the Slavey tongue. Mena Orford described how she had first learned the thirteen symbols of Inuktitut as well as the added accents. It seems that her teacher Etonah had pointed to common objects and named them; she then progressed to reading symbols on paper. "The endings," she added, "finished me." But she made up her mind to learn those too, because "obviously no chances could be taken with a language where, by the simple changing of a vowel ending, you found yourself discussing that part of female anatomy lying squarely in the field of gynaecology, when all you intended was to procure a part of the seal that went well with bacon."[75]

Mena Orford, it will be remembered, had had some difficulty eating that part of the seal which went well with bacon – an attitude towards country food and its preparation that shows the vacillation with which the white women in the north approached issues of culture and race. No pattern of behaviour can be firmly delineated, which leads to the conclusion that women's reactions to cultural contacts were individual rather than universal. The white women's interpretation of the other culture depended initially on their preconceptions, usually developed from misconceptions about Dene and Inuit customs. This was a barren and largely inhospitable land. Supplies were difficult to obtain. Women knew they would be isolated from women of their own culture; they understood that civilized people lived in houses, had some knowledge of personal hygiene and modesty, and lived apparently moral lives in the fear of God. There is every reason to assume that they met the challenge before them with some trepidation, often retreating back to the culture with which they were most accustomed.

The ultimate question about white women and cultural arrogance has to be whether their sex made a difference. And the answer has to be that it did. The white women's attitudes were principally shaped by their conditioning as women and mothers, and the social sensibilities of the time. Motherhood and the traditional occupations of women dictated a very different life than that of their male counterparts. Elements of life in the north were shared by men and women alike, yet the employment of men more often determined where the women were, and why they were there. The differences that society imposed between the sexes accounted for an alternative level of interaction, even though that may have been an adjunct. Remote location, physical and psychological isolation from their cultural sisters, and personal initiatives needed to deal with their environment were important influences at this other level.

Any discussion about racial and cultural attitudes inevitably raises a more vexing inquiry. What culpability can be assessed because these women refused to use native midwives, or because they insisted indigenous children learn their lessons in English, or even because they attempted to impose their own canons of sanitation? White women's views about race in the north have been presented here, in the knowledge that those attitudes cannot be changed, even if the current political climate demands it. It would have been remarkable if these women had arrived in the north, shed their cultural biases, and worked within the local society rather than imposing new ideas and concepts that were seemingly out of place. If they had been in the north in the later part of the twentieth century, instead of the first decades, they might well have been able to overcome some of the exigencies of geography, or the realities of their circumstances, and worked towards reforms in keeping with a more enlightened era. What these women did and how they lived their lives was not unusual for their time. That their white skins set them apart from their native neighbours does not mean cultural and racial conflicts were inevitable, in the same way that conflicts did not necessarily arise because the Inuit considered themselves as *the people*, and whites as inferior. In the NWT, race relations were played out by rules often bent by remoteness, climate, and the necessity to adapt, not to mention the possibility that the native people of the north may have made decisions about what was of value to them, and discarded what they did not want – without the white women's knowledge.

"A Certain Amount of Unpleasantness": One Woman's Encounter with the Holy Trinity of the North

Occasionally, research will uncover documents which even though they raise a number of questions, explain a whole range of issues under one theme. Sometimes, small details culled from a number of sources can serendipitously find themselves in a common file, making complete sense of an otherwise incoherent situation. Lucky historians know that every once in awhile both situations will come together fortuitously to create a singular example for their research. Such is the case of Mary Lyman and her winter at Herschel Island.

The pieces of the Mary Lyman puzzle were scattered across Canada at archives in Ottawa, Edmonton, Yellowknife, Winnipeg, and White-horse. Because of the nature of her experience, they were accumulated almost independently and in seemingly unconnected places. In many ways these discoveries exemplify the nature of the research for the entire project: the details are representative of the themes raised previously, and their significance lies not just in the location of the sources themselves.

The dismissal of Mary Philomena Lyman, the HBC cook at Herschel Island in the winter of 1924-25, offers insights into the unique circumstances of women's employment in the Arctic, but in a job defined by southern standards and the socialized views of European men, not by northern realities. Her employment and the ensuing circumstances permit the infusion of details relevant to northern history and gender relations that might otherwise not have emerged. Her employment confirms that the HBC hired single, white European women in what has always been considered a man's domain, which in itself adds to knowledge about the Company and its adventurers. And the events of one winter in a woman's life – seemingly insignificant events – suggest several compelling questions about the white men at the settlement.

What happens to a woman who crosses the lines of legal and social subordination at an isolated northern settlement? Inspector T.B. Caulkin, officer commanding the Arctic Sub-District of the RCMP, wrote with some understatement to his Commanding Officer James Ritchie at "G" Division in Edmonton in April 1925, that he had "the honour to report a certain amount of unpleasantness" that had arisen at Herschel Island.[1] That winter has been described as an "unusually rowdy one" on the island,[2] a relatively sheltered haven in the Beaufort Sea off the Arctic coast of the Yukon Territory. The population of the island had suffered from the loss of the HBC supply vessel *Kindersley*. The sinking had left a detachment of men from the Canadian Army Corps of Signals stranded, their kit and equipment having gone down with the ship.[3] Herschel Island was also home that winter to American trader Christian Klengenberg and his crew,[4] whose vessel was frozen in at Herschel.

The shipwrecked and stranded men had to be supplied from meagre rations, and fuel had to be found to keep them warm – a not inconsiderable task on an island where the only supply of wood came from what was washed ashore during the short Arctic summer. While their presence probably shortened tempers and added burdens to the men who directed the scene at Herschel, these sailors and soldiers were just actors on the periphery. Like all Arctic outposts in Canada in the twenties, the institutional power remained with what northerners and northern historians pointedly refer to as the "Holy Trinity of the North": the Bay; the Church; and the RCMP.

It was rumoured that the letters on the Hudson's Bay Company standard actually signified "Here Before Christ," which of course, practically speaking, it had been, in the Arctic and in northern Canada generally.[5] There were independent traders in the north – some of them quite successful – but the Company's network was ubiquitous. The HBC men had explored and opened up the region; explorers became traders; and the Company's posts became the focus for Arctic settlements and missions.

Despite the strength of both the church and the HBC in the region, it was the Royal Northwest Mounted Police, and later the Royal Canadian Mounted Police, that represented the real power. The detachment at Herschel Island was established in 1903, in response to repeated requests from the Anglican missionary for some form of law enforcement to police what that missionary termed the "general drunkenness" of the American whaling crews. Charles Whittaker was convinced that the sailors had a bad influence on the Inuit and, in particular, was worried about the debauchery of Inuit women and the apparent misuse of alcohol. By 1926, Inspector Vernon Kemp reported that at the Herschel Island Post (and at virtually every other northern RCMP detachment), the officer-in-charge acted officially in a vast number of roles: as law enforcement officer, coroner, mining recorder, magistrate, and postmaster; as inspector of radio licences, enforcer of hunting and trapping regulations, and deputy sheriff; as immigration and naturalization officer, customs collector, deputy of the public administrator, welfare officer, and registrar of vital statistics; and, inexplicably at Herschel Island where there were no trees, as timber agent. Unofficially, he also often acted as priest, undertaker, physician, and dentist.[6] How anyone could remember all those regulations is unknown, but with all those duties and, more importantly, with the power they embodied over the native and white population, the RCM policeman was entrusted with authority, second only to God himself, over all the Inuit and Dene of the region, as well as over all the white Europeans.

White European women had been present at Herschel for almost as long as white European men. Since 1895-96, the captains of a number of American whalers had been sailing to Herschel from San Francisco with wives on board and wintering over at Pauline Cove. Sophie Porter, wife of the captain of the *Jessie H Freeman*, published a number of stories about her life at Herschel Island.[7] Sarah Ann Stringer accompanied her husband, Isaac, to the Anglican mission in 1897, where they remained until 1901. Emma Whittaker and Christina Fry, wives of Anglican missionary clergy, also lived there. But Mary Lyman was the first unmarried white woman to be engaged to work at Herschel Island.

Mrs Lyman had been employed at the Fort MacMurray HBC Post as a housekeeper. When her employer, having been promoted, moved to Edmonton in the spring of 1924, Mary Lyman followed him; there she was hired on as stewardess aboard the *Distributor*, the HBC stern wheeler that supplied the Mackenzie District. Little is known about her position on board. Because this job, like the one at Fort MacMurray and later, at Herschel, was considered a "local hire," no personnel records exist, but essentially, Mary Lyman would have been a waitress whose special duties included the care of female passengers. (There were always female passengers on the steamers, notably Grey Nuns moving north to establish new schools and hospitals, nurses and teachers for the Anglican missions, and wives of clergymen and the RCMP.)

On 8 August, the *Distributor* arrived at Aklavik, the turn-around point at the Mackenzie Delta. Here she was hired by V.W. West as housekeeper for the Herschel Island HBC Post, where West was manager and the Western Arctic District accountant. At the time, Mary Lyman was a widow of about fifty years of age, with sufficient experience for the job at hand. Fort MacMurray was hardly a roaring metropolis in 1924, so Mary Lyman must have had some understanding of northern outpost life and the consequent isolation. All things considered, working as a housekeeper at Herschel Island was within her capabilities. Indeed, everyone seemed satisfied with her performance. However, by early November, Thomas Umoak the Inuit lay missionary at the Anglican mission wrote to Isaac Stringer saying that "she had become very troublesome."[8] On 6 December, Mary Lyman quarrelled with West over what was described as "the use of the Company's sitting room," a request which Umoak said the Post manager had refused. In retaliation, Mrs Lyman then refused to cook, and West asked for her resignation.

Obviously, animosity between white residents at an isolated point such as Herschel Island was better avoided. Conditions unique to the Arctic could complicate what might otherwise be a simple situation. Personal isolation, added to geographical remoteness, could cause misery for any resident. In this case, the island's limited accommodations were already overcrowded. It was December, and Mrs Lyman had nowhere to go until break-up enabled travel to Aklavik, estimated by Inspector Caulkin to be in seven months. It was cold and dark. No doubt the white population had begun to suffer from cabin fever. Inspector Caulkin was called in to mediate and reported that Mrs Lyman was willing to return to her duties. West, though, was adamant, and paid her off. West wrote to the Inspector that he wanted Mrs Lyman removed from the premises because her presence "jeopardized the Company's property"[9] and she was no longer his concern.

Caulkin took pains to inform West of his responsibility under Section 241 of the Criminal Code of Canada. The section entitled "Duties Tending to the Preservation of Life," states:

Every one who has charge of any other person unable by reason either of detention, age, sickness, insanity or any other cause, to withdraw himself from such charge, and unable to provide himself with the necessities of life, is, whether such charge is undertaken by him under any contract, or is imposed upon him by law, or by reason of his unlawful act, under a legal duty to supply that person with the necessities of life, and is criminally responsible for omitting, without lawful excuse, to perform such duty if the death of such person is caused, or if his life is endangered or his health has been, or is likely to be permanently injured by such omission.[10]

Caulkin confirmed that West then made an effort to provide for Mrs Lyman's welfare. To this end, West went to see Umoak, who provided what he described as the mission warehouse, really a shed that had been "fixed up extensively for quite a sum."[11]

The most extensive records of the events involving Mary Lyman originate with Inspector Caulkin, who noted that he never actually enquired what the problem was at the Post between employer and housekeeper, although he did know that the break was over the demands for use of the sitting room.[12] Contemporary readers with knowledge of labour relations in a domestic setting might imagine lurid scenarios for the sitting room at Herschel Island, perhaps some form of sexual harassment by Mr West, or even some indiscretion on the part of Mary Lyman. There is always the possibility of a lover's quarrel, although it should be noted that no hint of such a relationship appears in any of the sources.

There is some evidence that Mrs Lyman had a reputation among some of the men in the north that might account for the dispute between herself and V.W. West. Caulkin noted in one report to his commander that he had "heard considerable relative to the disposition of Mrs Lyman, and [he] anticipated that she would cause some commotion by her stay at Herschel Island, however, [he] was prepared to take the woman as he found her."[13] Irving Howatt, Mrs Lyman's solicitor, who was engaged on her return to Edmonton, echoed the same sentiment when he wrote to "G" Division headquarters on her behalf saying that he knew "perfectly well when she went to Herschel Island that there was going to be trouble."[14] Superintendent Ritchie replied that it was easier to discuss the problem at hand because the solicitor was "aware of the peculiar characteristics of the complainant."[15] The "peculiar characteristics" were never actually defined, but Richard Bonnycastle, who later stayed at Mary Lyman's boardinghouse at Aklavik in 1928, recorded in his diary that although a superb hostess, Mrs Lyman "never stops talking."[16] Her nature also included a propensity for gossip, revealed Bonnycastle, and she freely dispensed information about the local traders' alcohol consumption and other improprieties.

Consider this disposition in light of the situation at the Post. It should be understood that the HBC house at Herschel was only twenty-eight by thirty-four feet and that an error in construction – the rafters had been cut to thirty-four feet – had caused the long side of the roof to be placed along the shorter length, leaving the upper floor an overly high-pitched roof. The stairway was not well constructed, and residents had to climb half the stairs on hands and knees so their heads did not hit the ceiling. There were five bedrooms in the upper storey, each measuring six feet by eight feet and furnished with only a small bed. The hot kitchen was the only place where the year's supply of food could be stored and the beaverboard walls allowed no privacy. The house was described in an HBC report as "inconvenient,"[17] providing insight into the consequences of Mrs Lyman's inability to use the sitting room during long, dark, winter months. Imagine how it must have been when, in the darkest of Arctic winter, a chatterbox with a strong personality was cooped up in the Herschel Post's close quarters with three single men. Undoubtedly, the men would view their situation as insufferable.[18]

Caulkin, Ritchie, Bonnycastle, and Howatt never once mention the reputation of the male involved in the dispute – the one who had the power to fire the cook and banish her from the HBC Post. Their comments support an assumption that the dispute was over Mrs Lyman's request for the use of the room for herself. But subsequent research in vaguely relevant sources, coupled with a knowledge of the power structure at work, suggests that there may have been an alternative explanation. What happens, for instance, if the focus is reversed, and Mr West's use of the room becomes the focal point of the argument?

There are no personnel records left at the HBC Archives that describe the employment of V.W. West, save a single half-page in a miscellaneous search file that lists his appointment as Western Arctic District accountant. This omission is curious. The Western Arctic District was under careful scrutiny at the time by the Fur Trade Commissioner's office because of poor management in the posts of the Mackenzie and Western Arctic regions. However, several useful comments can be gleaned from reports filed about the HBC's business in the area; they are useful for the purpose of appreciating the dynamic in the sitting room. In one report, Angus Brabant, the HBC Fur Trade Commissioner, describes West as having many good points to qualify him for the position as District Accountant and Post Manager, but as at times showing "poor judgement in his management of the staff; being somewhat overbearing he [was] not altogether popular with them."[19] However, it is Hugh Conn's inspection report of the Western Arctic District in October 1925 that provides the important clue to West's disposition, and perhaps to the situation in the sitting room.

In this financial report assessing the economic strengths and weaknesses of the Herschel Post and commenting on Post management, Conn does not mention the manager by name, although the "cook" does appear fleetingly in a reference to salaries and expenditures. Conn notes that expenditures over the winter were less than budgeted because the cook's salary was not fully paid out. In addition, he appraises the duties of Mr Watt, the apprentice clerk. As for West, Conn concludes his report by suggesting that for future reference "it will be necessary to have a man in charge of the Post with good personality: he should be a good mixer, yet with enough strength of character to keep away from all gambling and drinking parties. In a word, he should be an all round good man."[20]

A new light is shed on the dispute in the sitting room. While there is only innuendo to suggest that V.W. West was himself "misusing" the room, the placement of this comment in Conn's report has to be viewed as significant. No similar comments about gambling, alcohol, and managers appear in Conn's reports about other HBC locations. It is conceivable that Mrs Lyman did not approve of alcohol and gambling in what was her home as well as Mr West's. It explains why Caulkin never enquired about the specifics of the dispute in the sitting room: the closeness of the white community at northern outposts and Caulkin's position within it were such that he would have had no need. The dispute over the sitting room, however, was only the beginning; it simply set the stage for Mary Lyman's real affront to the HBC, the Anglican Church, and the RCMP.

The warehouse shed which West had arranged for Mrs Lyman's accommodation at the Anglican mission was not a palace, even by comparison to the HBC house. No doubt everyone concerned hoped that spring would come quickly and uneventfully and that Mrs Lyman would stay quietly at the Anglican mission and try to keep herself amused throughout the long months still to come. They were to be disappointed. Mary Lyman did settle herself into the shed at the Anglican mission; then she announced she would set up a school, which meant that she lost any support she might have had from Thomas Umoak. Initially, Umoak had no objection to the school. After all, he recognized Mrs Lyman had to keep busy and make some kind of living. Umoak was one of the first Inuit in the region converted and trained by Isaac Stringer;[21] as a result he was well versed in Anglican dogma, including the part that viewed Roman Catholics as Papist competition not to be trusted. Imagine his consternation, then, when he discovered "how strong a Roman Catholic she was, and what her idea in having [a] school" meant.[22] The competition presented by a Roman Catholic school was difficult enough, but its operation on Anglican property was altogether an embarrassment. Because Umoak was unable to extricate the Anglican mission from its Christian undertaking to provide some dwelling for Mrs Lyman, Umoak told Stringer that he felt obliged to warn his flock at Herschel about Mrs Lyman. She became further isolated.

That Mary Lyman was a Roman Catholic is significant – there was no RC mission at Herschel. If there had been, her circumstances might have been different. Herschel was one of the few places among the Arctic and Mackenzie settlements where the two denominations had not set up centres in the community in active competition. This was primarily due to the difficulty of supplying the out-of-the-way island. It was also because the indigenous population consisted of transient Inuit. The Grey Nuns had been moving steadily northward along the Mackenzie River, building schools and hospitals with the OMI. They had yet to reach Aklavik, the largest centre closest to Herschel. Construction on the RC hospital and school at Aklavik did not begin until several years later, when Mrs Lyman herself would provide financial and personal support to the Grey Nuns.

While Mary Lyman apparently decided to establish an RC school and herself rectify the denominational imbalance at Herschel Island, there is no indication that she was asked to vacate the shed. After all, West had made financial arrangements with Umoak to ensure that she would not move back into the Post. West's dilemma was solved when Mrs Lyman gave up the school of her own accord and decided to take up duties as a private nurse. Women with nursing skills were always in demand in the north, where medical facilities were scattered and physicians few in number, and where there was constant danger from the environment and from diseases carried on-board supply vessels. Professional nurses, however, were normally members of religious orders or a missionary society, or they were the wives of missionaries or police.[23] No record exists of professional, private nurses in northern communities at this time.

Perhaps even more noteworthy was that on the northern frontier there was little surplus cash to pay women to nurse, and nowhere to spend any earnings except at the trading posts. Merchandise was scarce, but there were furs and, like all northern visitors, Mary Lyman no doubt wanted to take home a souvenir of her stay in the north – which is why she found herself in trouble again. If she had stayed put in her shed and eked out some existence until spring arrived, probably no record of her experience would ever have survived. But she did not confine herself to her residence, and it is the ensuing crime report filed by Caulkin that generated the official file.

On 1 May 1925, Mary Philomena Lyman was charged with trading fur without a licence, contrary to the Yukon Game Ordinance. The report, which is lengthy and descriptive, cites the testimony before Magistrate Caulkin. The plea was not guilty. Caulkin noted that the defendant refused to give testimony under oath, and that there was no explanation for her decision. Corporal Belcher, who arrested Mrs Lyman, testified that she had sold a shotgun to Phillip Nowyak for the sum of five dollars and a single fox skin. Nowyak, under oath, substantiated Belcher's account.

Mrs Lyman offered a slightly different story in her own defence. She told the court that she had gone to the Nowyak house on either the 26th or 27th of April to care for Nowyak's wife. She said that she and the Inuk had talked about the shotgun, and that Nowyak had expressed an interest. Visiting her the next day, he offered fur in exchange for the shotgun; she said that she refused but offered to sell the shotgun for what she had paid for it. When Nowyak agreed to shoot some ducks for Mary Lyman and offered some shoes made by his wife in addition to the $5.00, the deal was closed. Mary Lyman said she then suggested that Nowyak give her fox skins in return for nursing his wife.[24] This story made no impression on the magistrate. Mary Lyman was found guilty as charged and given a suspended sentence of one year. The fox skin was confiscated by the court and forwarded to Edmonton for final disposal.

There was more to it than that, of course. It was not until February of the next year when Caulkin expanded on the situation. By that time, Mary Lyman had returned to Edmonton, laid a complaint, and requested the return of her fox skin. Caulkin wrote that a "few details" were omitted because he did not "consider it necessary to quote them, in the face of the evidence produced at the trial."[25] He did not elaborate on how the missing evidence might have affected the outcome. What is apparent is that he believed that trading without a licence was more serious than the lesser charge of theft.

After comments about Mrs Lyman's disposition, Caulkin defended the hearing as fair and pointed out that Phillip Nowyak gave his evidence "under oath, of which this native [was] fully conversant, being a member of the Anglican Mission, and acquainted with all the beliefs of the Bible, the same as we are in civilization."[26] A photograph taken of Nowyak and his family in 1926 shows the Inuk dressed in European-style clothing, indicating that he had some connection with the white men in the community; perhaps he worked as a guide for the RCMP, or in some capacity for the HBC or the church. This would explain why Caulkin was prepared to accept Nowyak's statement over one made without oath by a troublesome woman. Caulkin did acknowledge that Mrs Lyman's skills and devotion as a nurse were admirable and that he was personally aware of her ability; he did not add that this was because Mrs Lyman had probably saved the life of his son.[27] The evidence never given at Mrs

Lyman's trial included essential background to the events leading up to the crime for which she was arrested. It involved an independent trader named William Seymore. An Australian with American citizenship, Seymore (Seymour), was an agent of Christian Klengenberg, which according to one HBC source meant he enjoyed the favour of the RCMP.[28] Seymore had lodged a complaint about the theft of a shotgun from his home. He reported that Mary Lyman had come to him wishing to trade the shotgun for a white fox skin, and that he had told her to pick one out from a bunch hanging from the rafters of his warehouse. Apparently she did not do so at that time, and instead tried to make a better deal with the local Inuit. It was then that Mary Lyman made her deal with Nowyak. She then returned to Seymore's house while he was absent and removed the shotgun.

On the surface, this appears to be a simple problem of communication. If Mary Lyman had been trading for rations or fuel it might well have stayed that way. But there were complicating factors, notably the fox skin, trading territories, and the RCMP's credibility. As Caulkin explained, the two trading posts on the island, both of which had secured licences at $25.00 each, no doubt expected some protection from illegal competition. If he allowed just anyone to trade "under their noses," he feared that he would leave himself open to criticism from legitimate traders.[29] Because Caulkin and the RCMP in the region were already open to criticism from traders in the area, he was likely sensitive about the subject.

At the time, the HBC was unhappy about the decision of the government in the summer of 1924 to allow American traders Klengenberg and Pederson into Canadian waters along the Arctic coast. Because they had missed the 1924 season, Caulkin permitted the traders to proceed east in 1925, despite instructions from Ottawa to the contrary. Writing from Aklavik on an inspection trip in June 1925, Angus Brabant accused Caulkin of taking this step for the personal gain available from his execution of duties as customs inspector. More importantly, Brabant also suggested that the RCMP officers east of the Mackenzie had been trading and trapping considerable numbers of white fox, and that by trading these furs to the American traders, there would be no official record of the trade in Canada.[30]

Mary Lyman's predicament over the fox skin just served to bring the issue to the fore. Indeed, she herself had suggested while still at Herschel that RCMP officers were trading illegally. Through her solicitor, she accused one RCMP corporal of attempting to "come out" of the area with $1500 worth of furs. Her motive was personal rather than patriotic: she felt it was her accusation that had identified the officer, and that a reward should have been forthcoming. Superintendent Ritchie pointed out to Howatt that no charges had ever been laid, although Caulkin had been aware of the accusation because he told Ritchie in his 1926 report that news of a possible illegal trade had reached him by the first steamer in 1925 – but not from Mrs Lyman. He did note that Mrs Lyman had informed V.W. West by letter about several persons trading illegally, and had offered to provide information if he came to her shack at 11 pm on a certain night. Caulkin recorded that Mr West was "apprehensive as to the idea" and sent him a letter asking for an investigation. Caulkin said that he had requested the same information from Mrs Lyman on four occasions, but that she had refused. Despite the situation between West and Mrs Lyman, West was the obvious choice to supply information about possible RCMP indiscretions. As the local HBC man, he would have had access to the Fur Trade Commissioner, who would have been more than happy to obtain concrete information supporting the Company's suspicions.

At any rate, rewards were never offered under either the Yukon or Northwest Territories Game Ordinances. But Ritchie's closing remark to Howatt raises some suspicion about what exactly was going on at the RCMP detachments in the area. He wrote, "I may say for your information that our men in the far North have certain few privileges in the matter of furs and souvenirs."[31] He added that the fox skin had been sent to Dawson City and could not be returned.

Perhaps Mrs Lyman's knowledge and, more importantly, what the men may have seen as her unwillingness to keep quiet about what she knew made Caulkin realize that everyone would be better off if Mrs Lyman went south. Whatever the reason, after the trial Mrs Lyman's removal from Herschel Island became a priority for Caulkin. She had wanted to leave Herschel Island right after the dispute with West, when she had asked to be taken to Aklavik by dog team. West informed Caulkin that he would in no way be responsible for Mrs Lyman's health or for any accidents on such a journey. Caulkin wrote that "he never thought Mrs Lyman would care to go out over the trail in winter time," and that he believed she would prefer travel in safety and comfort by boat. "It must be understood," he added, "that a woman of Mrs Lyman's age [is] hardly capable of withstanding some of the inconveniences prevalent in travel by dogteam." By the time of her arrest, Caulkin had decided that Mrs Lyman "seemed to be suffering slightly from a mental point of view, brought about by a lack of employment,"[32] and because she thought she was being detained against her will – which in a way she was.

Caulkin reported that Mrs Lyman had requested a Native to take her to Shingle Point, then Aklavik, by dog team. He pointed out that no Native would undertake the journey until after break-up; he also noted that V.W. West had sent messages to both those posts, saying that Post Managers should not, under any circumstances, allow Mrs Lyman to stay in a Company dwelling because of her conduct at Herschel. Of necessity, the journey had to be fairly direct and by the shortest route.[33] Both men seemed concerned about Mrs Lyman's age and that she might have to withstand some privations on the trip. Caulkin also recognized that West was guarding against any possibility of civil action against the Company. Having become resigned to the notion that he had to get Mrs Lyman away from Herschel Island, Inspector Caulkin made arrangements to take her to Aklavik, accompanied by him and his wife. He provided the supplies and conveyance himself and accepted full responsibility. They left on 11 May.

It could not have been a comfortable trip for anyone. Mary Lyman had a sled to herself and refused to converse. She would not share food and would not "bury the hatchet," despite Caulkin's request. The party arrived at Shingle Point, where the Post Manager and his wife provided a shed. Mrs Lyman told Howatt, her solicitor, that she was put up in a small building with barred windows. During her six-night stay, her bed was just a hard bunk; her only visitor was Mrs Blake, the Post Manager's wife. Howatt asked the RCMP to explain this lack of hospitality, suggesting it would be in the best interest of Inspector Caulkin to come up with a reasonable account that would "keep her quiet, because the way she tells the story it would lead people who do not know the circumstances of the country, into much criticism of the police, which is unjustified and unwarranted and we are quite sure you do not want that."[34]

Caulkin naturally disputed the accusations. He argued that the shed had been scrubbed clean, the bunk was the common variety provided to travellers in the north, and the Caulkins themselves had made use of a mission shed with similar accommodation. He noted that although one window of Mrs Lyman's shed had wood nailed across it, it was untrue to say it was barred. Moreover, it was warm outside – there being twenty-four hours of sunlight a day – and they had only stayed at Shingle Point for four days. He pointed out, too, that the Post Manager, his pregnant wife, three children, and a hired man lived in the Blake's small, two bedroom house. The shed, he contended, provided Mrs Lyman with a measure of privacy that no one else enjoyed. He insisted, too, that Blake had refused Mrs Lyman the use of the house on West's orders. Caulkin also described the trip to

Aklavik as uneventful, although they had been forced to camp for several weeks until break-up because ice conditions prevented travel.

Mrs Lyman apparently made it back to Edmonton, where she went to see her solicitor and lodged her informal complaint. Howatt must have provided his client with some useful counsel, because in November 1925, Mary Lyman wrote to the "Chief Game Guardian" of the Northwest Territories, requesting information on how to obtain a licence "for trading only." She was going north again in the spring, she declared, claiming to have spent two years at Aklavik. She said she had returned south as a companion to an insane woman[35] and planned to return to nursing for four or five years, saying that she would be a resident and demanding to know what it would cost her. She conceded that she had once taken "a fox skin for nursing and the police took it from [her], saying it was trading." She wanted "to be protected, and at the same time be on the square."[36]

Since it is known that Mary Lyman had worked only one summer on the *Distributor* and one winter at Herschel Island, she was not exactly "on the square." Her letter left out a few other important details, such as the theft of the shotgun. But she certainly got her trading licence. And she did return to Aklavik, where the Grey Nuns took her picture smiling in front of the new convent, in 1926. She was identified as Madame Kost, *notre benefactrice*, although strangely, her name does not appear in any of the correspondence from the Grey Nuns at Aklavik to the Mother House during that period. Government trading-licence records show Mrs Vincent Kost as holder of licence number 324 at Aklavik, first issued in 1928.[37] In 1939, the licence passed to Vincent Kost. Margaret Oldenburg's record of her trip to Aklavik in 1944 notes the passing of Mrs Kost in that year.[38]

It would be easier to understand the events of the 1924-25 at Herschel Island if all the gentlemen concerned had been more specific about what it was in Mrs Lyman's character that disturbed them, if they had acknowledged West's personality, and if Caulkin had related exactly what had gone on in the sitting room. It is possible that the men concerned worked together to prevent liability being assessed against the HBC. It is also possible that they were trying to protect Mary Lyman. Nevertheless, they presented Mary Lyman's character as the issue, and it is illuminating to see how they worked around this through innuendo and asides. More importantly, Mary Lyman's reputation provided bureaucrats in the north with a cover for their own petty indiscretions and shortcomings. Not surprisingly, and even if he *did not* gamble or drink, V.W. West never figured as part of the problem in any of the correspondence, crime reports, or letters of defence.

Because of the dearth of sources from the woman herself, any understanding of Mary Lyman's predicament meant a search through documents generated solely by these same men. It also meant reading between the lines in an array of sources not specifically labelled with her name, and not about her at all. It was an exercise in deciphering a woman's life from official documents awash with stereotypical images. With the exception of a single letter written from the south when the momentous winter was over and she had returned to civilization, there are no personal comments from Mrs Lyman herself – a not uncommon occurrence. What these records do show is that coupled with the prevailing myth among men in the north that conditions were too hard for a woman was the possibility of collusion to protect themselves. It was *their* north, and they were able to preach *their* gospel. A woman with what they saw as "peculiar characteristics" was the misfit, not themselves. Since conditions were hard for a man, they were by extension, and to their minds, harder for a woman. Yet consider that Inspector Caulkin thought nothing of plunking his wife into a *komatik* to travel to Aklavik under the same conditions as Mary Lyman. Consider, too, that he apparently gave little thought to the fact that Mary Lyman had made her way north independently of the RCMP and or perhaps despite them. Women had been able to handle the travails of Herschel Island for some time; marriage, however, provided them with a buffer between themselves and the men and institutions of power which those men themselves represented and which Mary Lyman lacked. Mary Lyman may have been responsible for some of her situation, but it would be a mistake to think her predicament developed because she was a woman who made errors in judgment. White men had been doing peculiar things in the north long before Mary Lyman arrived at Herschel Island, and these men have been immortalized by the romantic history of the region, along with the venerable institutions they represented.

Conclusion

The pieces of the Mary Lyman puzzle represent only one small part of the jigsaw I described in the introduction. I noted there how pieces were missing – and my resolve to assemble enough of the puzzle to illustrate how white European women in the Canadian north met the challenges posed by the climate and geography, and the southern institutions to which they were in some way attached or dependent upon. I pointed out, however, that drawing concrete conclusions proved to be an impossible task even though there were some notable findings.

I outlined in the first chapter how the climate of the Arctic regions only exacerbated the problems of supply in a northern home, affecting the ways in which women coped with those hardships. The women's ingenuity and patience were tested daily – just like the Dene and Inuit women with whom they lived, but on a parallel track, because the expectations were entirely different. The white women's experience resembled that of the women keeping house in a prairie soddie, although their tribulations were more often self-induced. Missionaries by vocation, travellers by choice, and working women looking for opportunity, these women shared lives that despite the conclusions of current academic discourse about imperialism and feminism, were made up of little pieces that fit together to form a whole. The final picture was not entirely suited to making generalized conclusions, but they do come together to form a collective memory. Some readers may find it troublesome to distance the personal details of people's lives from their intentions, whether their goal is the pursuit of self-accomplishment, or the spread of Christian knowledge. But to set aside people from the greater political understanding underlying the ideas of racial superiority, makes them seem more like individuals caught up in the philosophies of their time. Which was, of course, just what they were. They got hungry, they were often cold, and they were lonely and despondent or happy and capable of coping with their lot in life because they had faith in a force beyond their own lives.

The issues of race and racial superiority may be of some concern to analysts of white, European expansion. I was more interested, though, in the question of how to measure the impact of missionary forces in the Canadian north on the Dene and Inuit who found themselves subject to the ministrations of both the Oblate and Anglican missionaries, as well as the Grey Nuns and the Anglican women who assisted them. Since much of the documentation about early missions in the north is derived from the missionaries themselves, I knew that any historical assessment of the ultimate absorption of Christian values should be done with care. The missionaries, for example, would have southern observers believe that a certain success otherwise undocumented was achieved. The same applies to the imposition of southern culture fostered by white European women. That white European men thought of the north as a man's world is obvious from documentary sources as well. By exposing details of women's personal experiences, I discovered that the female contemporaries of these men were willing to challenge male hegemony, albeit with mixed success. The same finding applied to missionary accomplishments.

It is not possible, of course, to measure courage or independence against the backdrop of necessity. The current train of thought would have it that singling out these women in any way only valorizes their imperialist pursuits. This is, at best, a fatuous assumption. These women were not heroines in any sense; rather they were heroic on a personal level, using the true meaning of the word. Take Mary Lyman; she was one woman on an isolated island who exhibited courage, ingenuity, defiance, compliance, and assertiveness all at once in the face of a personal fiasco. Or take Isobel Hutchison, who could accept her situation, apparently dispense with the formalities, remain unconcerned about the proprieties, and write a book about her experiences. Adelaide Butler, on the other hand, saw her situation as tolerable because she had a meaningful, if trying, job. It nevertheless would be wrong to assume that these women were just ordinary and their fortitude simply the stuff of hardy pioneers. In every case, there was one element of the experience that held true for virtually all the white women: living in the middle of nowhere was sharpened by the simple finality of the situation, as well as the realization that they could not easily go home if something went awry. It required an acceptance impossible to imagine in a world of modern communication technologies.

It was an acceptance that differed in context from that of aboriginal women, who considered the north as both the home from whence they came and where they lived. Some of what is missing from the

puzzle, then, is the significant number of pieces that could be supplied by Inuit, Dene, and Métis women in the north whose lives inter-
twined with those of the white European women. That story remains
to be told. It must be told with the same understanding – that white
women left home with their bags packed not only with ideas of racial
and cultural primacy, but also with the social expectations of a
culture that dictated specific and well-schooled gender roles. It was
never my intention to see if white women could force custom and
change on another society without their compliance and receptivity,
because I have never believed that the indigenous people of the north
were that easily manipulated. Nor was that even possible in the
Canadian north – given the expansive geography, the scattered population, and the communication problems of the era. Nevertheless,
there can be no doubt that white women demanded the same cultural
norms of *themselves* in this strange environment as had been taken for
granted at home. And, ultimately, that expectation remains most
meaningful.

Abbreviations

ACC	Anglican Church of Canada
AD	Archives Deschâtaulets
CMS	Church Missionary Society
DIAND	Department of Indian Affairs and Northern Development
DOA	Diocese of the Arctic
DOMR	Diocese of Mackenzie River
DOY	Diocese of Yukon
GMA	Glenbow Museum Archives
GSA	General Synod Archives
HBC	Hudson's Bay Company
HBCA	Hudson's Bay Company Archives
MHS	Minnesota Historical Society
MSCC	Missionary Society of the Church of England in Canada
NA	National Archives
NWTA	Northwest Territories Archives
ODHS	Old Dartmouth Historical Society
OMI	Oblates of Mary Immaculate
PAA	Provincial Archives of Alberta
PABC	Provincial Archives of British Columbia
PAM	Provincial Archives of Manitoba
RCMP	Royal Canadian Mounted Police
RNWMP	Royal North West Mounted Police
SHM	Soeurs Grises de Montreal
SGME	Soeurs Grises de Montreal – Edmonton
SGMSB	Soeurs Grises de Montreal – St. Boniface
YTA	Yukon Territorial Archives

Notes

INTRODUCTION

1 Florence Hirst, Journals, 1933–1938. ACC, GSA, DOA, M71–4 (hereafter cited as GSA/Hirst).

2 Remember there were not many white *men* either.

3 *The Letter Leaflet of the Woman's Auxiliary to the Missionary Society of the Church of England in Canada*, later *The Living Message*.

4 Readers interested in the general history of the Canadian North should read Zaslow, *The Opening of the Canadian North*, and Zaslow, *The Northward Expansion of Canada*.

5 See for example: Callaway, *Gender, Culture and Empire*; Knapman, *White Women in Fiji*; Trollope, *Britannia's Daughters*; Davin "Imperialism and Motherhood"; Bulbeck, *Australian Women in Papua New Guinea*; Strobel, *European Women and The Second British Empire*; Gouda, "Nynonas on the Colonial Divide: White Women in the Dutch East Indies, 1900–1942"; and Rutherdale, "Revisiting Colonization Through Gender." For a slightly different slant consult Mills, *Discourses and Differences*; Pratt, *Imperial Eyes*; and Spivak, "Imperialism and Sexual Difference."

6 I have taken this information from two sources, written from two different perspectives. Purich, *The Inuit and Their Land*, and Damas, ed., *Handbook of North American Indians: Volume 5, The Arctic*.

7 Orford, *Journey North*, 9.

8 Winifred Marsh, Donald B. Marsh Papers, GSA, DOA, M74–4, box 16 series 5–1, Circular Letters.

9 Mhairi Fenton DiCastro, NA, MG29 C119, 26 August 1937 (hereafter cited as NA/DiCastro).

10 Gilbert, *Arctic Pilot*.

11 Rokeby-Thomas, "Married Under the Midnight Sun," 19.

12 Gwen Ross, 1937 circular letter, GMA, M 4745, file 46.

13 "The Most Northerly School in the British Empire," *Echoes*, October 1931, no. 124. This was probably Addie Butler because of the date.

14 Rokeby-Thomas, "Arctic Darkness," 17.

15 *Chroniques de la Mission de Chesterfield Inlet,* Hôpital Ste Thérese de l'ènfant Jesus, 12 Mai 1937, SGMSB. (Translation: The radio carried the sounds from the coronation festivities of our new King George VI. There was universal rejoicing. For our part we hoisted flags and requested that God bless this new reign. God save the King.)

16 MacLaren and LaFramboise, eds., *The Ladies, The Gwich'in and the Rat.* Quoted in Appendix 1, field notes 29 May, 201.

17 Attributed to Sister Marie Piché, quoted in Duchaissois, *The Grey Nuns,* 101.

18 Klim — milk spelled backwards — was a brand of milk powder commonly supplied to northern posts.

19 As W. Gillies Ross explains in *This Distant and Unsurveyed Country,* the term "Husky" probably evolved from the European habit of shortening "Esquimaux" to Esqui or Esque.

CHAPTER ONE

1 Secretary of the Diocese of the Arctic to Foster, 8 April 1935. NA, RG 85, vol. 883, file 630, part 219–2.

2 NA, RG 85, vol. 630, file 214–2 (no date, but probably 1920s).

3 Christina Fry, Herschel Island, *Letter Leaflet,* October 1918.

4 Adelaide (Addie) Butler, *Living Message,* April 1935.

5 Adelaide Butler, Letters 1932–1935, 6 September 1932, Private Collection.

6 Rokeby-Thomas, "Christmas, 1938," 54.

7 Finnie, *Canada Moves North,* 188.

8 GSA/Hirst, book 4.

9 Fleming to Arctic workers, 27 May 1932. Archibald Fleming Papers, GSA, DOA, M71–4, series 3–B, box 3, file 18 (hereafter cited as GSA/Fleming).

10 GSA/Hirst, book 1.

11 Ibid., book 4.

12 This description is Richard Finnie's, but it is surprising how often the word "swarm" is used to describe the visits to the ships on either side of the Arctic. There is a certain visual quality to that word which suggests those on board were overwhelmed.

13 Augusta Morris, Diaries 1881–1883, 27 January 1882. PAM, HBCA, E78(4M72) (hereafter cited as HBCA/Morris)

14 Manning, *Igloo for the Night,* 79.

15 Christina Fry to Bishop Lucas, Herschel Island, 5 January 1917. GSA, DOA, M71–4, series 5–3, box 19. Fry explained that the mail had to be ready for the tenth.

16 Munday, *A Mounty's Wife*, 156.

17 Orford, *Journey North*, 122.

18 Mrs Harcourt at Aklavik, *Living Message*, June 1928.

19 Porter, "An Arctic Winter," 353–8.

20 Cameron, *The New North*, edited by David Richeson,162

21 Christina Fry to Sarah Stringer, 2 December 1912, ACC, DOY, YTA, COR 251.

22 Miss Wilgress at Hay River, *Letter Leaflet*, May 1911.

23 Dorothy Page, *Letter Leaflet*, April 1914. These are Fahrenheit readings.

24 Rose Spendlove, *Letter Leaflet*, August 1903.

25 Ibid., January 1903.

26 Munday, *A Mounty's Wife,* 140. The term "deerskins" refers to caribou. This may have been an *atigi*, an *artegee*, or even a *parka*. The terminology and spelling changes from era to era, and place to place. With exceptions for regional variations in style, the women mean the same thing.

27 Sadie Stringer, Address to the American Women's Club, Winnipeg, Manitoba, 24 October 1934. Isaac Stringer Papers, GSA, DOA, M74–3, series 2–B, #28, box 13 (hereafter cited as GSA/Stringer).

28 O'Kelly, "A Woman's Log of an Arctic Adventure," Typescript, PABC, Add Mss 2636, 33. (hereafter cited as PABC/O'Kelly).

29 Manning, *Igloo for the Night*, 46.

30 Marsh, *Echoes from a Frozen Land*, 16.

31 Bompas, "Our Women in the North," 5.

32 Susan Quirt, Diary, Shingle Point, 1929–32, GSA, DOA, M71–4, 17.

33 The captions around Miss Fenton's drawing indicate that this was likely a duffel parka covered with an outer shell, as opposed to one fashioned from furs.

34 Mhairi Fenton DiCastro, Papers, Lake Harbour, 20 September 1937, NA, C119 (hereafter cited as NA/DiCastro).

35 Porter, "An Arctic Winter," 355.

36 Craven and Webster, *Arctic Adventure*, 84.

37 Munday, *A Mounty's Wife*, 155.

38 Butler letters, 20 January 1934.

39 Bompas, "Our Women in the North," 1908, 6.

40 Christina Fry, from Herschel Island, *Letter Leaflet*, October 1918.

184 NOTES TO PAGES 23–28

41 Rokeby-Thomas, "Arctic Darkness," 16.

42 Ibid., 15.

43 Butler letters, 6 September 1932.

44 Munday, *A Mounty's Wife*, 166.

45 Marsh, *Echoes from a Frozen Land*, 35.

46 Vyvyan, *Arctic Adventure*, 66.

47 Manning, *Igloo for the Night*, 24.

48 Mrs Trevor Jones, Typescript, "Journey to Aklavik," GSA/Fleming, series 3–B, box 3, file 18.

49 Sarah Stringer, Address, 6 November 1931, GSA/Stringer, series 2–B, no. 10, box 13.

50 Gladys Clarke, *Letter Leaflet*, July 1922.

51 Rose Spendlove, *Letter Leaflet*, August 1903.

52 Reita Latham, Shingle Point, *Living Message*, 1932.

53 Mildred McCabe, *Living Message*, July 1933.

54 Christina Fry to Sadie Stringer, Herschel Island, 2 December 1918. YTA, ACC, COR 251.

55 Hutchison, *North to the Rime-Ringed Sun*, 153.

56 GSA/Hirst, book 2.

57 Rose Spendlove, Fort Norman, *Letter Leaflet*, August 1902.

58 Thomas, "Kindly Dispatch Miss Gadsby," 13.

59 I am not sure if this is entirely true. For example, there were wives of whaling captains at the Herschel Island during Mrs Stringer's stay.

60 Sarah Stringer, Address, 6 November 1931, GSA/Stringer, series 2–B#10, box 13.

61 "A Woman in the Wilderness," *Letter Leaflet*, October 1914, 378.

62 Munday, *A Mounty's Wife*, 138.

63 Mary Ferguson to H.H. Rowatt, Commissioner, NWT Branch, 12 July 1933, NA, G 85, vol. 847, file F7774 (hereafter cited as NA/Ferguson). The legal situation and the bureaucratic progress of the actual request will be explored in another chapter.

64 Ferguson, *Mink, Mary and Me*, 95.

65 Annie Card, Interview, Philip Godsell Papers, GMA, file 311, box 23.

66 "The Detachment Man's Wife," *RCMP Quarterly:* editorial for January 1948, typescript. NA, RG 18, vol. 3301, 1924–HQ–660–G–1–Clay.

67 NA, RG 18, vol. 3301, 1924–HQ–660–G–1–Clay. All documents quoted are available in this file.

68 Munday, *A Mounty's Wife*, 195

69 Ibid., 192.

70 Manning, *Igloo for the Night*, 117.

71 Hutchison, *North to the Rime-Ringed Sun*, 76. RSPCA – The Royal Society for the Prevention of Cruelty to Animals.

72 Valenis Ottaway, *Living Message*, February 1926.

73 Butler letters, 6 September 1932.

74 Butler letters, 8 January 1933.

75 Thomas Melling, "A Study of the General Health of the White Residents of the West Coast of Hudson's Bay" (sic), GMA, M832, 1937.

76 O'Kelly, "A Woman's Log," 30.

77 Although I could not substantiate this comment with the Grey Nuns records or indeed with some nurses who had worked in the region at the time, Clara Vyvyan insists that she met a Mother Superior en route to northern posts who told her that the nuns had the real solution to the tooth decay problem: they had all their teeth drawn before going north. *Arctic Adventure*, 44.

78 GSA/Hirst, book 2.

79 Canada, Reports of the Royal Northwest Mounted Police, Sessional Papers (Ottawa: King's Printer, 1906).

80 NA, RG18, RCMP, "G" Division, 1925, HQ681–G–1–Oulton.

81 There is an intriguing footnote to this incident. Mrs Oulton was committed to the Alberta hospital at Ponoka. Her incarceration generated considerable paperwork because of the costs involved for Ottawa. In 1945, R.A. Gibson wrote to the hospital to ask why current accounts had not been rendered. He wondered if Mrs Oulton had died. The hospital wrote back with the astonishing revelation that she had eloped on 1 December 1944 and had not been seen since. "Eloped," a euphemism commonly used in facilities that treat the insane, simply means that she escaped.

82 *Chroniques*, Aklavik, 13 January 1926, SGME. Translation as provided by the archivist.

83 Reita Latham, *Living Message*, 1932.

84 Taylor, "A Women Explorer in the Mackenzie Delta," 229.

85 O'Kelly, "A Woman's Log," 47.

86 Hutchison, *North to the Rime-Ringed Sun*, 199.

87 Winifred Marsh, Circular Letters 1935, D.B. Marsh Papers, GSA, DOA, series 5–1, M71–4 box 16.

88 Rokeby-Thomas, "Anna's Diary: Arctic Honeymoon," 31.

89 Orford, *Journey North*, 136.

90 Bompas, "Our Women in the North," November, 1908, 6.

91 HBCA/Morris, 26 September 1882.

92 This is a paraphrase of the pseudo-scientific explanation provided by the NWT *Data Book*, p. 17.

93 Christina Fry, at Herschel Island, *Letter Leaflet*. October 1918.

94 Munday, "The Beauty of the Arctic," 242.

95 Morton, "The North in Canadian Historiography," 229.

CHAPTER TWO

1 "Woman Gives Vivid Picture," *Quebec Chronicle*, 18 September 1934, 4. The article is about Leota deSteffany, wife of the captain of the *Kindersley*.

2 Strobel, *European Women and the Second British Empire*, 10. This theme is examined in studies dealing with western women and imperialism.

3 One point of clarification is needed. This statement refers to women who lived in the north, and were employed by missions or were married to traders and policemen. This does not necessarily apply to transients, although it does not necessarily exclude them either.

4 Addie Butler described fog berries as similar to blackberries, but orange coloured and with larger drupes. They were watery and had a smoky, sour gooseberry flavour. I have no idea how they might taste when eaten with seal meat.

5 Christina Fry to Sadie Stringer, Herschel Island, 2 December 1918, YTA, ACC, DOY, COR 215. Sadie Stringer would certainly have understood.

6 Sister Elizabeth Ward, Fort Providence, 1885, quoted in Duchaussois, *The Grey Nuns*, 132.

7 Miss M. Hackett, Aklavik, *Living Message*, October 1928. This means for about three months of the year.

8 Louisa Camsell Mills, Typescript of interview, PAA 74.1/88.

9 Card, with Rutherford, "An Indian Agent's Wife," 22.

10 Vyvyan, *Arctic Adventure*, 129.

11 Munday, *A Mounty's Wife*, 174.

12 Orford, *Journey North*, 109.

13 Vyvyan, *Arctic Adventure*, 129.

14 Rokeby-Thomas, "Christmas 1938," 52.

15 Rokeby-Thomas, "Arctic Darkness," 15.

16 Christina Fry to Bishop Lucas, Herschel Island, 5 January 1917. GSA, DOA, M71–4, series 5–3, box 19.

17 Charles Edward Whittaker, "Autobiographical account as a missionary," Typescript, GMA, M5960, 32.

18 Munday, *A Mounty's Wife*, 152.

19 Hackett, *Living Message*, October 1928.

20 Duchaussois, *The Grey Nuns*, 134.

21 Winifred Marsh, 1 July 1936, GSA/Marsh, box 16.

22 Orford, *Journey North*, 85.

23 Ellis, "A Business Woman in the Far North."

24 GSA/Hirst, book 4.

25 GSA/Hirst, book 2.

26 Elizabeth Howard, *Letter Leaflet*, January 1915.

27 Hutchison, *North to the Rime-Ringed Sun*, 154.

28 Christina Fry, *Letter Leaflet*, October 1918.

29 Ferguson, *Mink Mary and Me*, 57.

30 Mary E. Crocker, *Living Message*, March 1938, 70.

31 Rokeby-Thomas, "Christmas Living," 9.

32 Bessie Quirt, Shingle Point, 14 June 1930, *Living Message*, October 1930, 308. She seemed pleased that *hours* was all it took.

33 Soper, "A Nurse Goes to Baffin Island," 33.

34 YTA, ACC, DOY, COR 250, box 2, file 11.

35 GSA/Marsh, Winifred Marsh, Eskimo Point, 1 August 1937, box 16.

36 Ibid., 27 August 1937.

37 Christina Fry to Sadie Stringer, Herschel Island, 2 December 1918. YTA, ACC, DOY, COR 251.

38 Munday, *A Mounty's Wife*, 145.

39 Irene Biss Spry, Diaries. NWTA N92–139, Western Trip, 1935 (hereafter cited as NWTA/Spry).

40 Winifred Marsh, Eskimo Point, no date, GSA/Marsh.

41 Cameron, *The New North*, 64.

42 Godsell, *I Was No Lady*, 21, 27.

43 Stringer, "My Husband Ate His Boots," 45.

44 In all the sources surveyed, only two brief mentions refer to toilet facilities. Many women described their homes, their living rooms, their kitchens and even the bath. Did they just assume that everyone knew about the pail in the corner or the outhouse?

45 Manning, *Igloo for the Night*, 43.

46 Winifred Marsh, Circular letters, GSA/Marsh.

47 Orford, *Journey North*, 82.

48 GSA/Hirst, book 2.

49 Middleton, "Christmas at Fort Rae," 8.

50 Rokeby-Thomas, "Christmas 1938," 55.
51 Winifred Marsh, 1938. GSA/Marsh.
52 Ibid., probably 1936.
53 Ibid.
54 Ibid.
55 HBCA/Morris.
56 Sadie Stringer, 12 July 1897, Peel River, series 2–A–1, GSA/Stringer.
57 Rose Spendlove to Miss McCord, Montreal Diocese, *Letter Leaflet*, August 1903.
58 Frances M. Harvie, Hay River, 1918, "Annual Reports of the Missionaries," *Letter Leaflet*, March 1918.
59 Munday, *A Mounty's Wife*, 151–2.
60 "Interesting News from Shingle Point," *Living Message*, August 1930.
61 Reita Latham, *Living Message*, April 1931.
62 Butler letters, 9 January 1933.
63 Ibid.
64 Ethel Hewer, "Christmas at Shingle Point," *Living Message*, May 1936.
65 *Chroniques, Mission de l'Immaculate Conception*, Aklavik, 1925–1944, 15, SGME. Translation as provided by the archivist.
66 Hutchison, *North to the Rime-Ringed Sun*, 220.
67 Rivett-Carnac, *Pursuit in the Wilderness*, 279.
68 Fleming, "Nearest the North Pole."
69 Card, "An Indian Agent's Wife," 7.
70 Mrs Vale, Hay River, *Letter Leaflet*, October 1921.
71 Finnie, *Canada Moves North*, 140. Of course, Finnie's comment refers to the presence of prostitutes in what was a solid mining community. I have one personal letter written in 1933 that suggests a prostitute worked out of a tent outside the Yellowknife townsite, but there is no way of knowing if this was just a cook at the mine who offered her services after working hours. Curiously, Irene Spry's diaries recording her trip through the area in the '30s never mention prostitutes; however, Spry was never shy about identifying other social problems like domestic abuse and alcoholism in her notes. None of the women's personal papers surveyed ever mention prostitution, even though they comment regularly on miscegenation. Neither is there any evidence in the form of arrest or court records. It would be naive to believe that there were no women working as prostitutes in a mining town, but

the lack of documents makes it impossible to ascertain the true situation.

72 Sophie Porter, Journal. *Log of the Steam Bark Jesse H. Freeman, 1894–1896,* ODHS, New Bedford, Massachusetts.

73 Beatrice Mason, Typescript, "Treasures of the Snow," YTA, MSS 169 (81/72), f–166.

CHAPTER THREE

1 "Remarkable Journey of Two Women to the Arctic," *Globe,* Toronto, 6 February 1909.

2 For analysis of the genre see for example: Birkett, *Spinsters Abroad;* Middleton, *Victorian Lady Travellers;* Miller, *On Top of the World;* Robinson, *Wayward Women;* Russell, *The Blessings of a Good Thick Shirt;* and Stevenson, *Victorian Women Travel Writers in Africa.*

3 Attributed to Rudyard Kipling by Agnes Deans Cameron, *The New North,* edited by David Richeson, 3.

4 Ibid., 5.

5 Elizabeth Taylor, "When I Knew the Far North in Canada," unpublished article, Elizabeth Taylor Papers, James Taylor Dunn Papers, MHS, St Paul (hereafter cited as MHS/Dunn), Canada file.

6 This was the *Wrigley* which was built by the HBC to supply its fur trade. Later, Taylor would change her description and recall the *Wrigley* as a "staunch little steamer."

7 Elizabeth Taylor, Paris, 27 January 1892, Correspondence 1892, MHS/Dunn.

8 "In the Far North," *Manitoba Free Press,* 1 October 1894.

9 The marriage was short-lived; they separated in 1897. Emma was travelling during most of her marriage.

10 "I Saw These Things," Providence, RI *Evening Bulletin,* 10 September 1932.

11 At the time of the trip, Lady Clara Vyvyan was Miss Clara Coltman Rogers. Her earlier works were published under that name.

12 Vyvyan, *Roots and Stars.*

13 Brabant to Governor and Company at London, 5 January 1926, HBCA, PAM, A92/19/4986; also A92/19/5125 and A92/19/5107.

14 These were not the only travellers, but they were the ones who published some significant material. Gladys O'Kelly prepared a manuscript that dealt with her voyage around Alaska and into the Northwest Passage on the HBC schooner *Kindersley.* Miriam Ellis travelled

the Mackenzie in 1925; but I could locate only one short article written by her, and one photograph in a missionary's collection. Isobel Hutchison sailed from Vancouver around Alaska; she wintered at a cabin off the Yukon coast near Herschel Island, then flew back south. Miss Hutchison was an amateur scientist and her book on the trip falls outside the scope of "lady travellers" (see chapter four). Undoubtedly, others made the trip but never published their records.

15 Agnes Cameron's untimely death from appendicitis in 1912, prevented further exploration.

16 A copy of Miss Taylor's journal is in the holdings of the Minnesota Historical Society. The published work is not substantially different from this diary. There are also numerous unpublished typescripts in the same records. It is not known if any attempts were made to have these published.

17 Winnipeg, 21 January 1892, Typescript, correspondence 1892, MHS/Dunn.

18 Montreal, 7 March 1892, James Wickes Taylor Papers, microfilm, PAM, MGS B2. Original in MHS.

19 1892 Correspondence file, MHS/Dunn. See also Dunn, "To Edmonton in 1892," 4.

20 Elizabeth Taylor, Paris, 6 September, 1891, Correspondence 1892, MHS/Dunn.

21 Taylor, "A Woman Explorer in the Mackenzie Delta," part 1.

22 Elizabeth Taylor, Winnipeg, 21 January 1892, Correspondence 1892, MHS/Dunn.

23 Taylor, "A Woman Explorer," part 1, 51.

24 Ibid., part 2, 122.

25 Taylor, "Up the Mackenzie River to the Polar Sea," 562.

26 Taylor, "A Woman Explorer," part 3, 229.

27 Ibid., 232.

28 Ibid., part 2, 125.

29 Ibid.

30 Ibid.

31 The current preferred term is Gwich'in.

32 Ibid., part 3, 230.

33 Ibid., 233.

34 Ibid., 231.

35 Colcleugh, "I Saw These Things." The other locations included the Mississippi, the Lake Champlain area, Alaska, Hawaii, the Rockies,

en route to Winnipeg (to view the scene of the Rebellion), Labrador, Samoa, Fiji, Australia, Uganda, the West Indies, and Cuba.

36 Colcleugh, "Missions and Mission-Workers in The Great Lone Land."

37 Elizabeth Taylor Papers, letter dated at Smith Landing, 21 June 1894, correspondence 1892, MHS/Dunn.

38 Elizabeth Taylor Papers, 22 June, 1894, MHS/Dunn. There are three handwritten letters of Emma Colcleugh's filed into the Elizabeth Taylor letters collection. There is no explanation for this. The Rhode Island Historical Society is not aware of any other private papers that can be attributed to Emma Shaw Colcleugh.

39 Ibid.

40 Colcleugh, "I Saw These Things."

41 Edmonton *Bulletin*, 28 May 1894.

42 "In the Far North," *Manitoba Free Press*, 1 October 1894.

43 Miss Taylor merited a single line in Morris Zaslow's *The Opening of the Canadian North*. Mrs Colcleugh just disappeared.

44 Cameron, "Canada's Farthest North," 705.

45 For more details see Pazdro, "Agnes Deans Cameron."

46 Agnes Deans Cameron, 1906, NAC, RG 18, vol. 323, file 759–06. This is Agnes Cameron's only letter that was located. According to David Richeson writing in his introduction to the reprint of *The New North*, none of her personal papers have survived.

47 In addition, the following articles were published: "Arctic Host and Hostess," "Beyond the Athabasca," "From Winnipeg to the Arctic Ocean," "Sentinels of Silence: Canada's Royal Northwest Mounted Police," and "Two Thousand Miles to Deliver a Letter."

48 The Reverend C. Whittaker, Fort McPherson, October 1911, *Letter Leaflet*, May 1912, 213.

49 Cameron, *The New North*, 29.

50 Ibid., 29.

51 Ibid., 31.

52 Ibid., 110–12.

53 Ibid., 159.

54 Ibid., 209.

55 Ibid., 202.

56 Ibid., 205.

57 Ibid., 215.

58 Ibid., 241.

59 Ibid., 169.

60 Ibid., 170.

61 Ibid., 168.

62 Ibid., 174.

63 Ibid., 204.

64 Ibid., 48.

65 Vyvyan, *Arctic Adventure*, 95, 97, 100, 111. See MacLaren and LaFrambroise, eds., *The Ladies, The Gwich'in and The Rat*, for Vyvyan's field notes of the trip.

66 Clara Vyvyan also published "On the Rat River," *Roots and Stars*, "Sunset on the Yukon," and "The Unrelenting North."

67 Middleton, *Victorian Lady Travellers*, 5.

68 Vyvyan, *Arctic Adventure*, p. 112, 113.

69 Ibid., 25.

70 Ibid.

71 Ibid., 30.

72 "To the Arctic and Great Bear Lake," HBC Pamphlet, 1933, YTA, PAM 1933–8C, 15.

73 Ibid., 46.

74 Cameron, *The New North*, 58.

75 Vyvyan, *Arctic Adventure*, 60.

76 For an interesting discussion about natural history and travel writing, see Pratt, *Imperial Eyes*, 27.

77 Vyvyan, *Arctic Adventure*, 122.

78 Ibid., 102, 124.

79 Ibid., 57.

80 Cameron, *The New North*, 299.

CHAPTER FOUR

1 Dickerson, *Whose North*, 57.

2 The window would no doubt be small, too small to crawl through. One of my colleagues who offered this analogy suggested that the dirtier the window, the more likely that a woman would have to clean it.

3 Mark Dickerson explains the hierarchy of the Northwest Territories Council and how the NWT was administered as a branch of the Department of Interior, then the Department of Mines and Resources. Although the Department of Indian Affairs was responsible for native welfare in the NWT, it was common for policy makers to serve in other roles within those departments. This did

not necessarily confuse programs as much as consolidate ideas. It also indicated how unimportant the NWT was in the overall administration of the country. Dickerson suggests that those who ran the NWT had their own agenda that charted two divergent courses for the north. The intention was to develop the natural resources of the NWT, to maintain the traditional life of the Aboriginals, and to keep the two separate.

4 "Artistic Canadian Records," Typescript, 26 July 1937, HBCA A/102/2217, Kathleen Shackleton (hereafter cited as HBCA/Shackleton).

5 This was the title eventually given to the showing of the drawings when they were displayed in Britain.

6 F.A. Stacpole, London manager to Kathleen Shackleton, 12 August 1937, HBCA/Shackleton.

7 "Artist Going to the Arctic," *Gazette*, Montreal, 11 December 1937.

8 K. Shackleton to Hudson's Bay House, Winnipeg, 7 November 1937. HBCA/Shackleton.

9 "Feels Indians, Eskimos are Suffering Injustice," *Star-Phoenix*, Saskatoon, 20 February 1938.

10 "English and Christian are not Synonyms Says an Artist," *Globe*, Toronto, 25 February 1938.

11 "English Culture of No Use to Nanooks of the North," *Winnipeg Tribune*, 28 February, 1938.

12 *Winnipeg Tribune*, 29 February 1938.

13 Ibid.

14 The Right Rev A.L. Fleming, Bishop of the Arctic, to Ralph Parsons, HBC, 10 March 1938. HBCA/Shackleton.

15 "Miss Shackleton Replies to Bishop Fleming," *Winnipeg Tribune*, March 1938.

16 Brooks to Shackleton, 1 April 1938, HBCA/Shackleton.

17 "English Culture," *Winnipeg Tribune*, 28 February, 1938.

18 Shackleton to Brooks, 15 April 1938, HBCA/Shackleton.

19 Ibid.

20 Ibid. She pointed out that Fleming had got cross and shouted at her after the lecture.

21 Ibid.

22 Addie Butler, 9 September 1934.

23 Things have not changed that much. This is still a common refrain.

24 The custom was, in fact, only one year old.

25 Gibson, Director, Lands, Parks and Forests, Department of Mines and Resources, to Marion Grange, 29 June, 1938, NA, RG 85, vol.72, file 201–1, Marion Grange (hereafter cited as NA/Grange)

26 McKeand to Gibson, 22 March 1938, NA/Grange.

27 McKeand to Gibson, 30 September 1938, NA/Grange. However, a letter to Mrs Grange from Ralph Parsons, Fur Trade Commissioner of the HBC praises Mrs Grange's reports and thanks her for her kind references to the Company.

28 "The Women of Pangnirtung," Calgary Herald, 12 November 1938.

29 Interestingly, Agnes Cameron made a similar observation. See chapter on women travellers in the Arctic.

30 Marion Grange, "On the Eastern Arctic Patrol: Birth, Death and the Arctic Circle," Typescript, NA/Grange.

31 NA/Grange.

32 Addie Butler, 1 April 1933.

33 NA/Grange.

34 McKeand to Gibson, 22 November 1938, NA/Grange.

35 McKeand to Gibson, 23 November 1938, NA/Grange.

36 Fur Trade Commissioner HBC to Miss McEuen, 16 April 1937, NA/DiCastro. The EAP in 1937 undertook an incursion into waters farther north than previously penetrated by the supply vessel.

37 See Inglis, The White Women's Protection Ordinance.

38 Miss Hutchison would later be awarded an honorary doctorate from St Andrew's University, which is why one of her books is published using Dr Hutchison as her designation.

39 I think it fair to say that male adventurers and explorers were usually allowed free rein across the region, often at taxpayer's expense. All they had to do was convince the government they were worthy.

40 Isobel Hutchison to Secretary of the NWT, Vancouver, 9 June 1933. NA, RG 85, vol. 850, 7834, Isobel Hutchison (hereafter cited as NA/Hutchison).

41 J.F. Doyle to Department of Interior, 24 August 1933, NA/Hutchison.

42 An Ordinance Respecting Scientists and Explorers.

43 Masik and Hutchison, Arctic Nights' Entertainments, x.

44 Aklavik Post to OC, "G" Division, Edmonton, 6 October 1933, NA/Hutchison.

45 Rivett-Carnac, Pursuit in the Wilderness, 271.

46 Hutchison, North to the Rime-Ringed Sun, 306.

47 Gordon Sinclair, "Wife-Swapping Now Obsolete in the Arctic," *Daily Star*, Toronto, 24 February 1934.

48 Ibid. He obviously meant if there were women there too.

49 "Woman's 1,000 Miles in Arctic," *Daily Mail*, London, 8 March 1934.

50 Anna Rokeby-Thomas recalls how conscious she was that her husband had taken no long trips during her first winter in the Arctic. She wanted to go with him, but could get no support for her plans. "You're a woman was the reasoning," she explained. (Rokeby-Thomas, "Arctic Darkness," 18.) Her first long sled trip to Bathurst Inlet from Cambridge Bay had involved some controversy. "The police didn't like" her travelling native-style, and the "Eskimos gave her silent and dubious looks" (Rokeby-Thomas, "On an Arctic Trail," 26). Wallace Manning recalled how on general principles, no one wanted her to go north either. People told her that "no white woman had ever gone to the Arctic to live away from the Posts; it was madness to keep up with the travels and share the hard life of a man who had asked me to go ... so they made excuses. Mr Manning had not been heard of for a long time, and they didn't know where he had gone" (Manning, *Igloo for the Night*, 12).

CHAPTER FIVE

1 For example, see Boon, *The Anglican Church From the Bay to the Rockies*, Craven and Webster, *Arctic Adventure*, and numerous works cited in the bibliography by the Venerable Archibald Fleming.

2 Stanley, *The Bible and the Flag*, Introduction.

3 These included Julia McDonald, who was of mixed blood, wife of then Archdeacon McDonald from Red River and who had been in the north since 1862. They were married at Fort McPherson in 1877.

4 Coates, "Send Only Those Who Rise a Peg."

5 See Peake, "From the Red River to the Arctic," 46.

6 Quoted in Thomas, "Kindly Dispatch Miss Gadsby," 10.

7 Autobiographical account, the Rev Charles Edward Whittaker, Typescript, GMA, M5960.

8 William Fry to Isaac Stringer, 10 December 1916. YTA, ACC, DOY, COR 251, file 16, Herschel Island.

9 Lucas to Fosterjohn, 31 January 1922, PAA, ACC, DOMR, 70.387/MR200/52 (hereafter cited as PAA/Fosterjohn).

10 Fosterjohn to Lucas, 23 February 1922, PAA/Fosterjohn.

11 Fosterjohn to Lucas, 5 December 1922, PAA/Fosterjohn.

12 Quoted in Hallenby, *Anglican Women's Training College,* 69.

13 *Enlisting for Service,* PAA, DOMR, MR200/123/ box MR12.

14 Ibid., 12.

15 Butler letters, January 1934.

16 Susan Elizabeth Quirt, Personal Diary, 1929–1932. GSA, DOA, M71–4, 11 and 12 (hereafter cited as GSA/Quirt).

17 Butler letters, 8 January 1933.

18 Helen Sowden, *Living Message,* April 1931.

19 Geddes to Stringer, Aklavik, 7 January 1927, YTA, ACC, DOY, COR 251, file 22.

20 Geddes to Stringer, Aklavik, 6 February 1928. Ibid.

21 PAA, DOMR, 70.387/MR200/75, 1922 and 1923.

22 Lucas to Stoddart, 6 September 1923. Ibid.

23 Stoddart to Lucas, 4 January, 1924. Ibid.

24 Ibid.

25 Finnie, *Canada Moves North,* 57.

26 See Peake, "From Red River to the Arctic: Policy and Personnel," 51.

27 See Headon, "Women and Organized Religion in Mid-Nineteenth Century Canada," 3–18.

28 It should be pointed out that a number of attempts have been made. Bishop Donald Marsh, for example, continually quoted unreliable census statistics to insist that the Anglicans had 82 percent of the Canadian Inuit in his flock.

29 *Letter Leaflet,* May 1898.

30 GSA/Quirt.

31 *Letter Leaflet,* July 1922.

32 *Living Message,* June 1929.

33 See Headon, "Women in Organized Religion."

34 *Living Message,* September 1935.

35 Westgate to Vale, 8 May 1926, GSA, DOA, St Peter's, Hay River, Correspondence, M71–4, series 2–1–d, box 7 (hereafter cited as GSA/HayRiver).

36 Bompas to Secretaries CMS, 3 January 1895, quoted in Coates, "Send Only Those Who Rise a Peg," 7.

37 Isaac Stringer to William Bompas, 3 April 1906, series 1–A–1, GSA/Stringer.

38 Bompas, "Our Women in the North," 8.

39 Fleming to Westgate, 31 March 1938, Indian and Eskimo Residential School Commission, file 17, GSA/Fleming.

40 Fleming, "Nearest the North Pole," 14.

41 J.R. Lucas to Mrs Bedford-Jones, 21 December 1921, PAA, ACC, DOMR, 70.387/MR200/161. Interestingly, Lucas worked with a number of single women at the turn of the century who served for long terms. He does not mention these women in his list.

42 Westgate to Marion Harvey, 16 June 1928, GSA/HayRiver

43 Butler letters, 15 August 1932. Addie Butler had previously worked at an Indian Residential School.

44 Edith Carter, WA of the MSCC, to Archdeacon Lucas, 1 May 1913, PAA, DOMR, MR200, item 18, box MR10.

45 Westgate to Carter, January 1916, Ibid. This high cost of travel would account for the stipulation in contracts that employees were responsible for paying travel expenses should they not fulfill the entire contract.

46 Return of agents employed at the Hay River NWT School, GSA, DOA, M71–4, series 2–1–d, box 6.

47 T.B.R. Westgate to Fleming, 5 October 1933, file 17, GSA/Fleming.

48 GSA/HayRiver.

49 Fleming to Westgate, 31 Mar 1938, file 17, GSA/Fleming.

50 The Missionary Society of the Church of England in Canada, "Report of the Medical Examiner," Form D, PAA, ACC, DOMR, 70.387/MR200/117.

51 Cummings, *Our Story,* 78.

52 *Enlisting for Service.*

53 McKeand to Gibson, 6 November 1940, NA, RG85, vol. 907, file 10533.

54 MSCC Candidate's Committee, Minutes, 27 April 1926, GSA, GS75–103, series 2–5, box 10.

55 Scott to Finnie, 11 February 1931, NA, RG 85, vol. 907, file 10533.

56 G. Rowley, DOA to T.G. Murphy, 24 September 1934, NA, RG 85, vol. 856, file 8115.

57 Wardle to Turner, Ministry of the Interior, 28 February 1936, NA, RG 85, vol. 862, file 8248.

58 For example, the MSCC notified the Deputy Superintendent General of Indian Affairs on 9 November 1926 that Miss Dorothy Bradford would replace Valenis Ottaway at Hay River. The forms were forwarded through the winter mail and were returned to Winnipeg on 24 February 1927, GSA/HayRiver.

59 The 1933 salary for a matron qualified as a nurse was $50.00 per month. The government paid a graduate nurse (Grade 1, attached

to an Indian residential school or stationed at a reserve with a population of up to 300) between $960 and $1200, plus maintenance allowance (10 April 1930, NA, RG 85, vol. 907, file 10533). In 1928, Miss Beatrice Rose Terry was appointed at $1080 per annum, plus maintenance allowance. (McKeand to Finnie, 15 June 1928, NA, RG 85, vol. 783, file 5299). In 1931, these salaries were raised. The range then was $1380 to $1560 (Heagerty, Pensions and National Health to Finnie, 2 February 1931, NA, RG 85, vol. 907, file 10533).

60 Field Secretary, MSCC to E. Goddard, 8 July 1935, series 2–1–d , GSA/HayRiver.

61 Opinion attributed to Dr Urquhart, Assistant Deputy Minister, Ministry of Interior, to Lorne Turner, 11 July 1935, NA, RG 85, vol. 907, file 10533.

62 McKeand to Gibson, 6 November 1940, ibid.

63 Mimeograph copy of Privy Council minutes, 14 December 1922, NA, RG 85, vol. 783, file 5921. Whether this view had anything to do with the use of uniforms by Anglicans cannot be determined.

64 Fleming to Arctic workers, 27 May 1932, file 18, GSA/Fleming.

65 *Living Message*, July 1933.

66 Margaret Currie, "Work Among the Eskimos Satisfies the Soul," *Montreal Daily Star*, 4 February 1933.

67 Lindbergh, *Hour of Gold, Hour of Lead*, 171.

68 YTA, ACC, DOY, COR 263, series 1–1c, box 15, file 3, no date.

69 *Living Message*, September 1934.

70 Journals, St Matthew's Mission, 2 July 1920, NWTA, N79–027, ACC, 197 and GSA, DOA, M71–4 series 2–2–c, box 10.

71 Mackenzie River Diocesan Branch of the Woman's Auxiliary, Annual Report of All Saint's Aklavik Branch of the WA, 31 December 1927, YTA, ACC, DOY, COR 263, series 1–1c, box 15, file 3.

72 *Living Message*, March 1933.

73 "The Arctic," *Living Message*, October 1938.

74 *Living Message*, September 1935.

75 *Living Message*, October 1938.

76 GSA/Hirst, book 1.

77 GSA/Hirst, book 2.

78 Orford, *Journey North*, 169.

79 Excerpts from Diary of Florence Giles, Pangnirtung, *Living Message*, July 1938.

80 GSA/Hirst, book 3.

81 Sarah Stringer, "Address to the Canadian Club," November 1931, GSA/Stringer.

82 Lindbergh, 6 August 1931, *Hour of Gold, Hour of Lead*, 166.

CHAPTER SIX

1 *Arctic Angels*, pamphlet, probably 1940s.

2 Drouin, *Love Spans the Centuries*, 195.

3 See for example: Choquette, *The Oblate Assault on Canada's Northwest*; Huel, *Proclaiming the Gospel to the Indians and the Metis*; and McCarthy, *From the Great River to the Ends of the Earth*. In McCarthy, the Grey Nuns figure as part of the contingent, in Choquette, the women simply do not exist.

4 There is one set of exceptions. The necrologies published in the annuals of the order do describe some family life and service, but the hagiographic nature of the necrologies makes them suspect. As well, it appears that the necrologies used the same primary documents as I did for sources.

5 See McCarthy, *From the Great River to the Ends of The Earth*.

6 Literally, the five victims (or sacrifices) that the Good Lord requires me to send to you. But the actual meaning is more subtle.

7 (Translation: Give our dear sisters the strength to perfectly preserve the spirit of their vocation.)

8 "Fondation de l'hôpital du Sacre–Coeur," 1866, Providence *Historique*, document 10, W242 reel 86, AD, OM, SGM. (hereafter cited as AD/Grey Nuns).

9 Drouin, 190. Both Drouin and Duchaussois reproduce parts of this letter in English. Some pages of the original are still readable. Original document is AD/Grey Nuns, W242, reel 85, Providence *Historique* document 3.

10 See Drouin, and Duchaussois. Drouin's version appears to be a simply updated account of Duchaussois. Both cite the same letters in translation – some of which are now unreadable, but the translations are slightly different.

11 Duchaussois, 125.

12 See Abel, *Drum Songs*, 139 for a discussion.

13 J.S. Camsell, Fort Chipewyan, Athabasca, 15 February 1882, W242, reel 102, Providence *Historique* document 117a, AD/Grey Nuns.

14 5 October 1885, W242, reel 102, Providence *Historique* 130, AD/Grey Nuns.

15 "École et Hôpital St. Joseph, Fort Resolution, NWT," SGME. (Translation: Their habit would have been nicer if it was red, remarked one of the Natives.)

16 Ibid., page 12–1. (Translation: We finally arrived at dear Resolution, our promised land. Our first visit was at the church to pay homage to our Divine Mother, and to offer our humble selves to work for Him with open hearts. We had many thanks to offer to God for protecting us against the elements which we had to face to arrive at our destination. But fatigue, the cold especially, and bad weather, far from weakening our resolve, seemed to provide it to those who did not have any [resolve], and renewed it for those who had. The tiny Sr Ernestine was the only exception. She was sick throughout the long voyage, not being able to take even a little soup. She appeared to recover when we reached St Albert, but a slight infection, which we took to be a mosquito bite, gave her the shivers. The redness increased and it became an open wound. I made the dear sister lie down and cared for her the best that I could.)

17 *Résolution Historique,* document 36, 17 September 1915, w242, reel 172, AD/Grey Nuns. (Translation: My Mother, I am afraid of the Monseigneur.)

18 Sr Delphine Giroux-Pinsonneault – Fort Resolution, (1906–10, 1918–19, and 1928–330). The rest of her time was spent at Fort Smith (1919–27, 1928–30, and 1933–35). For someone not attached to the region she gave long service.

19 Ibid.

20 Pamphlet date April–October 1912, supplied by the archivist, SGM, no publishing information.

21 "Fort Providence" *Historique,* typescript. Translation provided by the archivist, SGME, Edmonton.

22 "St. Ann's Hospital et Maison Provinciale, Fort Smith, NWT," typescript, SGME.

23 Lucille Lévesque, SGM, "The Sacred Heart Mission: Fort Simpson – NWT," Fort Simpson *Historique,* document 1–A, SGME.

24 15 September 1918, w242, reel 88, Simpson *Histoire,* document 15. AD/Grey Nuns.

25 OM, Aklavik, 10 July 1924, w242, reel 1, AD/Grey Nuns. (Il y a en donc declaration de guerre, et nous avons ouvert les hostilitiés en elevent en face de leur place fort, un petit araouillet de 20 par 20 qui les met tout en moi. Il semble qu'ils se sentent vaincus avant de

combattre. Mais cette arme vielle [maison en boulin superposes] c'est vraiment trop couteuse et trop grossière pour en conserver l'usage. Le frère Becshoeffer et moi avons décidé sur-le-champ de prendre d'autres moyens d'attaque.

26 *Chroniques*, Grey Nuns, Aklavik 1925–1941, SGME. Translation provided by the archivist.

27 Ibid., 5 September 1925.

28 29 January 1926, W242, reel 1, *Aklavik Histoire* Document 12, AD/Grey Nuns.

29 *Chroniques*, Grey Nuns, Aklavik 1925–41, SGME. Translation provided by the archivist.

30 Paquin, "Fifty Years Ago," 5–8.

31 Paquin, "In Those Days...," 9–13.

CHAPTER SEVEN

1 Butler letters, 1933. It should be remembered that this study embraces three racial groups: White, Dene, and Inuit.

2 See Bulbeck, *Australian Women in Papua New Guinea*, 40, for a discussion of this theme.

3 Said, *Culture and Imperialism*, 96.

4 Rokeby-Thomas, "Farewell With Memories," 56.

5 Manning, *Igloo for the Night*, 19. I have used Manning's spelling in the quotation.

6 Godsell, *I Was No Lady*, 35.

7 Porter, "An Arctic Winter," 358.

8 See Abel, "Of Two Minds," 77.

9 Munday, *A Mounty's Wife*, 147.

10 As one later missionary suggested, "Utopia only exists in the abstract – the packaging is as valuable as the contents and is inseparable from the contents – [she] arrives with the handicap of not understanding the language and since this is the only way [she] gets [her] message across, [she] has to use it and [her] own cultural biases until something better comes along." Lechat, "Evangelization and Colonization," 4.

11 Munday, *A Mounty's Wife*, 173.

12 Rokeby-Thomas, "Anna's Diary," 31.

13 Taylor, "Up the Mackenzie to the Polar Sea."

14 Taylor, "A Woman Explorer in the Mackenzie Delta," part 3, 230.

15 Craven and Webster, *Arctic Adventure*, 85.

16 Christina Fry to Lucas, Herschel Island, 5 January 1917. GSA, DOA, M71–4, series 5–3, box 19.

17 "Fort Providence," typescript history, SGME.

18 This element of Inuit etiquette is explained in Moore, *Privacy: Studies in Social and Cultural History*. In chapter one, Moore examines the experience of Jean Briggs, an anthropologist doing fieldwork in an Inuit community, who learned that despite the constant visiting by Inuit to her tent, she was not under any obligation to act as hostess.

19 Beatrice Mason, YTA, 69.

20 Card, "An Indian Agent's Wife," 22.

21 PABC/O'Kelly, 34. ·

22 "A Woman in the Wilderness," *Letter Leaflet*, October 1914, 378.

23 Sadie Stringer, Herschel Island, 25 January 1898, series 2, 2–a–1, GSA/Stringer.

24 Romig, *The Life and Travels of a Pioneer Woman in Alaska*, 74, 54.

25 Soper, "A Nurse Goes to Baffin Island," 34.

26 Orford, *Journey North*, 76.

27 Rokeby-Thomas, "Sadness and Joy," 16. The implication, of course, is that Mrs Rokeby-Thomas considered childbirth as a sickness that required medical attendance.

28 Ibid.

29 One notable exception seems to be the birth at Arctic Bay of Evelyn Scott in 1938 (first baby born the farthest north in the British Empire). Mrs Scott was apparently attended by two Inuit women. Two reasons account for this change in attitude. The first is the late date, reflecting a change in view. But it is more likely that since Mr Scott was an HBC trader, he had not received the "medical" training given missionary men sent into the north. That meant that Mrs Scott did not even have the benefit of a husband/midwife. Marriot, "Arctic Bay Baby," 46.

30 Catherine Hoare to Sadie Stringer, Aklavik, 11 January 1922, YTA, ACC, DOY, COR 252, file 3, box 4.

31 Thomas, "Kindly Despatch Miss Gatsby." This article was written from Mrs Spendlove's diaries.

32 Whittaker, "Autobiographical Account," GMA, 33.

33 Mills, "Seventy Years Ago," GMA/Godsell.

34 Ibid.

35 William Fry to Isaac Stringer, 12 January 1919, YTA, ACC, DOY, COR 251, file 16.

36 "Journals of St Matthew's Mission," Fort McPherson, NWTA, N79–027, St Matthew's Mission 37, 1 June 1919.
37 See the essays in Arnup, Levesque and Pierson, eds., *Delivering Motherhood*.
38 Inuit mothers, of course, often did succumb to the rigours of childbirth on the trail. Just because women in "primitive" societies had managed childbirth for centuries without European medical assistance does not mean that it was a safe enterprise.
39 Reita Latham, *Living Message*, October 1932.
40 "Work Among Eskimos Satisfies the Soul," *Montreal Daily Star*, 4 February 1933.
41 Porter, "An Arctic Winter," 355.
42 PABC/O'Kelly, 39.
43 Ibid., 31.
44 Munday, *A Mounty's Wife*, 184.
45 Ibid., 28.
46 Cameron, *The New North*, 168, see chap. 3.
47 Rokeby-Thomas, "Some Notable Inuit," 16.
48 Jenness, *The People of the Twilight*, 53–4.
49 Tims, *Historical Sketch of the Origin and Work*, 12.
50 Manning, *Igloo for the Night*, 36.
51 Munday, *A Mounty's Wife*, 147.
52 Bompas, "Our Women in the North," 85.
53 Reita Latham, *Living Message*, December 1932.
54 Rokeby-Thomas, "Arctic Life, 1937," *Living Message*, March 1938, 71.
55 Tims, *Historical Sketch of the Origin and Work*, 8.
56 Catherine Hoare to Bishop Lucas, 15 January 1921, PAA 70.387, DOMR 200/85.
57 Priscilla Shepherd, Shingle Point, *Living Message*, July 1931.
58 16 September 1921, PAA, DOMR, MR200/142/box MR12.
59 Reita Latham, *Living Message*, December 1932.
60 4 March 1922, PAA, DOMR, 70.387/MR200.
61 *Living Message*, May 1930.
62 Hutchison, *North to the Rime-Ringed Sun*, 198.
63 *Living Message*, August 1930.
64 Fleming to Rowat, 4 Jan 1933, PAC, RG85, vol. 1883, file 630/219–2.
65 GSA/Hirst, book 2.
66 *Living Message*, January 1936. Since this program was offered to girls in residence at the boarding school, this comment suggests

204 NOTES TO PAGES 157–163

that Miss Sowden believed that their former mode of living was now in the past.

67 GSA, DOA, M71–4, series 2–1–i.

68 Before being enrolled as a Girl Guide, the new recruit was required to learn the history of the three flags that made up the Union Jack and the protocol for maintaining and flying the flag. She also had to memorize and show some understanding of the Guide Law and Promise. For those uninitiated in the mysteries of Guides and Brownies or Kipling, Kim's Game is a memory game. Objects are placed on a tray and exposed for a set period of time; the goal is to identify as many items as possible when the tray is covered again. As late as the 1960s, these aspects of the program were still an integral part of Guiding, and this game was used to teach observation as well as memory skills. The program has now changed.

69 In his 1944 report, Richard Finnie was somewhat more cynical about the purpose of Girl Guide companies and Boy Scout troops at northern missions. The children were "drilled to signal with flags such messages as 'Welcome to our Bishop," he said, while others were "robed in scarlet cassocks, white surplices, and ruffs." This made the demonstrations attractive subjects for missionary publicity – a sort of early northern photo opportunity. *Canada Moves North*, 59.

70 *Living Message*, June 1937.

71 GSA/Hirst, book 1.

72 Helen Merritt to Mrs Lucas, Bernard Harbour, 17 November 1921, PAA 70.387, DOMR200/111.

73 *Letter Leaflet*, September 1921.

74 *Chroniques*, Chesterfield Inlet, SGMSB, 26 November 1935.

75 Orford, *Journey North*, 68, 92.

CHAPTER EIGHT

1 Caulkin to J. Ritchie, 11 April 1926, NA, RG18, Mary Lyman (hereafter cited as NA/Lyman).

2 Ingram and Dobrowolsky, *Waves Upon the Shore*, 85.

3 Herschel Island was supplied from the west coast and through the dangerous conditions of the Beaufort Sea, and not from the Mackenzie River as were posts along that river.

4 Often referred to as Charlie Klinkenberg, particularly in HBC documents.

5 This was not the case for Herschel Island. The Anglican Church mission was established by William Carpenter Bompas in 1893 and the HBC Post was not built until about 1915.
6 Kemp, *Without Fear, Favour or Affection.*
7 See for example, Porter, "An Arctic Winter."
8 Thomas Umoak to Isaac Stringer, 15 January 1925, YTA, ACC, DOY, COR 257 file 6. (hereafter cited as YTA/COR 257).
9 Caulkin to Ritchie, 11 April 1925, NA/Lyman.
10 *Revised Statutes of Canada*, 1906, vol. 3, chap. 146.
11 Umoak to Stringer, 15 January 1925, YTA/COR 257.
12 Caulkin to Ritchie, 6 February 1926, NA/Lyman.
13 Ibid.
14 Irving B. Howatt to Supt James Ritchie, 1 September 1925, NA/Lyman.
15 Supt James Ritchie to Irving Howatt, 5 September 1925, NA/Lyman.
16 Richard Bonnycastle, Diaries, HBCA, E154/6, 19 September 1928.
17 Western Arctic District, March 1925, HBCA, A102/1042 (hereafter cited as HBCA/Western Arctic).
18 HBC papers suggest W. Murray acted as assistant to V.W. West. There is also evidence of an apprentice clerk named Watt, 1925, A102/1043, HBCA/Western Arctic.
19 Ibid.
20 Hugh Conn, Inspection Report, A/102/1044, "Herschel Island," 14 October 1925, p. 7, HBCA/Western Arctic.
21 Umoak was ordained the first Inuit Deacon in 1927.
22 Umoak to Stringer 15 January 1925, YTA/COR 257.
23 On occasion, nurses like Carolyn Soper would accompany their scientist husbands on expeditions, or long-term postings. They would then offer their services as nurses at isolated posts.
24 RCMP, Arctic Sub-District, Herschel Island, NWT, 1 May 1925, Crime Report. NWTA, Mary Lyman.
25 Caulkin to Ritchie, 6 February 1926, NA/Lyman
26 Ibid.
27 This report notes Mrs Lyman was a "middle-aged woman with experience in nursing, and it is probably due to her untiring efforts that several natives who were very ill with influenza and pneumonia are alive today," A102/2629, June 1925, p. 7, HBCA/Western Arctic District.
28 Report, A102/1042, p. 7, March 1925, HBCA/ Western Arctic District.
29 Ibid., p 2.

30 A. Brabant to Winnipeg, Aklavik, 30 June 1925, HBCA/Western Arctic District.

31 Ritchie to Howatt, 5 September 1925, NA/Lyman.

32 Caulkin to Ritchie, 6 February 1926, NA/Lyman.

33 Radio contact had been established between Western Arctic District stations the previous year.

34 Howatt to Ritchie, 1 September 1925, NA/Lyman.

35 This was probably Minnie Oulton. See chapter one.

36 Correspondence to O. Finnie from Hudson's Bay Junction, Saskatchewan, 11 November, 1925, NA, RG85, vol. 1388, 405.

37 Ibid.

38 Margaret Oldenburg, NWTA, N79–550.

Bibliography

ARCHIVAL SOURCES

PRIVATE COLLECTIONS
Butler, Adelaide. Letters.

ARCHIVES DESCHÂTAULETS, OBLATES OF MARY IMMACULATE,
OTTAWA (OMI)
Records of the Grey Nuns in the Mackenzie Valley.

GENERAL SYNOD ARCHIVES, ANGLICAN CHURCH OF CANADA,
TORONTO (GSA)
Anglican Women's Training College.
Diocese of the Arctic Collection:
   Candidate's Committee, Missionary Society of the Church of England
   in Canada.
   First Hay River Girl Guide Company, Log Book.
   Fleming, Archibald. Papers.
   Hirst, Florence. Journals.
   Indian and Eskimo Residential School Commission, Correspondence.
   Jones, Mrs Trevor. Typescript. *Journey to Aklavik*, 1938.
   Marsh, Donald B. Papers (includes Winifred Marsh).
   Peck, Edmund James. Papers.
   Quirt, Susan Elizabeth. Diaries.
   St Peter's Mission, Hay River. Reports and Correspondence.
   Stringer, Isaac O. (includes Sarah Alexander Stringer).
   Vale, A.J. Typescript. *The Story of the Hay River Woman's Auxiliary.*

GLENBOW MUSEUM ARCHIVES, CALGARY (GMA)
Dawson, Clair. Papers.
Godsell, Phillip. Papers (includes Jean Godsell).
Hockin, Prudence. Papers.

Melling, Thomas. Papers.
Ross, Gwen. Correspondence.
Whittaker, Charles Edward. Typescript. Autobiographical account.

HUDSON'S BAY COMPANY ARCHIVES, WINNIPEG (HBCA)
Bonnycastle, Richard H.G. Diaries.
Hoare, Catherine. "Adventures Unlimited." Unpublished manuscript.
Morris, Augusta. Diary.
Records of the Fur Trade Commissioner:
    Correspondence
    Shackleton, Kathleen.

MINNESOTA HISTORICAL SOCIETY, ST PAUL (MHS)
Colcleugh, Emma Shaw. Letters. James Taylor Dunn Collection.
Dunn, James Taylor (includes Elizabeth Taylor).

NATIONAL ARCHIVES OF CANADA, OTTAWA (NA)
Canada. Records of the Department of Indian and Northern Affairs
    (DIAND), Northern Administration Branch, RG 85:
    Cameron, Agnes Deans.
    Ferguson, Mary.
    Grange, Marion. Official historian of the Eastern Arctic Patrol.
    Greenwood, Tom (includes Isobel Greenwood).
    Hutchison, Dr Isobel.
Canada. Records of the Royal Canadian Mounted Police. RG 18:
    Clay, Margaret.
    Lyman, Mary.
    Oulton, Minnie.
Fenton [DiCastro] Mhairi Angela MacLeod. Papers.

NORTHWEST TERRITORIES ARCHIVES, YELLOWKNIFE (NWTA)
Buffum, Louise, and family. Papers.
Lyman, Mary.
Metis Association of the Northwest Territories.
St. Matthew's Mission, Journals.
Spry, Irene Biss. Diaries.

OLD DARTMOUTH HISTORICAL SOCIETY, NEW BEDFORD,
MASSACHUSETTS (ODHS)
Porter, Sophie. Log of the Steam Bark *Jesse H. Freeman.*

PROVINCIAL ARCHIVES OF ALBERTA, EDMONTON (PAA)
Anglican Church of Canada, Diocese of Mackenzie River.
Mills, Louisa Camsell. Typescript.

PROVINCIAL ARCHIVES OF BRITISH COLUMBIA, VICTORIA (PABC)
O'Kelly, Gladys (Grace). Typescript.

PROVINCIAL ARCHIVES OF MANITOBA, WINNIPEG (PAM)
Taylor, James Wickes. Papers

ROYAL CANADIAN MOUNTED POLICE CENTENNIAL MUSEUM,
REGINA (RCMP)
Geraldine Moodie File.
Margaret Clay File.

SOEURS GRISES DE MONTREAL, EDMONTON REGIONAL CENTRE
(SGME)
Chronicles:
  Aklavik
  Fort Providence
  Fort Resolution
  Fort Simpson
  Fort Smith
Historical Sketches from Chronicles and Lists of Sisters Attendant at
  Convents in the North. Typescript.

SOEURS GRISES DE MONTREAL, MONTREAL (SGMM)
Published Material.

SOEURS GRISES DE MONTREAL, ST BONIFACE REGIONAL CENTRE
(SGMSB)
Chronicles:
  Chesterfield Inlet 1931–1937.
Codex Historicus, Chesterfield Inlet.

YUKON TERRITORIES ARCHIVES, WHITEHORSE (YTA)
Anglican Church of Canada, Diocese of the Yukon, Corporate Records.
Foster, Frank. Papers.
Mason, Beatrice. Typescript.
Woodall, R. Papers.

NEWSPAPERS AND PERIODICALS

Arctic Circle
Arctic News (ACC Diocese of the Arctic)
The Calgary Herald
Eskimo (OMI)
The Gazette, Montreal
The Globe, Toronto
The Letter Leaflet of the Woman's Auxiliary to the Missionary Society of the Church of England in Canada, replaced by the *Living Message*
The New York Times
North
Northern Lights (ACC Diocese of Yukon)
The Prospector, Yellowknife NWT (1938–39)
Saskatoon Star-Pheonix
Star Weekly
The Winnipeg Tribune
The Yellowknife Blade (1940–42)

PHOTOGRAPH COLLECTIONS*
NWTA:
N87-020   Anglican Church of Canada, Diocese of the Arctic
N86-006   Buffum Family
N91-041   Cook, Dr AJ
N79-008   Cook, Henry G
N91-045   Day, Harry L
N79-033   Finnie, Richard Sterling
N79-050   Fleming, Archibald Lang
FPGN   Grey Nuns of Fort Providence
N88-008   Henderson, Helene and Mildred Hall
N87-033   Learmonth, LA
N79-006   Yellowknife Museum Society
N79-053   Yellowknife Museum Society
N79-054   Yellowknife Museum Society
N79-057   Yellowknife Museum Society

YTA:
PHO 379 Anglican Church of Canada
PHO 29   Sharp, Bob

* These collections were a rich source for identification purposes. Many of the women could only be found in photographs.

Hudson's Bay Company
National Archives of Canada

PUBLISHED MATERIAL

Abel, Kerry. *Drum Songs: Glimpses of Dene History.* Montreal and Kingston: McGill-Queen's University Press, 1993.
– "Of Two Minds: Dene Response to the Mackenzie Missions, 1858–1902." In *Interpreting Canada's North*, edited by Kenneth Coates and William R. Morrison.
Archer, S.A. *A Heroine in the North: Memoirs of Charlotte Selina Bompas (1830–1917) Wife of the First Bishop of Selkirk.* Toronto: Macmillan, 1929.
Arnup, Katherine, Andree Levesque, and Ruth Roach Pierson. *Delivering Motherhood: Maternal Ideologies and Practices in the 19th and 20th Centuries.* London: Routledge, 1990.
Bailey, Susan F. *Women and the British Empire: An Annotated Guide to Sources.* New York and London: Garland Publishing, 1983.
Bethune, W.C. *Canada's Western Northland: Its History, Resources, Population, and Administration.* Ottawa: King's Printer, 1937.
Bockstoce, John R. *Whales, Ice and Men: A History of Whaling in the Western Arctic.* Seattle: University of Washington Press, 1986.
Bompas, Charlotte Selina. "Our Women in the North." *Imperial Colonist*, October 1908, 7–9 and November 1908, 4–9.
Bonnycastle, R.H.G. *A Gentleman Adventurer: The Arctic Diaries of R.H.G Bonnycastle.* Edited by Heather Robertson. Toronto: Lester & Orpen Dennys, 1984.
Boon, T.C.B. *The Anglican Church From the Bay to the Rockies.* Toronto: Ryerson, 1962.
Boswell, Hazel. "Voluntary Educational Work in the Canadian Labrador." *Echoes* (The Official Organ of the IODE) (March 1930): 15.
Boyd, Josephine W. "On Some White Women in the Wilds of Northern North America." *Arctic* 27, no. 3 (1974): 168–74.
Cameron, Agnes Deans. "Arctic Host and Hostess." *Canadian Magazine*, no. 35 (1910): 3–12.
– "Beyond the Athabasca." *Westward Ho Magazine*, 1909, 743–50.
– "Canada's Farthest North." *Geographic Journal* 35, no. 6 (1910): 705–8.
– "From Winnipeg to the Arctic Ocean." *Manchester Geographical Society* 26 (1910): 97–101.

- "God Save the King, The Empire's Anthem." *Educational Journal of Western Canada* 3, no. 4 (1901): 106–9.
- "The Idea of True Citizenship – How Shall We Develop It?" *Educational Journal of Western Canada* (Brandon) 1, no. 8 (1899): 229–35.
- "Sentinels of the Silence: Canada's Royal Northwest Mounted Police." *Century* 79 1909, 289–99.
- "To Success – Walk Your Own Road." *Educational Journal of Western Canada* 4, no. 1 (1910): 10.
- "Two Thousand Miles to Deliver a Letter." *Harper's Weekly,* no. 52, (1908): 16.

Cameron, Agnes Deans, David Richeson, eds. *The New North: An Account of a Woman's 1908 Journey Through Canada to the Arctic.* Saskatoon: Western Producer Books, 1986.

Canada. Northwest Territories Council. Department of the Interior. *An Ordinance Respecting Scientists and Explorers.* Ottawa: King's Printer, c. 1926.

Card, Annie (with Helen Rutherford). "An Indian Agent's Wife." *Beaver* 270, no. 2 (1939): 21–4.

Choquette, Robert. *The Oblate Assault on Canada's Northwest.* Ottawa: University of Ottawa Press, 1995.

Clevette, Wilma, Freda Heacock, Great Routledge, and Gwen Skelley. *Red Serge Wives.* Edmonton: Lone Pine, 1974.

Climate of the Northwest Territories. Northern Information Series. Yellowknife: Government of the Northwest Territories, Culture and Communications, 1987.

Coates, Kenneth. *Best Left as Indians: Native-White Relations in the Yukon Territory, 1840-1973.* Montreal and Kingston: McGill-Queen's University Press, 1991.

- *Canada's Colonies.* Toronto: Lorimar, 1988.
- "Send Only Those Who Rise a Peg: Anglican Clergy in the Yukon, 1858–1932." *Journal of the Canadian Church Historical Society* 27, no. 1 (1986).

Coates, Kenneth, and William R. Morrison. *Interpreting Canada's North.* Toronto: Copp Clark Pitman, 1989.

- , eds. *For Purposes of Dominion: Essays in Honour of Morris Zaslow.* New York: Captive Press, 1989.

Colcleugh, Emma Shaw. "I Saw These Things." *Evening Bulletin,* Providence, RI, August 30 to September 21, 1932.

- "Missions and Mission Workers in 'The Great Lone Land'." *Catholic World* April 1895, 108–20.

Cook, Terry. "Paper Trails: A Study in Northern Records and Northern Administration." In *For Purposes of Dominion*, edited by Kenneth Coates and William R. Morrison. New York: Captive Press, 1989.

Copland, A. Dudley. *Coplalook: Chief Trader, Hudson's Bay Company, 1923–39*. Winnipeg: Watson and Dwyer, 1985

Craven, Edna, and The Reverend J. Harold Webster. *Arctic Adventure*. Ridgetown, Ont.: GC and HC Enterprises, 1987.

Cummings, Emily. *Our Story: The Women's Auxiliary of the Missionary Society of the Church of England in Canada, 1885–1928*. Toronto: Glity Press, 1928.

Damas, David, ed. *Handbook of North American Indians, Arctic*. Vol. 5. Washington: Smithsonian Institution, 1984.

Decoursey, Duke. *The Yellowknife Years*. Squamish, BC: Parkview Publishing Ltd., n.d.

DeStaffany, Lileotta. "A Woman Adventurer in the Arctic." *The Illustrated Canadian Forest and Outdoors*, December 1930, 690–2.

Dickerson, Mark O. *Whose North: Political Change, Political Development and Self Government in the NWT*. Vancouver: UBC Press, 1992.

Diubaldo, Richard J. *Stefansson and the Canadian Arctic*. Montreal: McGill-Queen's University Press, 1978.

Dobin, Michael. "Iron Will and Arctic Men: The Last of the Whaling Men." *Up Here* (Aug./Sept. 1992): 27–30.

Drouin, Clementine, SGM. *Love Spans the Centuries: Origin and Development of the Institute of the Sisters of Charity of Montreal, "Grey Nuns"*. Translated by Antoinette Bezaire, SGM. Montreal: Meridian Press, 1990.

Duchaussois, Rev. Father P., OMI. *The Grey Nuns in the Far North*. Toronto: McClelland and Stewart, 1919.

Dunn, James Taylor. "Nipigon Fisherwoman." *Beaver* 280, 1949, 20–4.

– "To Edmonton in 1892." *Beaver* 281, 1950, 3–5.

Ellis, Miriam Green. "A Business Woman in the Far North." *The Canadian Countryman*, 1925: 1669, 1710.

Enlisting for Service: Information for Prospective Candidates. Woman's Auxiliary to the Missionary Society of the Church of England in Canada, n.d., n.p.

Ferguson, Chick. *Mink, Mary and Me: The Story of a Wilderness Trapline*. New York: MS Mill Company, 1946.

Ferland, Leonie, SGM. *Une Voyage au Cercle Polaire*. Montreal: Les Soeurs Grises de Montreal, 1939.

Finnie, Richard. *Canada Moves North*. New York: Macmillan Company, 1944.

– *Lure of the North*. Philadelphia: David McKay Company, 1940.

Fleming, Ven. A.L. *Baffin Land Revisited*. Reprint from *The Canadian Churchman*, NWTA Library.

– *Brief History of Missions to the Canadian Eskimo*. Toronto: Missionary Society of the Church of England in Canada, 1929.

– *Flying Beyond the Arctic Circle*. London: Society for the Propagation of the Gospel in Foreign Parts, 1933.

– "In Journeyings Oft." *Arctic News*, 1930.

– "The Last Great North." *Arctic News*, 1934.

– "Nearest The North Pole." *Arctic News*, 1931.

Francis, Daniel. *Arctic Chase: A History of Whaling in Canada's North*. N.p., Breakwater Books, 1984.

Frost, Georgie (as told to Wilbur Granburg). "Home 12x14 Feet Lat 62'45'N." *Beaver* 265, no. 2 (1934): 23–6.

Gibbon, John Murray. *Three Centuries of Canadian Nursing*. Toronto: Macmillan, 1947.

Gilbert, Walter E. (as told to Kathleen Shackleton). *Arctic Pilot: Life and Work on Northern Canadian Air Routes*. Toronto: Thomas Nelson & Sons, 1942.

Godsell, Jean W. *I Was No Lady ... I Followed the Call of the Wild*. Toronto: Ryerson, 1959.

– "Radio's Bow to Silent Places." *Manitoba Calling*, July 1940, 3.

– "Those Good Old Days." *Liberty*, 9 October 1937, 6.

Godsell, Philip H. *Pilots of the Purple Twilight*. Toronto: Ryerson, 1955.

Goldring, Philip. "Religion, Missions and Native Culture." *Journal of the Canadian Church Historical Society* 26, no. 2 (1984).

Grange, Marion. "The Women of Pangnirtung." *Calgary Herald*, 12 November 1938.

Grant, John Webster. *Moon of Wintertime: Missionaries and the Indians of Canada in Encounter since 1534*. Toronto: University of Toronto Press, 1984.

"Grey Nuns of Fort Smith to Leave the North." *The Native Press*, 8 June 1979.

Griffis, E.M. "Lady of the Bay." *Beaver* 291 (winter 1960), 46–50.

Hail, Barbara, and Kate C. Duncan. *Out of the North: The Sub-Arctic Collection of the Haffenriffer Museum of Anthropology, Brown University*. Providence, RI: Brown University Press, 1989.

Hallenby, Grace. *Anglican Women's Training College: A Background Document*. Toronto: Centre for Christian Studies, 1989.

Hamelin, L-E. "Images of the North." In *Interpreting Canada's North*. Kenneth Coates and William R. Morrison.

8

Headon, Christopher. "Women and Organized Religion in Mid and Late Nineteenth Century Canada." *Journal of the Canadian Church Historical Society* 20, no. 1–2 (1978).

Hill, Meredith. "The Women Workers of the Diocese of Athabasca." *Journal of the Canadian Church Historical Society* 28, no. 2 (1986).

"Historical Sketch of the Origin and Work of the Hay River Mission, Great Slave Lake." N.p.: Missionary Society of the Church of England in Canada, n.d.

Hoare, Catherine. "Edmonton to Aklavik, 1920." *Beaver* 269, no. 1 (1938): 40–3.

– "Herschel Island to Aklavik, 1923." *Beaver* 269, no. 3 (1938): 42–5.

Hodgins, Bruce W., and Margaret Hobbs, eds. *Nawstawgan: The Canadian North by Canoe and Horseshoe.* Toronto: Betelguese Books, 1985.

Huel, Raymond. *Proclaiming the Gospel to the Indians and the Metis.* Edmonton: University of Alberta Press, 1996.

Hutchison, Dr Isobel W. *North to the Rime-Ringed Sun: Being the Record of an Alaska-Canadian Journey Made in 1933–34.* London: Blackie, 1934.

"In the Far North." *Manitoba Free Press,* 1 October 1894.

Inglis, George. "The Grey Nuns in the North." *North* 14, no.1 (1967): 12-15.

Ingram, Rob, and Helene Dobrowolsky. *Waves Upon the Shore: an Historical Profile of Herschel Island.* Whitehorse: Department of Tourism, Heritage Branch, 1989.

Jenness, Diamond. *People of the Twilight.* Chicago: University of Chicago Press, 1928.

Kemp, Vernon, A.M. CBE. *Without Fear, Favour or Affection: Thirty-Five Years With the Royal Canadian Mounted Police.* Toronto: Longmans, 1958.

Kitto, F.H. *The North West Territories, 1930.* Ottawa: King's Printer, 1930.

Krech, Shepard. *The Subarctic Fur Trade: Native Social and Economic Adaptations.* Vancouver: UBC Press, 1984.

Latham, Barbara, and Cathy Kess, eds. *In Her Own Right.* Victoria (BC): Camosun College, 1983.

Lechat, R., OMI. "Evangelization and Colonialism." *Eskimo* (spring/summer 1976): 3–9.

Lesage, Rev. F.S., OMI. *Sacred Heart Mission, Fort Simpson: An Historical Sketch, 1858–1958.* N.p., n.p., 1958.

"Life at a Trading Post: An English Woman's Experience." *Beaver* 4, no. 6 (1924): 205.

Lindbergh, Ann Morrow. *Hour of Gold, Hour of Lead: Diaries and Letters of*

Ann Morrow Lindbergh, 1929–1932. New York: Harcourt Brace Jovanovitch, 1973.

– *North to the Orient.* New York: Harcourt, Brace and Company, 1935.

Longstreth, T. Morris. *The Silent Force.* New York and London: The Century Company, 1927.

McCann, Edward. "Geraldine Moodie." *Canadian Women's Studies* 2, no.3 (1980):12–14.

McCarthy, Martha. *From the Great River to the Ends of the Earth: Oblate Missions to the Dene, 1847–1921.* Edmonton: University of Alberta Press, 1995.

Mackenzie River Diocesan Branch of the Woman's Auxiliary to the Missionary Society of the Church of England in Canada and to the Diocesan Missions. *Reports of the First, Second, and Third Meetings of the Diocesan Board.* 1914, 1927 and 1928.

MacPherson, N.J., and Roderick Duncan MacPherson, eds. *Dreams and Visions: Education in the NWT From Early Days to 1984.* Yellowknife: Government of the Northwest Territories, Department of Education, 1992.

Manning, E. Wallace. "Chimo Days." *Beaver* 270, no. 2 (1939): 30–4.

– *Igloo for the Night.* London: Hodder and Stoughton, 1943.

– "The Long Trail." *Beaver,* Parts 1 and 2, no. 273 (1943): 46–50; no. 274 (1943): 16–19.

Marriott, Richard. "Arctic Bay Baby." *Beaver* 270, no. 3 (1939): 46–7.

Marsh, Donald. *Echoes from a Frozen Land.* Edited by Winifred Marsh. Edmonton: Hurtig, 1987.

Masik, August, with Isobel Wylie Hutchison. *Arctic Nights Entertainments.* Glasgow: Blackie & Son Ltd., 1935.

Merrill, Anne. "Wings in the Wind." *Globe and Mail,* 17 June 1950, 8.

"The Most Northerly Residential School in the British Empire." *Echoes (The Official Organ of the IODE)* 124 (1931): 4.

Middleton, Nancy. "Christmas at Fort Rae." *Citizen Magazine* (Ottawa), 24 December 1965, 8.

Mills, Sara. *Discourses and Differences: An Analysis of Women's Travel Writing and Colonialism.* London: Routledge, 1991.

Moore, Barrington, Jr. *Privacy: Studies in Social and Cultural History.* Armonck, NY: M.E. Sharpe Inc, 1984.

Morrison, William R. *Showing the Flag: The Mounted Police and Canadian Sovereignty in the North, 1894–1925.* Vancouver: University of British Columbia Press, 1985.

Morton, W.L. "The North in Canadian Historiography." In *Selected Essays of W.L. Morton,* edited by A.B. McKillop. Toronto: Macmillan, 1982.

Munday, Luta. "The Beauty of the Arctic." *National Review* (London) February 1934, 240–5.
– "Children of the Igloos." *Echoes* 38, no. 47 (1945): 3.
– *A Mounty's Wife.* London: Sheldon Press, 1930.
Murphy, Mrs A. "Northern Pioneers." *Canadian Magazine* 32, December 1913, 170–4.
– "Northern Vistas." *Canadian Magazine* 32, April 1914, 615–20.
North, Dick. *Arctic Exodus: The Last Great Trail Drive.* Toronto: MacMillan, 1991.
Northwest Territories Data Book. Yellowknife: Outcrop, 1991.
Nute, Grace Lee. "Down North in 1892." *Beaver* 279, 1948, 42–46.
– "Paris to Peel's River in 1892." *Beaver* 278, 1948, 19–23.
O'Kelly, Grace. "A Woman's Arctic Log." Parts 1, 2 and 3. *Beaver* 4, no. 6 (1924): 210; 4, no. 7 (1924): 245; 4, no. 8 (1924): 295.
Orford, Mena. *Journey North.* Toronto: McClelland & Stewart, 1957.
Pazdro, Roberta J. "Agnes Deans Cameron: Against the Current," In *In Her Own Right*, edited by Barbara Latham and Cathy Kess. Victoria (BC): Camosun College, 1983.
Peake, Frank A. "From the Red River to the Arctic." *Journal of the Canadian Church Historical Society* 31, no. 2 (1989).
Peary, Josephine. *My Arctic Journal (A Year Among the Ice Fields and Eskimos).* New York: Contemporary Publishers, 1893.
Peters, Mary Crocker. "Aklavik of the Arctic." *Beaver* 276, 1943, 28–31.
Piché, Mère Marie-Anne. *De Montreal a Mackenzie: Notes de Voyage.* Montreal: Soeurs Grises de Montreal, 1912.
Porter, Sophie. "An Arctic Winter: A Woman's Life in the Polar Seas." *Overland* 29, n.d., 353–9.
Price, Ray. *Yellowknife.* Toronto: Peter Martin Associates, 1967
Purich, Donald. *The Inuit and Their Land: The Story of Nunavut.* Toronto: James Lorimer & Company, 1992.
Quirt, Susan Elizabeth. "On the Way to the Arctic." *Living Message* 40, no. 10 (1929): 336–7.
Ray, Arthur J. "Periodic Shortages, Native Welfare, and the Hudson's Bay Company 1670–1930." In *The Subarctic Fur Trade*, Krech. Vancouver: UBC Press, 1984.
"Remarkable Journey of Two Women to the Arctic." *Globe* (Toronto), 6 February 1909.
Rivett-Carnac, Charles. *Pursuit in the Wilderness.* Toronto: Little Brown & Company, 1965.

Robinson, Jane. *Wayward Women: A Guide to Women Travellers*. New York: Oxford University Press, 1991.

Rokeby-Thomas, Anna. "Anna's Diary: Arctic Honeymoon." *North* 21, no. 5 (1974): 26–31.

- "Arctic Darkness." *North* 22, no. 1 (1975): 15-21.
- "Christmas, 1938." *North* 22, no. 6 (1976): 52–7.
- "Christmas Living Under the Mid-Day Moon." *North* 21, no. 6) (1974): 8-15.
- "Farewell With Memories." *North*, 22, no. (1976): 52–7.
- "Married Under the Midnight Sun." *North*, 21, no. 4 (1974): 14–21.
- "On An Arctic Trail," *North*. 22, no. 4 (1975): 26–31.
- "Sadness and Joy," *North*. 22, no. 2 (1975): 16–23.
- "Some Notable Inuit," *North*. 22, no. 5 (1975): 16–21.

Romig, Emily Craig. *The Life and Travels of a Pioneer Woman in Alaska*. Colorado Springs: privately printed, 1945.

Ross, W. Gillies. *Whaling and Eskimos: Hudson Bay 1860–1915*. Ottawa: National Museum of Man, 1975.

- *An Arctic Whaling Diary: The Journal of Captain George Comer in Hudson Bay, 1903–1905*. Toronto: University of Toronto Press, 1984.
- *This Distant and Unsurveyed Country: A Woman's Winter at Baffin Island, 1857–1858*. Montreal & Kingston: McGill-Queen's University Press, 1997.

Rourke, Louise. *The Land of the Frozen Tide*. London: Hutchinson and Company, 1928.

Rutherdale, Myra. "Revisiting Colonization Through Gender: Anglican Missionary Women in the Pacific Northwest and the Arctic, 1860–1945." *BC Studies* 104 (1994).

Soper, Carolyn. "A Nurse Goes to Baffin Island." *Beaver* 295, 1964, 30–8.

Stafford, Marie Ahnighito Peary. "Child of the Arctic." *Beaver* 275, 1944, 8–13.

Stanley. Brian. *The Bible and the Flag: Protestant Missions and British Imperialism in the Nineteenth and Twentieth Centuries*. Leicester: Apollos, 1990.

Stanwell-Fletcher, Theodora. *Clear Lands and Icy Seas*. New York: Dodd Mead, 1958.

Stringer, Sadie. "My Husband Ate His Boots." *Maclean's* 68, 1955, 10–11, 44–9.

Strobel, Margaret. *European Women and the Second British Empire*. Bloomington: Indiana University Press, 1991.

Strong-Boag, Veronica. *The New Day Recalled: Lives of Girls and Women in English Canada, 1919–1939*. Markham (Ont.): Penguin, 1988.

Taylor, Elizabeth. "A Woman Explorer in the Mackenzie Delta." *Outing,* October, November, December, 1894–95.
– "Up the Mackenzie to the Polar Sea." *Travel* 3 (1899): 559–64.
Thomas, Mrs P.A. "Kindly Dispatch Miss Gadsby." *North* 17, no. 2 (1969): 6–19.
"To Photograph the Frontier" *Archivist* 5, no. 1 (1978): 1–5.
Turner, Dick. *Nahanni*. Saanichton, BC: Hancock House, 1975.
Vyvyan, Lady Clara. *Arctic Adventure*. London: Peter Owen, 1961.
– "On The Rat River." *Canadian Geographical Journal* (January 1931): 48–57.
– *Roots and Stars: Reflections on the Past*. London: Peter Owen, 1962.
– "Sunset on the Yukon." *Cornhill Magazine* 153, 1936, 206–16.
– "The Unrelenting North." *Cornhill Magazine* 152, 1935, 176–83.
Watt, Maud. "Nascopie Honeymoon." *Beaver* 268, no. 4 (1938): 18–26.
"Woman Gives Vivid Picture." *Quebec Chronicle*, 18 September 1934, 4.
The Yearbook and Clergy List of the Church of England in the Dominion of Canada, 1920–1926. Toronto: The General Synod of the Church of England in Canada, 1920–1926.
Yellowknife NWT: An Illustrated History. Sechelt (BC): Nor'West Publishing, 1990.
Zaslow, Morris. *The Northward Expansion of Canada 1914–1967*. Toronto: McClelland and Stewart, 1988.
– *The Opening of the Canadian North 1870–1914*. Toronto: McClelland and Stewart, 1971.

Index